Twenty Gallons of Milk

And other columns from the El Dorado News Times

JOAN HIBBARD HERSHBERGER

WestBow
PRESS
A DIVISION OF THOMAS NELSON

WestBow Press books may be ordered through booksellers or by contacting:

WestBow Press
A Division of Thomas Nelson
1663 Liberty Drive
Bloomington, IN 47403
www.westbowpress.com
1-(866) 928-1240

Scripture quotations marked (NIV) are taken from the Holy Bible, New International Version®, NIV®. Copyright © 1973, 1978, 1984, 2011 by Biblica, Inc.™ Used by permission of Zondervan. All rights reserved worldwide. www. zondervan.com The "NIV" and "New International Version" are trademarks registered in the United States Patent and Trademark Office by Biblica, Inc.™

ISBN: 978-1-4908-0668-6 (sc)
ISBN: 978-1-4908-0669-3 (hc)
ISBN: 978-1-4908-0667-9 (e)

Library of Congress Control Number: 2013915660

Printed in the United States of America.

WestBow Press rev. date: 10/01/2013

For my number one fan,
Joseph

Table of Contents

Acknowledgment

This book of my columns was made possible with the permission of general manager Betty Chatham, the years I wrote under managing editors George Arnold, Shea Wilson, and Chris Qualls, and my faithful readers who continue to sustain interest. I also want to thank those who helped me edit this book of selected columns: my daughter Sharon Schulte, and my friends John Day, Janice McIntyre, and Kay Shaddock. Especially I must thank my family and friends for their permission to share their stories.

Introduction

I never set out to work at a newspaper and write a weekly column. In my thirties, I went back to school to become a high school math and science teacher, graduated with honors, and quickly landed a teaching job.

While teaching did not turn out to be my calling, I did appreciate the administrative support I experienced at a local high school. I wrote a letter to the editor of the El Dorado News-Times, George Arnold, about my favorable experience at the local school. That letter caught his attention. He called and asked if I would be interested in writing a weekly column for the newspaper while working as the office news clerk.

After I said, "yes," he asked me to fill out an application and as an afterthought asked, "do you know how to type?"

I told him I did. For years I had typed a weekly letter to my mother about my children. She wrote back with news of my extended family. Our correspondence ended in 1992 when cancer cut her life short at sixty and left me bereft of my weekly correspondent.

With Arnold's invitation to work for the paper and write a column in 1993, I returned to my weekly report on the family. This time I wrote for a community of interested parents, grandparents and friends eager to hear about the antics of my children, my husband's periodic projects, family trips, and our grandchildren.

Through the years, my responsibilities at the newspaper expanded. I have written feature stories, hard news stories, editorials, travelogues, public service announcements, special sections, and education news of students in academic settings. But always, no matter how full my schedule might be, no matter what our current family crisis, I always wrote a weekly column. In January 2013 I tallied my one thousandth column. As my responsibilities have expanded, so have the topics of my columns as I wrote other people's stories and my personal opinion of current topics or community events.

At the request of faithful readers, I have compiled this book of columns. After some consideration I chose primarily columns about my family. Although I have organized the columns in chapters and chronologically according to their date of publication, each stands alone.

Bread crumbs

A Loaf of Bread in the Road

I HARDLY EVER SAW MY son as he rushed to after-school band practices, an evening class in Camden, his part-time job, and various church activities.

"I know you're growing up, but I'd like to see you sometime," I said wistfully as he headed out the door again.

He turned warily, "I would like to see me sometime, too."

After a couple of days of seeing that same weariness in my usually hyper energetic teenager, I urged him to quit the job and offered to drive him to class.

One night as we left El Dorado, I interrupted his reading, "Looks like the bread truck had an accident." Squashed plastic sacks of bread and packaged snack cakes littered the blacktop. He looked, mumbled something, and went back to reading.

A few miles down the road, I nudged him, "Somebody must have left the backdoor of the bread truck open." Yellow, plastic-wrapped loaves of bread rested neatly on the asphalt shoulder as on a store shelf.

"We ought to pick them up."

"Mo-o-o-om," he protested. I drove on silently.

The next time I saw a loaf of bread I slowed down and headed for it.

"Come on, all you have to do is open the door, bend down, and pick it up."

He sighed in exasperation but opened the door. The bread was out of reach. He got out, picked up the loaf, and jammed it in the back seat.

"There are you satisfied?" He whacked his book open. A few miles down the road, I saw a familiar patch of yellow against the black asphalt.

"I'll bet that bread truck driver is as fed up with life as you are," I said as I slowed down beside the loaf. "He is showing the world what he thinks with each loaf he tosses out."

He looked at me and grinned as he picked up the loaf. "Yeah, maybe he is," he agreed, dropping the loaf and his book in the backseat.

He spotted the next one. I slowed down and he scooped up the loaf in a perfect *Dukes of Hazzard* swoop.

For the next half hour we had a grand time as we rescued the bread from its roadside fate.

My son's weariness dissolved as he was swept away in our tracking of the bread trail from El Dorado to Camden-Tech.

"What are we going to do with all this bread, Mom?" he asked as he made a hook shot to the back seat with yet another loaf.

"I don't know. It's just fun."

As we turned off the highway to head for Camden-Tech, we sat back confident the game was over. "Where do you suppose that bread truck was going?" he mused.

"I don't know," I shrugged then veered the wheel to the right, "but he took this road, too."

As another loaf flew into the back seat with the rest, I wondered which had more bread, our car or the bread truck.

Maybe we should have left them where they lay beside the road.

Maybe it was a modern version of Hansel's trail of bread crumbs to show the way back to El Dorado.

Maybe they were manna in the wilderness. At least on the trip home we didn't see any of the loaves we had missed, and our bit of fun nourished the soul because we grabbed it where we found it.

February 7, 1994

What's In a Name?

As a new bride, I was writing the information on the envelope used to hold film for processing. I started to spell out my husband's name and stopped as I realized I would be the one picking up the film. I wrote my first name instead. I haven't been Mrs. M.J. Hershberger since.

After encouraging my husband to earn his degree, I went back for mine. I was very aware of the sacrifices my husband and children made while I studied. However, as I filled out the forms for my diploma, I wanted to recognize the role my parents played in my education. So my diploma declares that Joan Hibbard Hershberger has satisfied requirements for graduation.

I didn't hyphenate our names. I never could figure out what would happen to the children's names. If the couple's hyphenated last name is given to the children, would that name be hyphenated to their future spouse's?

For instance, my mother used her maiden name "Waight" as a middle name. If she had instead hyphenated that name with my father's name and passed it along to me, I would have been Joan Marie Waight-Hibbard-Hershberger.

It seems reasonable to me that both sets of grandparents be recognized that way. They all effected my formative years. Grandma Hibbard sewed my clothes, and Grandma Waight mended them. Every Sunday afternoon for years we played in the yard while Grandpa Hibbard sat in his lounge chair watching ball games with his dad. Every Sunday evening we watched *Lassie* and *Disney* while Grandpa Waight slept in his lounge chair.

So both sets should be acknowledged which would make my initials J.M.W.H.H.

But wait, I still remember the thrill of being twelve-years-old and seeing a family genealogy that went back to the years of the Pilgrims and the Puritans. My maternal grandmother was a direct descendant of Roger Williams, founder of the first American colony with freedom of worship.

We all knew that my grandmother Hibbard was proud to have been a Holt. She always signed her name Harriet Holt Hibbard. Her father is the only great-grandparent that I knew.

So one day I decided if Grandma Hibbard always initialed herself as H.H.H. I ought to recognize her parents' contribution to my life as well.

Which all means that before I ever married, I was a hyphenated J.M.W.W.H.H.: Joan Marie Williams-Waight-Holt-Hibbard.

I believe in being fair. My husband's family is just as proud of their ancestry. We have three books of genealogies from his family gracing our bookshelves. His maternal ancestors deserve as much recognition as mine. So I married (unbeknownst to him) Mr. Mishler-Detwiler-Yoder-Hershberger.

These days when the little ones ask, "What's your real name?" I reply, "Joan Marie Williams-Waight-Holt-Hibbard-Mishler-Detwiler-Yoder-Hershberger."

The child is always impressed.

However, I'm not so sure that it will be acceptable as a byline for this column, so, I remain respectfully yours, Joan Hershberger.

May 9, 1994

Award Winning Work

"I MOWED THE YARD DIAGONALLY this week," gloated my husband during a lemonade break.

"Uh-huh. Very interesting."

"I feel pretty good about that."

"I'm sure you do."

While I was away as camp counselor, he cleaned house, picked blueberries, mowed the yard, and made his first piecrusts for fresh blueberry pie.

"After I mixed the flour, water, and shortening, it didn't look right so I worked it until it did." He had broken every rule and still produced a flaky, delicious pie shell.

"You did a good job, dear."

His piecrusts pleased him. His mowing satisfied him, and the pile of blueberries thrilled him. As we relaxed with the family Sunday afternoon, for the umpteenth time, he asked, "Weren't those pies good?"

"Yes, dear, the pies deserve a certificate of recognition."

My son grinned, "No, a plaque. They are good." He reflected a moment. "Could you imagine what it would be like if we handed out plaques for everything? We could redo a floor with little wooden plaques:

Kids: hung their clothes neatly, May 5, 1989.

Mom: great roast, July 27, 1990.

Dad: four fantastic piecrusts, June 23, 1997.

About then, it was time to dress for evening services. "I am going to change for church," my husband announced.

"And there's another one! Dad changed his clothes for church."

The next several weeks we handed out verbal certificates and plaques for daily deeds of accomplishment: dishes, grocery buying, making supper, and moving the sprinkler across the lawn.

Last week after a stop at the bread store, I turned the key in the car's ignition and heard the dismal click of a dead battery. The sun was hot, the car was hotter, and the concrete sidewalk was blistering.

I went back inside the bread store, borrowed their phone and called my husband. It was time for his lunch break.

"The car won't start and your daughter needs it to drive to work this afternoon."

He came, parked his car alongside mine, found the battery cables, and recharged the battery. He slammed the hood down, "Better have the battery checked before you go home."

I looked at him. When I take the car in for repairs, some guy asks a hundred questions that I have no idea how to answer. Besides, the car was running and our daughter needed it to get to work.

"You take it," I said. "I'll swap cars with you."

I grabbed the bread and left him on the hot parking lot with a funky car and the task of having it checked out. I went home to an air conditioned house. Guilt or thankfulness caused me to realize this deed deserved recognition.

With the computer's help, I made a certificate of recognition to a most noble and honorable husband who rescued his wife on a hot day, charged the battery, and took it to be checked for his humble and thankful wife.

He never said a word about what he had done. But he did leave his certificate tacked to the bathroom mirror for a very long time.

August 4, 1997

My Favorite Child

In June some of the children decided they knew which one I favored. I contended I had no favorites. After I talked with my friend at the library who also has four children, I decided to follow her example and agree with them.

In July we visited my favorite son, his wife, and five-month-old daughter. I insisted that everyone else had to yield car space to the pile of garage sale finds I had purchased for my pet. He said he could use a few of the things I laid at his feet.

The next week, my favorite child, a junior in college, phoned in ecstasy. "The professor says I have an 'A' going into the final test in Organic Chemistry II." After a big fat 'F' on the first test, he had studied organic Chemistry night and day. "So, Mom, is there any incentive for me to get an 'A' in this class?"

As an incentive for my cherished child, I would give him the world. So a few days later when I won a portable CD player, I knew exactly which child to give it to—if he got an 'A.' I called to tell him.

"A portable CD player! All right! I was studying chemistry when you called. That should keep me going." He got the A and the CD player.

The next week my favorite child needed the family minivan to move all his books, computer, and clothes to Indiana for his first year of graduate studies. Because he is my favorite, I talked his father into loading all his boxes into the car top carrier. I wanted to be sure he had everything he wanted in his new room. The weight left a dent in the roof, but my favorite's books arrived unscathed.

In Indiana my favorite one was moving his family from an apartment to their first home. All summer we had planned to help with his transition. For five days my husband put in ten- and twelve-hour days pounding nails, slapping up dry wall, and sanding. I made the kind of meals I thought my favorite would enjoy.

My husband enjoyed the work too much. We all pushed him to fulfill his promise to take my favorite child to the beach at the Michigan dunes. Once there, he led the charge up the mountain of sand while I supervised the lunch box. After eating sandwiches sprinkled with sand, everyone tiptoed into sixty-five degree water. My favorite child got an earache. I tried to warm it away with my hands. We did not leave until the favored child was ready.

On the way home we delivered the T-shirts I had carefully selected to reflect the personalities of my favorite's three daughters.

Later, as we again helped at the new house, one of my children asked me to go to town for something. I questioned the request until my heir said, "You know you want to do it. I'm your favorite child."

"Oh! I forgot. Today you're my favorite child. I'll get the keys."

One of the others overheard me. He stared at us strangely as we walked out until I explained, "Sometimes I forget which one is my favorite." I think he is still bewildered. He should be. After all, the listener is my favorite, and I would hate for him to hear otherwise.

August 25, 1997

The Sister Game

A SIMPLE HAIRDO UNDERSCORED FOR me the subtleties and longevity of sibling rivalry.

In the week before I reunited with my sisters, friends complimented me saying, "Nice hair." "Like your hairdo." I caught myself saying, "Thanks, I have been telling myself to go to the hair dresser, but when I realized I was going to see my sister whom I haven't seen in a long time, I had to do something now." Sometimes I added, "because we will be having the sister competition, if you know what I mean."

Women with sisters lit up with a smile of recognition, "Oh, yeah!"

The sister game is not said in so many words. It is not done with any obvious tallying of points scored, but it is played any time sisters get together.

The game goes something like this: As we warmly greet each other, we silently evaluate the other's clothes, hair, aging process, and overall health. As we politely ask about each other's children, we mentally analyze whose kids have done better, whose children's careers were glossed over, or who is doing, or did, a better job parenting their children.

After my visit I summarized my foray into the sister game: "Well, she always looks the best. She always wins for wearing the nicest clothes, and her hair always looks great because she's got the really thick hair that holds up, and I began turning gray first. But, I usually win for being the thinnest, even when I am at my shockingly highest weight, not because I work at weight control, but because my genes come from our tall Indian ancestor which gives me a few more inches to hide any weight gain."

The parenting aspect of the game is much more fickle. The score depends on who is awarding points, what aspects are most important to the judge, and in which phase of life the child happens to be.

Occasionally the game is played in the open as it was the day a proud mother asked her preschooler to tell another mother a newly memorized Mother Goose poem. "Lucy Locket lost her pocket. Kitty Fisher found it. Nothing in it, nothing on it, but the binding round it," the child rattled off. Immediately the second mother turned to her child saying, "You can learn that, can't you?" and began repeating the poem's lines, pushing her own child to catch up and even out the score.

A couple of small family reunions ago I watched my brothers play the brother's version of the sibling rivalry game.

Living on different sides of the country, they had not seen each other in quite a while. Each sized the other up quickly. Big brother had recently lost his spread around the middle. Little brother had found some of it, but by a fluke of nature, long past the time for the traditional last growth spurt, he had also grown a couple of inches taller. Suddenly their heights matched, but the weights did not, and this time the usual winner needed to lose.

From hours of listening to my only daughter, when one does not have sisters, close friends make great substitutes for playing the sister game.

When I mentioned the "sister game" to an acquaintance, she said, "I realized I could not win, so I worked on developing a quiet spirit instead."

"Oh, so you aim to win the personality contest," I responded before I realized saying that meant I lost the Miss Congeniality trophy for the day, which is why the contest is one of observation, a *mental* tallying of points, and a *silent* noting of the other person's score in the perpetual game of sibling rivalry.

March 8, 2004

How Many Make a Couple?

I TOLD MY HUSBAND a couple of guys were coming over to talk with us about staying for a few weeks.

A couple of guys—I expected two men.

Three showed up. They wanted to stay thirteen or fourteen weeks.

After they left, my husband mused, "How many would you say is a couple?"

"Usually I'd say, two, but sometimes a couple is three."

"If a couple can mean three, what is a few?" he asked.

"I guess three to five or six."

"Then how many are several?" he persisted.

"Several. Well, that would be seven to eleven."

"I always thought it was four or more," he said.

"No, definitely at least five."

"Then how many is some?"

"That would be less than several."

"So a couple can be two or three. Some is less than several, but more than a few. A few is three to five or six, maybe. But several can be six or seven to maybe eleven."

He took a deep breath, "And then you have a dozen which is twelve, unless you have a baker's dozen which is thirteen. If half a dozen is six, what is half of a baker's dozen? Six, six-and-a-half or seven?"

I just stared at him.

He did not notice. "And how much is a bunch?"

"Well, a bunch is more than some and several, so I would say it is fourteen, fifteen or more."

"But what about a group?" my torturous word definer persisted.

"Well, a group is more than several, so I would say maybe five to ten," I ventured.

"But isn't that also several? We had twenty in our Bible study group, so a group could be up to twenty or thirty," he concluded.

"Okay, you're right!" I threw my hands up in defeat.

He refused to quit, "If a couple can be two or three and a dozen is twelve or thirteen, then a couple dozen would be twenty-four to thirty-nine."

"Well, at least a pair is always only two," I sighed, wanting it all to end.

"A pair is two," he agreed, "yet a couple can be two or three, some is less than several, and more than a few. A few is three to five or six, maybe. But several are seven to eleven. A dozen is twelve or thirteen. So, if a group can be up to twenty or thirty, how many is a team?"

A team, I paused to think. "Well, five," I said thinking about basketball, "to whatever. It could be up to forty or fifty when you talk about a swimming team," I reflected.

"Or a team could be as little as two, as in tennis when people play doubles," he mused.

"Nah, the ones who play doubles are part of a team of players who make up the group of students that play. It's some of the bunch that showed up for tennis tryouts."

He wasn't listening. He had gone to the computer.

"In fact, a college football team can have up to eighty-five people, plus walk-ons," he said checking a college football website. "So, if a couple is two or three, and a couple of teams came to visit us, we could expect maybe three hundred people to show up," he summed up.

He had gotten out of hand. Our defining moment had to stop.

"I take it all back. A couple is always two. And two people like you and me make a really great team except when we try to define a few words."

May 29, 2006

Sounds in the Night

I LOVE HAVING THE HOUSE to myself on occasion. Then it's mine, all mine, and I relish every moment except when something goes bump in the night as it did the night I heard a beeping time bomb in my kitchen. Heart beating, I tentatively went to investigate. The sound stopped.

Barely breathing, I looked around.

Nothing.

Slowly my heart rate returned to normal, only to be jacked up again when the ominous beeping returned. I ran into the room and found a smoke alarm's battery announcing its dying experience.

I changed the battery.

No dying batteries required my attention last month when I had the house to myself. Only the scolding cat demanding her breakfast broke the silence of the house.

Then my husband came home and something broke the silence of the night as we slept.

We both woke up from a deep sleep to hear voices mumbling at the other end of the house.

"I thought I heard the phone ring," he said. I had not heard it even though we do have a phone at the head of the bed.

Silently, we lay in bed staring into the darkness, wanting to sleep, but we had to know what we heard.

"You better check that out," I said before I slid a bit deeper in the blankets, ever so happy it was not me going down that hall to investigate.

He rolled out of bed and turned on the hall light. The mumbling stopped.

"They stopped as soon as I turned on the light," he said.

Silently, he walked down the hall. I heard nothing. Waiting in the silence, I wondered how long it would take me to push aside the blinds, yank open the window, and climb out to the lawn.

I wondered how I would know if I needed to get out of the house.

He did not return. He did not call out anything. I thought about calling out and asking what he found, but what if those mumbling voices answered instead.

I waited.

Finally, he walked in, puzzled, and quiet, "Everything was turned off: the radio, the TV, the computer. They stopped talking as soon as I turned on the light."

Oh.

"Did you check all the closets and behind the couch?"

He sighed, put on a brave face, and went down the hall to look inside all those hiding places.

He came back, "Nothing."

We looked at each other.

Something had awakened us.

"I thought I heard the phone ring," he said again.

Standing up, he walked resolutely down the hall again. A couple of seconds later I heard the mumbling voices again.

"It's on the answering machine. That's what I heard," he said.

"Come here, listen to this, and see if you can understand it."

I emerged from the safety of the blankets, touched the bed lamp, and leaned over to study the plug for the bedroom phone. It had come loose. We had not had a working phone in the bedroom. He HAD heard the phone ring.

I plugged in the phone and went to listen to the messages. Garbled talk echoed through the house. It sounded like a not quite tuned in TV or radio station.

We deleted the messages and went back to bed to puzzle over our midnight alarm. Eventually, our hearts stopped racing. We slept, hoping nothing else went beep in the middle of the night.

September 28, 2009

The Grandparent Rule

"IT'S A RULE THAT GRANDPARENTS have to have interesting things."

I didn't know that, not until the Pennsylvania grandkids came last week and repeatedly told us that grandparent rule.

They said it shortly after they arrived and had spread out through the house in search of the interesting stuff which they quickly found and took down from shelves to study further.

The oldest grandson reappeared with a collection of pebbles, rocks, an arrow head, and shark teeth from the Crater of Diamonds via a yard sale.

"This is so cool," he kept exclaiming. His wanted to identify those rocks. He wanted to know enough that he pulled out the R encyclopedia, the M encyclopedia for Mohs Scale of Hardness of rocks and minerals, and finally logged onto the Internet for identification techniques.

Sorting the rocks, studying them, talking about them with me, his grin spread from ear to ear as he told me, "Grandparents have to keep interesting things around."

Their dad came prepared to add another study in stones. He planned a day trip to the Crater of Diamonds State Park. Gathering up shovels, a wheelbarrow, a rake, lunch, and the audio version of the second Harry Potter book, we enjoyed the drive and the day proved interesting even if we did swelter in the heat at the crater. We returned rich with memories and a few quartz crystals.

Disregarding any disappointment, back at our house the grandkids began sharing with me their collection of jokes. One, using names as puns, reminded me of the classical comedian skit "Who's on first?"

I called it up on YouTube and played it for them. The kids laughed and laughed and laughed. Then they replayed it a couple of times and searched for other Abbott and Costello videos on YouTube.

"I could listen to this a thousand times. It is not like the comedians on TV. They say something and that's it, but this I could listen to a thousand times," our grandson said.

The next day he and his sisters spontaneously reenacted bits and pieces of the skit. When someone did not know the answer to a question and said, "I don't know," they all chimed in, "Third base."

"So who's on first base?"

"That's right."

And they laughed just as hard at hearing the old lines in the twenty-first century kid voices as Abbott and Costello's audience did in the pre-WWII era of the twentieth century.

Their laughter lightened our day as well. For some reason, my husband pulled out the ladder to snag a stray pine branch stuck on our roof. The kids asked if they could climb up with him.

We looked at their dad. Sure, from personal experience he knows we have a low angled roof over our one-story ranch house surrounded by lots of bushes and shrubs close to the house. A dogwood tree overhanging the house provided a quasi-club house of protection from the sun. The children sat up there reading the interesting books I have reclaimed from my childhood and found online or at used book stores. From their perch they enjoyed an entirely different perspective of the world around them.

Late at night my husband took down the ladder and stored it away. However, before he sat down for breakfast, the ladder magically returned as the gateway to the roof. He could not believe they had done that without his help.

Building sets, the game of Life, books, trails of water from the pool lined with damp towels, and energy filled the house for a couple of days. They kept us as busy and interested in them as they were in us; then they loaded up and left us with an implied mandate to get busy and find more interesting things to show them the next time they come to visit.

June 7, 2010

Missing Items Went Here

I KNEW EXACTLY WHERE TO find the ingredients the day I wanted to make chocolate chip cookies with my preschooler. I pulled out flour, sugar, baking soda, eggs, butter, nuts, but no chocolate chips. They were not there beside the vanilla. They were not under the counter. They were not up high on the top shelf.

They were not anywhere. Opening cupboard doors, I muttered, "Where are those chocolate chips? I know I have some."

"I found them," my preschooler announced.

I turned and looked at him, "Where?"

He ran to the little closet built under the stairs, crawled way back where the ceiling met the floor, and pulled out a boot. "Here they are." He reached inside the boot and pulled out a nearly empty bag of chips

If he had not found the chips for me, I would never have known what happened to them. They would have simply been missing, inexplicably gone like the other half of a pair of socks on laundry day.

Finding half of a pair of socks in the laundry frustrated me so much I quit sorting socks and tossed them in a basket to wait for the other half to catch up. Every so often my husband amused himself sorting socks. The leftovers he bundled together and began imagining ways to use them: puppets, cleaning rags or mismatched pairs of socks to wear inside boots.

The year we had four boys who all wore the same size of socks, I simplified sorting and designated each child a specific color: blue, brown, black, and turquoise. Yes, I said turquoise. It was the only other color in

15

the boys' department that year. I never thought to simply buy everyone black socks and be done with the sorting; I thought each needed his own set of clothes.

I simplified sorting, but we still ended up with an odd number for each color of sock, and I never found the missing socks. But last week I finally figured out what happened to all those missing socks.

Last week I listened to an audio reading of *There's No Place Like Here,* by Cecilia Ahern. This fantasy book relates the life of Sandy Short, a tall, black-haired woman who becomes obsessed with finding the lost. She opens a detective business dedicated to finding missing people.

One day she goes missing and discovers 'Here' where all the inexplicably missing people and items landed. Socks hang from bushes. Lost luggage filled with vacation clothes shows up in the forest. Money means nothing because the folks find it everywhere. There in the woods of 'Here' Sandy reunites with her lost teddy bear, a notebook, and missing people she has sought for years. Even in 'Here' Sandy Short loses stuff. It shows up back home after days, weeks, and years of being lost.

I'm sure she found at least one turquoise sock in 'Here.'

I cannot say for certain that our child's missing black oxford went to 'Here,' but we did search the house, the yard, and our car for that shoe. We did not have a lot of money to buy multiple pairs of shoes for each person, so we looked for that shoe until we accepted it was missing. Then unexpectedly we found it in the car on the black carpet over the hump under the radio. We decided the black color of the shoe had blended in with the black carpeting and had been there all the time. But after reading *There's No Place Like Here,* we thought maybe it wasn't.

Or, maybe that's what happened to the completed cross stitch piece I could not find for a couple of years. It went to 'Here' before returning and settling between layers of our stash of poster board.

I never did understand what happened to my son's unique piggy bank, a dried gourd. We hunted everywhere for that gourd until we gave up and forgot about it, only to find it one day mysteriously tucked between the frequently worn slacks and dresses hanging in my closet.

Now I know. That gourd bank had been in 'Here.'

Last fall I lost my ring of office keys even though I knew I had put them into the glove compartment in the van. They were not there when I reached for them. I took everything out of the compartment two or three times looking for those keys.

I really needed those keys. I had to use the back door or simply not enter without those keys. Then last week I reached for something in the glove compartment and there were the long lost keys, exactly where I knew I had placed them.

They had obviously just returned from 'Here.' That's my story, and I'm sticking with it.

April 18, 2011

Driving the Hills of New York

WITH THE BACK OF THE van stabilized with a load of boxes of books we had agreed to transport across country as a favor, my husband drove up the long, rough dirt road to the family party on top of the steep hill. He pulled in and parked (as instructed) in the thick grass beside the rough dirt road. I took in the view across the valley then began to hike up to the top of the hill to the party. I was only a little bit out of breath from the climb and the higher altitude.

Near the end of the party my sister and I went back to our cars so I could get something I had to give her. Now that most of the company had gone, we decided we would move our cars closer to the house. She pulled out in her little car and disappeared up to the top of the steep hill.

My loaded van, with its rear wheels on the downside of the parking area, spun its front-wheel drive tires and dug deep into the wet grass to the soil underneath. I turned the wheel. I tried rocking the car. I tried backing up. It only left another rut in the grass. Fearing I would slide all the way downhill or worse yet turn sideways enough that the van would tip over, I stopped trying. I grew up in this hilly farming country. I've seen and heard of tractors tipping on these hills. Looking at the narrow confines of the mowed areas and the cars still parked near my van, I set the brake and walked back up to the house. My husband could move it later. Let him be the expert who drives on slippery roads and in and out of tight parking spots. I huffed my way up the hill to the house.

When the party was over, we went back down the hill and he confidently slid behind the wheel to show me how to drive out of a slippery situation. He pressed gently on the accelerator. The tires spun. He put it in reverse. The tires spun.

"We'll have to push," he said. I volunteered to get out and push. My brother came about that time and he put his considerable strength into the push. The tires spun, turned and did not move except to slide a bit further downhill.

"It's all those books in the back of the car," I said.

We unloaded books.

The car spun. We unloaded more books. The car refused to get on with the business of driving down the hill.

My cousin stopped on her way down the hill and jumped out to help. "We need to get something under the tire," she declared. I volunteered one of the boxes holding books.

She positioned the flattened cardboard in front of the tire. My husband revved the engine. The tires spun and the van stayed put.

"Let me try driving," she said and my husband got out. She has lived in snow country fifty-nine years and driven these steep hills for decades. She knows how to get out of slippery spots.

The wheels spun.

My husband got back in and tried again with the three of us pushing. Nothing happened. The van would not move forward.

My brother said, "Here, let me try." He has lived in Arizona most of his adult life in the desert, no snow and not too many steep roads and hills.

He looked at the dash, assessed the location of gears, and released the brake. Released from its bondage, the car turned, and obediently began moving down the hill.

We reloaded the books and left the party with another story for my brother and cousin to tell for many years.

July 14, 2011

Animal House

Houdini of Hamsters

I LEFT THE HAMSTER IN the washing machine the other night. It was his fault. He is the Houdini of hamsters. The first time he escaped we took the blame, the next time we wondered. The third time, my daughter saw him reach up to the air vent, unscrew it with his paws and teeth, and pull himself out.

We have always found him.

The first time, though, we battled tears at the certainty of his loss. The next day, when I was alone, I heard an awful gnawing and scratching behind the refrigerator. I figured it was the hamster.

I hoped it wasn't a rat.

Being a good mother, I slid the refrigerator forward on its casters and looked into the dark eyes of a fur ball hissing, "I'm one mean, wild critter."

I thought he looked like Houdini. As I grabbed a kitchen towel, in case he wasn't, I wondered where I could go to resign as a good mother.

My teenage son saw him sneaking across the floor after one escape. Teenage boys don't mind leaning over and scooping up moving fur balls with bare hands.

The longest escape began the night Houdini's squeaking exercise wheel got him exiled to the garage. I left the cage on the workbench without securing the escape routes, but I thought he lacked a way to climb down the tall work bench.

I was wrong.

The garage door was partially open. We assumed he had achieved his goal. I promised to buy another hamster when the summer trips were over.

Like a bad penny, he showed up in the middle of the summer as we were cleaning the garage. He had been living behind some sheets of plywood. My daughter had already prepared his cage for another hamster.

Houdini was furious! He hissed and puffed out his fur until he looked twice his normal size.

My husband and son captured him and fought him back into the cage. His paws kept grabbing the edge of the lid as he frantically resisted capture.

Over the next several weeks, he gnawed away a significant portion of the plastic cover. We replaced his plastic cage with an old glass aquarium, with heavy books to hold the cover in place.

He escaped through the hole beside his water bottle.

This time he hid under the dishwasher. That appliance is NOT easy to move. When the springs and electrical wires had to be reattached, my husband wondered where he could go to resign as a good daddy.

So the other night, when my daughter handed me Houdini to hold while she cleaned out his cage, I knew I had to keep him secure. Ten times he wiggled his way between my fingers looking for FREEDOM! I was trying to be a good mother when I noticed the empty, dry washing machine: deep sides, room to move, hard to chew. I dropped him in, watched him discover the impossibility of escaping, and left him there while I went to do some chores.

I didn't think about him again until the next morning when I started to stuff a load of towels in the washing machine. I hastily pulled out the towels and checked.

He wasn't in there.

I checked his cage. Whew!

My daughter saw me and said me she had heard him scratching at the metal tub, had taken him out of the washing machine, and returned him to his cage. He is still there, plotting, planning, preparing for his next great escape.

August 30, 1993

The Cat's Crooked Tail

OUR CAT WENT STROLLING IN front of the neighbor's dog. The dog went into red alert and attacked. With a loud yowl, our cat with its charcoal stripes and calico patches leaped into the nearest pine tree.

With her tail at full mast the cat turned to hiss her rage at being scared half out of her wits and fell out of the tree. At least that's what the neighbors said happened when they handed the limp pile of fur to my children.

The cat's pride was crushed. It was in shock from the fall, and its tail was limp. Between her sob and sniffs over the phone, I finally heard my daughter say, "The cat's tail is broken."

I called the vet. I understood him to say we could either have him amputate the tail or just wait and see.

I called home and explained the options. "Is the cat in any pain right now?"

"No, it's sleeping in my lap."

"Then let's just wait."

The next phone call, days later, was a duet of cat yowls and sobbing screams, "The cat's tail is broken."

"I know that."

"No, Mom, it got caught in the door. It's bent."

By the time I arrived home the cat was resting quietly. About two inches from the body, the tail had a kink. Below the kink was a limp rope of fur.

For days I debated between going to the vet for an amputation and hoping it would recover. Keeping the tail attached without that mysterious feline twitch, seemed pointless, but maybe it just needed time to awaken the injured nerves for it to quit looking like a rag.

The cat didn't even wash that rag of a tail. She seemed to think the rag was a toy mouse and began playing an "I'm going eat you" game with the mussed up fur. She chomped down HARD on her tail. The cat's yowl of pain, confusion, and dismay announced that life remained in the dead looking tail.

That bite began awakening the stunned nerves. The cat quit using her tail as a toy mouse. With her sandpaper tongue the cat perpetually cleaned the fur, massaging the nerves back into awareness.

The tail still hung like a flag on a windless summer day, but it was neatly groomed. The cat knew it was part of her.

The kink stayed, yet ever so slightly I noticed that the tip moved up off the ground.

A few days later I saw the tail make a gentle curve away from the door as it came inside.

A fraction of an inch at a time, the tail moved higher and wider. The day I noticed the tail giving a warning swish as the cat stalked my daughter, I almost applauded.

Then that cat crouched across the room from me. She watched my toes nervously tap out my impatience as I worked on some papers. Her eyes, paws, body, and tail twitched from side to side revealing her intent to attack. With a bounding leap she hurled herself across the room and pierced my bare feet with claws and teeth. I quit applauding.

When the cat wasn't aiming for my feet, I celebrated the signposts of healing as the tail swished its warnings, made a playful flip, or curled cozily around its sleeping head.

Retaining a now barely discernible kink, the cat has its tail. As much as I don't like having my toes attacked, I'm glad those few inches of fur-covered bones are still there to warn me when it's time to run for cover.

February 14, 1994

How to Catch a Cat

I DASHED INTO THE LAUNDRY room. Our old tom cat woke up, looked at me guiltily, and jumped off the blue jeans I was after. I opened the back door, "Scat!" He left.

I yanked on the jeans, smoothed my hair, and rushed out the door to visit a friend.

She greeted me at the door. Behind her, two sleek, well-groomed cats nervously prowled. They refused to be cuddled. They ignored us as we sat down and she told me about them.

"Shortly after I moved here," she said, "I decided I wanted a kitten. I saw an ad for free kittens. I went expecting to choose and pick it up after I had time to purchase cat supplies.

"The kittens were not healthy. They looked so miserable that I told the people I would take them both. I left them with the vet with instructions for him to do what he could. I did not expect them to live. I did not want to see them die. They survived. A week later, the vet called. He told me to come get them. With medicine, time, food, and love they'd live."

When they stopped their nervous prowling, I was amazed to see them lay on the towels placed on the couch and chair.

"How did you train them to that?"

She laughed, "I didn't. I put the towels where they slept."

I shifted to look at the one sleeping at the end of the couch where I sat. It opened its eyes, looked at me, and got up to leave.

As the cat passed my legs, its whiskers twitched forward. The cat looked up at me, started to move away, sniffed, and did a feline double take. It inched towards me. Step by step, whiskers alert, the cat came closer and touched its nose to the leg of my jeans. It stayed there, sniffing and walking around, looking at me but not moving away.

As it sniffed me, the other cat quit playing with its ball and came over to warn it away. The second cat did a double take and began nosing my jeans.

Their mistress watched, laughing in amazement. "You should have seen the last visitor. She loves animals. She has a couple of dogs and horses. She worked the whole time she was here to get them to come to her. They ignored everything she did to entice them."

"Probably the smell of dog on her clothes scared them away."

"Maybe, but they are always cautious around people. They never seemed to get over that home where I got them. What is your secret?"

I shrugged. I was amused, but I really did not know quite what to do with two cats moving in close and sniffing my legs so thoroughly.

"Wait a minute. I bet I know what it is. We have a male cat which has developed a strong odor. Sometimes it is almost like living with a skunk. I keep him outside now, but the kids let him in this morning. He sneaked into the laundry room and was sleeping on my pile of clothes when I went in there to get this pair of jeans. Those cats aren't attracted to me; they are attracted to his smell left on my jeans. I probably smell faintly as bad as he does." She politely said she had not noticed any smell.

As I left, I told her, "Tell the animal lover, next time rub up close to a tom cat before coming. It seems to be a surefire method with your cats."

June 20, 1994

Mothering Instinct

WITH A HOUSE FULL OF children since the day I married, I've learned to tolerate the critters they call pets. As long as the pets keep out of my way, they can stay. I have even fed some occasionally. Especially this fall, after my last son went off to college and left behind his only sister, something has changed. I'm not sure exactly what.

I noticed it recently when the black cat joined me as I started to wash the clothes.

This cat loves to watch the movement of water. At the sound of a flush or turning on of a tap, she becomes a black streak heading for the moving water. Shortly after she came, she stuck her head inside the shower curtain to watch the water spraying out of the shower head while another son, home for a visit, was taking a shower. My son did not care if that cat only wanted to watch the shower of water. He objected to her invasion of his privacy.

So when I started the washing machine recently, I knew what the cat wanted when it jumped up on the dryer and stared inside the wash tub. I held the button down to keep the machine running with the lid open so the cat could watch the water sloshing around the washing machine.

I actually asked my daughter to fix the switch so the cat could continue to watch the water. This is not the Joan of a houseful of children.

Worse are the silent fish my son left behind when he went to college. My daughter and I take turns feeding them. They may be limited to swimming circles in their tanks, but those fish have developed a staring technique that sends me rushing for their food, even when I've already fed them for the day.

Those cotton-pickin' goldfish swim to the end of the tank nearest to the door and stay there. All of them are lined up with their faces to the glass looking expectantly through the door, waiting for me to walk by, notice them, and toss them another handful of food.

If I am in the room reading a book or watching TV, they swim to the front of the tank and stare at me until I pitch in a few pellets to start a feeding frenzy. Their helpless look does it every time.

Until my son left them in my care, I ignored the things. Now I am at their every beck and stare.

I think with my sons gone and my daughter nearly full grown, I am looking for some poor helpless little ones needing my attention.

I can't believe I have written this column. Me! The one who has always scoffed at people who treat their pets as children substitutes! I am finding ways to entertain a cat and preparing snacks for goldfish with a starving stare.

It's so true. I actually caught myself asking our princely white cat as he waited at the back door, "Do you want to go outside?"

The cat gave me a scornful teenage stare and waited for me to slide the door open. Old age and my fast emptying nest have gotten to me. I need to get a life.

January 15, 1996

Rabbits are Cute...In a Cage

OUR YOUNGEST CHILDREN WERE RIDING the miniature train at the county fair several years ago, when my oldest ran up to me. "Where's Mert?" he panted frantically.

I blinked. "I don't know. I think he went in the exhibit building."

"I need him to toss the ring around the duck's neck so I can get a real live rabbit free. I tried six times, but I can't do it. Tell him I'm down there."

He pointed and ran that way.

The children's ride was over. We ambled around looking for Mert and found my husband. "Mark wants Mert at a booth with rabbits."

He went looking for Mert.

Mert emerged from the exhibit barn just as Mark charged back down the fairway. "Mert! Come on. I need you to throw the ring around the duck's neck. Then we can get a free rabbit."

Little brother asked no questions. He followed big brother through the crowd, past the cotton candy, to the game where they gave away stuffed or real rabbits as prizes.

I saw immediately why he had to have a rabbit. They were lop-eared rabbits. Long, soft, fuzzy ears drooped mournfully around the reflective, rabbit faces. They looked warm, cuddly, and pathetic. I wanted one, too. Mark shoved yet another ticket into the barker's hands, took the rings, and handed them expectantly into Mert's hands.

Unruffled, Mert looked at the calm pool of duck decoys. He aimed and dropped that ring over the duck's head. It fell smoothly down the bird's neck.

The barker called to the passing crowd. "Win a rabbit like this kid did with one throw. See what you can do."

Several took up the challenge. Tickets changed into rings, the crowd pressed in, the decoys swirled in the wading pool. Rings bounced off the duck's backs and heads, but none slid down the necks.

As Mark picked out a freckle-faced bunny, Mert tossed in the remaining rings. He aimed as carefully as he had the first time. He never made it past the beak. Game over.

As the man handed Mark the rabbit, its strong hind legs kicked him hard. A startled look spread over his face. He wanted that rabbit. It did not want him. It wiggled. It squirmed. It fought to escape his grasp. I reached over to help him. One lucky rabbit's foot gouged my arm.

My husband arrived and was drafted to carry the writhing rabbit. The harder it kicked and fought to escape, the tighter his grip. Proud, excited, all eyes on our new, free rabbit, we headed for the car.

The last couple of tickets were passed to friends we met on the fairway. No one noticed that they had traded their last ride at the fair for a very angry rabbit.

No one noticed the angry scratch marks on their arms as we bought rabbit food and a water bottle and built a cage.

We had that rabbit a couple of years. All four children petted and played with it, but it never became a cuddly bunny.

Interest waned. I advertised "rabbit with food and cage: free."

A little boy, who wanted a free rabbit, made sure his dad drove over to claim it that day.

I hope it didn't kick too much on the way home.

September 19, 1996

Don't Smash My Spider

THE CAT SAT AT THE patio door, meowed, and looked at me expectantly, asking to be let out.

I sighed, shoved away from the computer, and pulled the drape back from the glass door, revealing a web stretched across the top half of the doorway. Busily spinning her way around the web was a fat, ugly garden spider. I cringed as I slid open the door. The cat walked out oblivious to the spider's presence overhead.

I shut the door. "Look at this," I called to my daughter.

She came over looked through the glass at our personal *National Geographic* picture.

"Eeooouww, gross," she shuddered. "Let's smash it."

"It's on the other side of the glass. It can't hurt you. Watch the way she hooks the strands of web to the anchor lines with her legs."

My daughter looked at me skeptically.

"No, I mean it. Come and look at this."

She reluctantly wandered over and watched the spider as it quickly spun, hooked, latched, and spun again round and round the center of the web, filling in the spaces.

"All that work and she will take it all down and start in fresh tomorrow," I mused.

With the porch light behind it and our dining room in front of it, the spider had an ideal location to be watched and catch bugs.

A moth hit the web. With split second timing, the spider dashed across the fine strands, lassoed it, tied it securely, and left it hanging.

"Dad, come see this," the once reluctant watcher called. He came and watched, then went to the front porch, and caught a moth seeking to be burned by the porch light. He brought it to the back door and tossed it in the web. The spider interrupted her work to zap and wrap that moth.

The next morning as I let the cat out, I was relieved to see that the web was gone. But that night, the spider was back and weaving another web. When I did not see it the third night, I assumed it had moved on.

As my daughter let the cat in, though, she looked around the corner and discovered the spider had spun her web in front of the back porch light. She caught a couple of moths to toss to it before going to bed.

Our once caterpillar loving toddler had become a teenager who claimed yet another critter as a pet. For weeks she dished up cat food, sprinkled fish flakes, and caught moths every night to toss at the spider's web. After three or four weeks she pronounced, "That spider is getting fat."

I looked, shuddered at its size, and kept away from the back porch. "What do you expect after force feeding it?"

"Right, and when it gets fat enough, I'm gonna' smash it."

"After all this time of feeding it, come on. Besides, it is probably fat with eggs it's about ready to lay."

She shrugged, "Well, maybe not."

A couple of mornings later as I let the cat out, all I could see of the web had been reduced to a few strands and a brown egg sack. It will be swept down when I do fall cleaning to rid the outside of all the spider webs and egg sacks. A little natural science education is one thing. A chorus line of spiders vying to entertain us is quite another.

October 21, 1996

Mole Joins the Family

THE CAT SCRAMBLED OVER OUR colorful, hooked throw rug. It pounced to the side, eyes focused on the gray, wiggling ball of fur burrowing under the rug. I reached down and pulled back the rug, "Look, cat, catch your mouse and take it out of the house."

The cat just sat there watching, as a mole, not a mouse, dashed toward the wall, scratching frantically to pull itself under something, anything.

"Eeeuw, yuk! Come here," I yelled at our resident teenager. "Your cat caught a mole and brought it inside." I grabbed a paper sack to hold the mole against the wall. The mole's spade-like paws hooked onto the edge of the sack, pulled mightily, and escaped.

I shifted the sack to hold it. "Hurry up!"

Its shovel like paws fought to find the edge of the sack again. The cat wandered over, eyes alert to the mole's every move, waiting for me to pick the thing up just as it used to wait for me to capture escaping hamsters it had cornered.

My teenaged daughter came in. "A what?"

"A mole."

"Let me see."

I pulled the paper back, revealing the silky, rich fur of a sightless mole, feeling its way to safety with its wide paws.

She laughed, "Don't let it get away. I want to keep it."

"You what!"

"I want to keep it."

Sure, we had once kept a baby possum and an infant wild rabbit, but I thought the fuzzy critter stage had ended when the hamster died last year. "All right," I agreed, "but it stays outside."

She came back with a large paper sack. Between the two of us, we guided it into that sack.

When her dad came home, she proudly showed off her newest acquisition. He pulled out my blue enamel pan and added dirt to make a mole safe cage.

Next thing I knew, they were studying Mr. Mole burrowing into the loose soil they had provided. My teenager reached into the pot, shoved aside the moving dirt, and picked up the mole.

"Look, Mom," she set the mole on the grass. Using its oversized front paws and long snout, it nuzzled under a tuft of grass and headed down.

"You better not let it go too far," my husband warned her. "Once those paws get a grip, it will be very hard to pull out." She pulled it back, let the mole angle underneath the grass one more time, then picked it up, and dropped it in the pot.

At least Mr. Mole won't be like the hamster that climbed to the top of its cage to claw and chew every night, seeking to escape. His instincts for safety and escape keep him digging down under the dirt, out of sight and sound, and that's where he can stay.

While I was inside making our supper, she drafted the next door neighbors to help hunt worms for the mole's supper. After supper, they shoveled dirt into our car top carrier, converting it into the largest critter cage ever at our house.

So once again our household has another furry critter for a pet. I doubt that it is the last.

April 21, 1997

Creepy Crawlers

"You killed my baby!" the woman's voice on the phone cried in the ear of the man who had sprayed her home for creepy, crawly critters.

The pest control guy froze in disbelief as visions of the end of his career and business flashed before him, "No. This stuff does not harm mammals. It can't have hurt your baby."

"It was outside in the bushes on the corner of the house," she wailed.

"In the bushes? What is your baby?"

"A spider." A big, fat, juicy garden spider had entertained her with its nightly webs.

Understanding and relief flooded the pest man. "I'm sorry, ma'am, but you called me out to kill your pests, and spiders are pests."

The woman immediately canceled the rest of the contract. She refused to have that pest company, or any other, come to her house again. Only for the invasion of water bugs and at her husband's insistence did she relent—just once.

When the pest control agent returned to deal with the water bugs, he worked cautiously around the favored spider as he did for a few other customers who liked to watch their spiders at work, but didn't want termites eating the foundation out from under them. His precautions were in vain, the spider was already dead. The cat had killed it.

Even though his insecticide had not killed the spider, the agent said, "Look, if you really like this kind of spider, we see them all the time. I'll bring you a whole box of them."

She welcomed him and the box of spiders, but has not relented again about having her house sprayed for bugs, according to the pest man who recently treated our home.

A spider and its web intrigued my new son-in-love. During our first visit to my daughter's new home, she proudly showed off a huge spider web highlighted against the night sky by the flood light. Her husband and his friend sometimes spent their evenings catching moths attracted by the light, tossing them into the web, and watching the spider dash over to zap the free food, she said.

It wasn't spiders but ants which totally intrigued one of my granddaughters last summer. She crept along the ground gathering them up in any handy container, insisting she was going to be a veterinarian until my husband said, "Oh, I thought you looked like an entomologist."

"What's that?"

"A person who studies insects."

"That's what I want to be," her face lit up.

Creeping, crawling creatures fascinate children.

My daughter loved to pet the furriest of caterpillars. When she found one, she would pick it up, let it crawl up her arm or between her hands, and stroke its furry back and sides bald. She offered me the pleasure. I smiled, kept my distance, and said, "I think you need to let the caterpillar go outside for a rest."

My son didn't pet the fuzzy caterpillar he found on the way to his first day of school. He stuck the furry little teddy bear into his pocket.

As he walked through the classroom door, he proudly announced, "Guess what I have in my pocket?"

"What?" his sweet, little teacher asked.

He reached into his pocket, "A caterpillar!"

She did not miss a beat. From behind her desk she gushed, "That's marvelous. Why don't you put it outside to wait for you while you are in class?"

He marched proudly over to the door and put his caterpillar on the ground. The caterpillar did not wait for school to end. My son never noticed. He knew where he could find a whole box of caterpillars to replace it.

February 3, 2003

Persistence with Pets Pays

THE PART SIAMESE CAT LIVED for two years in a sterile cage at the local animal shelter before my daughter and her husband found it during their search for pets the winter after they married. They also found a kittenish tabby. They took the felines home.

Predictably, the younger more frisky cat quickly won everyone's attention at last year's holiday gathering. She played with bits of holiday ribbons and toys dangled in front of her, batted at the fish in the tank, and purred when petted. The Siamese mix shambled around the periphery of the crowd, oblivious to everything around it including its matted fur. It usually managed to get to the pad of newspaper around the cat litter pan. Sometimes it made it into the litter pan. Mostly it ignored any hand reaching out to stroke it.

Just before my daughter graduated and moved away from college the following spring, the younger cat went prowling outside one afternoon and never returned. Only the fish and the Siamese mix joined them in their post college life.

The day I spent helping my daughter, her husband, and others pack the moving van, the Siamese mix curled up in the middle of our path. Other than having a bit neater fur and occasionally glancing at the crowd of movers stepping over it, the Siamese mix continued to be oblivious to the wider world.

It never ventured toward the open back door or looked curiously out at the activity on the porch and in the truck. The cat lay there watching us until my daughter hauled it out of the way into an empty bedroom where it stayed, never moving, until she put it into the cat carrier.

I saw the old cat again last week during a holiday visit with the family. Except for the fact that it still was a Siamese mix, I would not have recognized it. It no longer looked like a frumpy, old, half-blind cat. It was sleek and alert, almost as regal as a purebred Siamese. At times it even hinted it wanted to be picked up and petted.

From having spent years watching my daughter with our cat, I know exactly what happened. Whether it liked it or not, that frumpy old Siamese was picked up and dragged over to the couch to be petted and stroked right above its nose on its softest of fur while my daughter watched TV, read, or talked on the phone. Anytime she had a treat to give it, she encouraged the cat to pay attention, reach up, and be petted before it received the treat.

As we watched the movie *Radio* one evening during the visit, the cat lay draped over my daughter's arm with the most blissful look on its face. Not even one muscle twitched to jump down and slink off to a dark corner.

In a small way the cat reflected the truth of the movie about a mentally disabled man who once shambled awkwardly around a small community, saying nothing, avoiding people who had often hurt him. During football season the head coach in this true story caught team members tormenting the man whom he nicknamed Radio. The coach decided to do something. He began inviting the man to join him at practice. Over time, as increasingly more members of the community reached out to him, Radio began talking, interacting, and contributing. He became an intricate, well-loved member of the community.

Persistent loving attention paid off for both the cat and the man. Both stories are inspiring, but the benefits emerge as especially rewarding for the whole community as each individual focused his care and concern on one whom they had once disregarded.

January 5, 2004

What Goes Up Will Come Down

CAT OWNERS DESPERATELY WANT TO help their treed pets.

Ken Sinclair of Portland, Ore., climbed thirty feet into a fir to rescue his kitten, Breather. The cat came down without any help. Sinclair had to be saved by firefighters, according to an Associated Press story last week

I understand Sinclair's impulse. We had not seen our cat Harusun for a couple of days. But, we did hear a loud, pathetic, feline plea in the backyard. It came from the top of a mature loblolly pine where our gray cat paced a branch about forty feet off the ground, too afraid to come down the way it went up. We've been through this before with this cat.

The first time, it climbed a curtain and froze at the top. I reached up and lifted it off the curtain and down to the floor. It never climbed another curtain.

Next he climbed a tree overhanging the house, jumped to the roof, walked over to the edge of the garage, and whined, "Help me down." I rolled my eyes and told him to find the tree. Someone took pity on the poor young thing, grabbed a ladder, and lifted him down.

A week later he did the roof routine again. It took him a couple of days, but he figured out how to get down.

So when the cat mewed from the tree top, we shrugged it off, at least initially. After twenty years of cats, we remember what the veterinarian said the first time we had a treed cat. "No one has ever found a cat skeleton in a tree yet. Put a dish of food at the base of the tree, call it, and see if it will come down."

My husband placed cat food at the base of the tree. He called to the cat. I called the cat.

Harusun looked at us, looked at the food at the base of the twenty-feet of branchless trunk, and gingerly made his way down three layers of branches before scrambling back up the tree.

After three days of intermittent cat pleas, my husband told me his plan for ascending the tree to rescue the cat. I told him we had a family trip planned that did not include a hospital visit.

My daughter came to visit and clicked her tongue invitingly at the cat. My husband told her his rescue plan. She told her dad he did not need to climb that tree to get that cat. It would come down. Her friend came to visit, listened to the cat, talked with her fireman husband and reported, "Firemen don't make cat runs."

The cat continued to mew and pace from branch to branch.

My granddaughter came to visit. She puzzled over the cat with her grandfather. With the granddaughter's help Mr. Fixit rigged up a rope and a basket to deliver food to the cat. The cat climbed down to the basket, ate the food, and settled down for a nap in the basket.

Grandpa and granddaughter did a celebration march, grabbed the end of the rope, and began easing the basket with the cat down.

Something happened to the rope. Cat, basket, and food dropped quickly. Harusun hit the ground on a run.

For the next several days when he wasn't eating, Harusun hugged the cement on the front porch, refusing to even go out on the lawn to stretch up with his claws and scratch his favorite climbing tree.

July 3, 2006

Never Let Them See You Sweat

OUR OLDEST SON SHRANK BACK in horror at the crawdad his father found in a ditch. "Just touch it. It won't hurt you," my husband urged the eight-year-old.

The child whined, refused, and wiggled away from it.

I knew that reaction well. I used to feel it all the time as a child but without the sounds or actions. I knew better than to let my brothers or cousins see or hear my repulsion and fear when they returned victorious from exploring the shallows of the mossy creek bed looking for crawdads. No way would I ever let them know I abhorred their collection of creepy critters.

As an adult I do not always have the luxury of fear. As an adult with children I had the onerous task of setting a good example, and this child needed to toughen up a bit. He needed to touch the crawdad. So, cringing inwardly I talked soothingly to him, reached out, and, for the first time in my life, touched a crawdad.

It felt kind of like a fingernail with long whiskery legs, waving its antennae.

Not that I volunteered to pick it up and let it crawl all over my hand, but, being the grown-up, I had set the example. I had touched it and had shown no fear. Seeing he was outnumbered by adults and younger siblings all contacting the crawdad, the squeamish child reached out his hand.

A few years later, again in the name of being a good example, I petted a snake for the first time. I didn't say I relished the experience. And, I only touched the creature because I was a chaperone of grade school aged children on a field trip when one girl whimpered, cried, and recoiled as the park ranger walked down the line of children towards her holding out a green garden snake for the kids to touch.

Other kids at least stretched out one tentative finger and touched it. She absolutely would not. The ranger did not even offer her the snake.

But there I stood, next in line, and that old "Adults Set the Example" rule dictated that I had to reach out and, for the first and last time, I stroked a snake discovering to my surprise that it felt like expensive ribbon.

Oh! So this is what I had been missing all those years. But, just because I adhere to the "Adults Set the Example" rule does not mean that I ever really quit the "I Hate Creepy Crawly Things" club.

A couple of years after touching that snake, I took the Anatomy and Physiology course mandated for science majors at Southern Arkansas University in Magnolia. The weekly lab included two sessions with live animals: a couple frogs one week, a live turtle the next week.

I won't go into the details, not out of sensitivity for my readers, but because after sitting way in the back and watching the preparation for the frog lab, I refused to stay and watch the other students and professor prepare the turtle for the experiment. I rationalized that as pre-med majors my fellow students needed the experience. I just wanted the credit to be certified to teach biology. I intended only to use preserved animals soaked in formaldehyde.

So that day I did not step up to the plate. I walked out and waited until we needed to take lab notes. Then I returned, sat on the other side of the room, took my lab notes, wrote my report, and maintained my dignity. I don't think I fooled anyone.

November 26, 2007

Foul Weather Friend

LAST WEEK'S COLD SNAP UNDERSCORED what a foul weather friend we have in our frumpy, old cat. In the heat of the summer she curled up in the middle of the concrete drive, soaking up the radiant heat. As the day waned, she aimed for her favorite perch of concrete slab in the back yard or climbed the fence to check out the neighbor's warm spots.

If we would leave the cat food dispenser outside in the garage as we used to do, the cat would rarely grace us with her presence from late spring to early fall. However, we quit serving the cat outside after we noticed critters flagrantly galloping into our garage to gulp down a week's worth of cat food. Neighborhood dogs, an opossum, and a feral cat or two treated our garage as a free buffet. So, we moved the food dispenser inside and our cat food bill dropped drastically.

Understanding our frugality and lack of hospitality to her distant relatives, the feline expects my husband to act as her personal lackey.

When she howls, he must come and turn the knob to open the door for her any time she beckons: 10 a.m. tea, 11 p.m. late night snack or 4 a.m. hunger pangs. Whatever the time, she wants service—NOW!

In the summer every few hours as hunger strikes, she lazily stretches, meanders up to the house, and commands her doorman to come to the front door.

My husband pulls himself out of his recliner and accommodates. She strolls in flicking her tail at him disdainfully, takes a few nibbles, and walks to the back door where she wails until her doorman puts his computer game on pause, stands up, and opens the door for her.

Day after day through the heat of summer, she treats our house like a fast food restaurant with a porter. In return, all summer she ignores my husband's invitations to come, sit on his lap, and purr while he pets her. She has no interest in being petted until the fall rains come. Cats don't like being wet. With soaking wet whiskers and her tail dripping, she begs to have the door opened. Once inside she stays until the rain stops or necessity forces her outside.

But it is the frigid days of winter that reveal the cat's true nature.

In the winter chill we double up on socks and layer on the clothes to keep warm.

Not the cat! She hollers at us to sit down on that couch, to get comfortable in that lounge chair and wait for her. The minute we stretch out after a long day, she walks over to us, scolds us for taking so long, and aims for the belly, the back, or a crook behind the knees.

She's not picky. She just wants our radiant body heat to warm her with a lot of petting to top off her pleasure. She demands to be petted. If we move our hands aside for the briefest of moments to turn the page of a book, pick up a phone, or just to rest, she lifts her head, looks around, and begins vigorously licking any bare skin she can find, especially any errant hand, arm, or fingers until we begin petting her again.

I can live the rest of my life without ever having another sponge bath from that cat, so I either pet her or show her the door.

The cat acts as if she can live the rest of her life without ever being held or petted as long the sun warms the dry cement. Let the temperature drop as it did last week and she is miffed if we refuse to sit down, roll over, or deny her room on our laps. The colder and wetter the weather, the more this cat cuddles up to us. She's such a nice cat, our feline, foul weather friend.

December 14, 2009

The Last Cat Leaves

I OPENED THE FRONT DOOR, instinctively took a quick half step back, and glanced down, keeping an eye out for a hungry cat dashing in for breakfast as I ventured out for the morning newspaper.

But no feline creature surged over the door step to tangle up my feet. Again I realized that after twenty-seven years of having a cat or two waiting for me at the front door, we no longer served any cat.

Earlier this year, courtesy of my daughter, we had two cats. The oldest, Kramer was, a sixteen-year-old tortoise shelled cat my daughter had adopted as a kitten and left with us when she went to college. Kramer loved our warm laps in the winter and shunned us for the heated cement driveway in the summer. We also had Pirate who was exiled to our house after he stretched luxuriously and left a scratch on the grandbaby's face.

"Nothing mean about what the cat was doing," my daughter assured me. "It was just being a cat." But her littlest one did not yet understand giving a real live kitty a break from her petting. We inherited cat, cage, litter box, and sack of food.

Our cat-in-residence sniffed, spat, and turned her back on the interloper, barely tolerating his intrusion at meal times. She sulked off to a corner and watched him take over the family and the house. If he was in, she was out; if she was in, he was out. She did not care for the intruder.

My door duties increased to monitoring the cat exchange as they switched places hissing and spitting as they swapped front porch and front room. They took turns demanding to be petted when my husband or I sat in the lounge chair. They took turns waiting by the front door in the morning for a game of "trip the lady of the house." I usually more or less missed them, but one morning no cat greeted my husband when he went out to pick up the morning newspaper. He quickly found the body of our elderly cat in the yard. He could not find any obvious reason for the end of its time with us. He buried it in the back yard and petted Pirate a bit longer that day.

The hot summer days warmed the cement for Pirate, our solitary feline who was sorely missed by our three-year-old grandson and his little sister who could now stand up for herself. We made no plans to move Pirate back home. They had plenty to do and we had no plans to visit. Then a late afternoon call sent us snatching up clothes, suitcases, and plane tickets for a family emergency.

Not knowing how long we would be gone, we told (we did not ask) my daughter that we would also be packing up the cat and all its trappings. That would be her contribution to helping out during the family emergency. Pirate entered his old home, sniffed, walked around to remap the house, and settled in for the long haul. After being there two weeks he proved as amicable as ever. By the time I returned home, he had settled in again with my daughter. She visited me a week later, without the cat, her kids, or her husband.

We shopped, cooked, and sewed together for several hours. Towards evening she commented, "It's quiet in your house." That is the sound of an empty nest devoid of even the presence of pets demanding to scamper inside for their 4 a.m. breakfast.

October 18, 2010

Pirate and the Blue Jay

CURLED UP ON THE FLOOR beside a toddler, the sleek, young cat filled the bill for a child friendly pet. Tolerant of hands poking his yellow eyes and ruffling his black fur, only the neighbors saw Pirate's dark side as he quietly prowled the seas of grass and overhanging trees searching for movement. A stealthy stalk, a quick pounce, and Pirate hooked another mouse, mole, or bird to present to his family with a posture that said,

"Look, what I caught!"

Cats will be cats until the backyard Mafia gets on their tail.

Last week in the back yard a cacophony of screeching birds interrupted the human adults' conversation and the preschoolers' play. They turned in time to see Pirate leap over the neighbor's fences with feline grace, carrying a half grown blue jay in his mouth followed closely by a flock of blue jays and three black birds.

The blue jays swooped down chattering, scolding, screaming and pecking their protest at Pirate's invasion of the nest. The Mafia of black birds attacked with a vengeance. No black soulless creature better try to steal a little bird when they are in town!

The bird's age did not matter to Pirate. He saw food and fun. He had legitimately stalked the nest and grabbed a fledgling to bring home to fulfill the old saw "The cat doth play and after slay."

Intent on his game before his meal, he ignored the extra humans in his back yard. Down still fluffed the chest of the kidnapped blue jay. It had flying feathers, but they needed another few days of growth before they would fly.

Preschoolers, toddlers, and adults stared at the black cat guarding the brightly colored blue jay lying limp as a corpse on the ground. The children wanted to check out this phenomenon.

The mother of the house believes the adventures of the Discovery Channel begin in the back yard. "You can look, but you have to hold your hands behind your back. Do not touch it or get too close. That's the cat's catch."

Pirate stood guard over his pile of feathers as the little tikes stepped forward to study it. The blue jays continued to dive and peck the cat, driving him away from the captive. The birds looked at the humans only long enough to see that they kept away before they fearlessly, incessantly screamed at the cat to let their little one go. The cat dodged the bird attacks and tried to guard his catch. It was no use. Considering his odds against a flock of protective blue jays and the black bird Mafia, Pirate left with as much dignity and speed as he could muster.

As quiet settled and the reserve force of blue jays and black bird Mafia left to protect their own nests, the momma and poppa bird chattered and walked around the young bird. It lifted its little head, looked around bleary-eyed and panting. Poppa bird stood in front of his offspring, coaxing, and prodding it. Momma bird chirped encouraging words to the fledgling, reassuring her offspring that it still could hop, skip, and jump.

The little fellow hopped; he flapped his too-small wings. The parent birds stayed on the ground near their fledgling, encouraging it to keep trying. Once, poppa bird glanced at his audience of toddlers, preschoolers, and parents. As long as those humans stayed away from him and his baby, he ignored their proximity and kept coaxing the little one to get away from this open space, to head for the bushes and trees.

The baby bird slowly took stock. He looked at momma and poppa bird and hopped over to the shelter of a nearby bush, then up a branch or two. Bit by bit, with his parents coaching him, he moved under, and then up into the safety of the bushes. It took time, time the humans did not have. They drifted off to play, fix supper or pick up their conversation, returning intermittently to check on the bird's progress.

Birds and people breathed easier when the fledgling found shelter from that Pirate sneaking up to steal from the family nest.

May 23, 2011

Live and Learn

Book Thief

HE'S BEEN AT IT AGAIN. The book thief has invaded my bookshelves, my piles and closets of books, sorting through the paperbacks and hard covers, quietly, unobtrusively shifting the books from my pile to HIS.

It started so innocently. I bought books at garage sales, book stores, and through the mail. We read some. Others were placed on the shelves to be read in the future. I even gave some to him, shrugging away my ownership at the joy of seeing him read.

He started out so young, so innocent, so interested in biology. I still haven't figured out what happened.

I thought I bought the books about trees for my botany class. Somehow they became his property.

The family subscription to *National Geographic* became his when everyone else only looked at the pictures. I actually read a couple of articles in each *Science News*, but he read everything else and fussed when the pile was not in chronological order and in his cupboard.

"You can have them!" I thought. "I'm through with those college courses anyway."

He became interested in religion: Historically, theologically, and inspirationally. Whole shelves of my books disappeared only to reappear on his bookshelves.

I know I recommended the books to him. I know I hadn't read them in years, but still!

I went on the defensive and bought used books in subjects I thought interested him. I left the new books near the books he owned but stored at home.

He came home from college, quietly smiled his thanks at my finds, and began cataloguing them. I relaxed until I noticed that the bottom shelf of my bookshelf was empty. The book thief had struck again.

I'll never know which ones he took. Some have sat there unread for years.

It's that awful college's fault; they made him purchase his own books. They told him to make notes in his books, to underline important passages, to make the books his. He discovered the power, the joy of reading and owning a book.

He discovered a used book store in the college town with out of print books that intrigued him. He discovered a book mail service and began buying books.

One day after receiving his latest shipment of books, he called to proudly announce, "My books take up seven feet of space!"

I resisted asking, "How many of those books began as MINE?"

Every time he comes home he brings more books that he has read and wants me and his brother to read. I'm only forty-three inches of books behind him. (His brother is at least fifty inches behind.)

He pores over his books like a miser over his gold. He counts them. He writes down each title, author, and synopsis of content. Then he puts them away in alphabetical order.

He knows what he has read. He knows which books he owns, but he can't remember which ones came from my bookshelf.

He's already promised to bring more when he comes back for Christmas. I have a couple I think he ought to read, but he better give them back when he is through.

December 13, 1993

Literary Diversion

I LIKE TO KEEP A book handy to read. Any old book will do. Since I only had a dozen left to read the last day of the used book sale at Magale Library at Southern Arkansas University, I filled a couple of grocery sacks with books, including an in-depth study of the physiology of fish reproduction. I thought someone might want it. At home I shoved aside the stacks of books in the linen closet to make room for my latest finds.

I was too late to buy anything except textbooks at the community college book sale, so I made sure I got to the public library's book sale at the mall soon after they opened. I found a couple of dozen other books for the closet. As I thrust them in, I vowed to sort through and straighten up the mess as soon as I got back from checking out the weekend garage sales for books and dropping off a dessert at church.

The problem with garage sales is that they tend to have stacks and stacks of formulaic romance novels and nothing on the physiology of fish reproduction. I did find a couple of children's books I hadn't read though.

My dessert made it to the church kitchen, but I did not make it home in time to sort books. I was too busy sorting through our church library's discards. The Christian education director had decided to get rid of them at a dime apiece.

Replacing our lost copy of the *Egermeier's Bible Story Book* for a dime was a steal. I stocked up on the old devotionals and Christian biographies that one of my sons had requested and left with fifty books. Those went on the floor in the bedroom with the bookshelves my husband built.

Sunday morning the rest of the leftover books at church were relabeled, "Free, help yourself." I added thirty to our overflowing pile.

I didn't bother to shelve anything. My son would do that when he came home from college in a couple of weeks. I knew he was bringing more to add to his books heaped in the bedroom closet.

Was it only two years ago when he called from college to proudly announce, "I have seven feet of books"? They now stretch out thirty-seven feet.

Later, when the bibliophile returned from college, we spent a half hour of quality time in front of the free books in the church in deep conversation.

"You have to read this one. That is a good author, take it."

Staggering in with our load of books, we decided it was time to sort books, organize shelves, and eliminate a few. He was overwhelmed with the number of biographies I had found. I sadly agreed it was time to kick out the Hardy Boys. For a week he hid in the bedroom sorting books by topics and authors, discarding ones he did not want, and some I did want. He helped himself to any book he wanted from my shelves. I started to protest until I realized he had to dust them and I could borrow them back. In the end two boxes of books made it to the garage. They held our Hardy Boys mysteries, the overflow of biographies, and the book on the physiology of fish reproduction. For some reason no one wanted to read it.

June 3, 1996

Reading is So Doing Something

SATURDAY I DID ABSOLUTELY NOTHING, zilch, zero, nada. Friday afternoon, before my daughter's piano lesson, I had dashed into the bookstore to pick-up a Torey L. Hayden book. It was the last of her nonfiction books on my to-buy list.

Daughter tickled the ivories; I began reading.

Half an hour later, I reluctantly put down my book and drove her to church to practice for Sunday's offertory with Linda, who promised to bring her home.

I sped home and plunged into bed with my book. I only left my nest of blankets to fix a simple supper and put clothes through the washing machine and dryer.

Hubby, busy as an elf, sanded his latest building project. When the piano player finally came home, we sat down to supper—my book close at hand.

After supper, I dropped onto the couch, read a couple of chapters, and fell asleep. I woke at 9 p.m., tried watching TV, and switched it off. It was tedious, predictable, and annoying. The rest of the family was in bed.

I picked up my book and read the rest of it. At half past midnight, I laid the book down with a happy sigh. There is absolutely nothing like a good book with a realistic but happy ending. I went down the hall to the bedroom, slid into bed, and slept contentedly.

The next morning I woke up enough to shove my daughter out the door at 9:30 to clean house with a friend. Her father was already busy slapping varnish on the smoothly sanded wood.

I had the house to myself. I grabbed the James Herriot book I had started before the holiday rush and read until I fell asleep.

I woke up from my morning nap, shifted a few clothes from the washing machine to the dryer, folded others, and began cooking beef for vegetable soup.

My feet chilled from walking barefoot on vinyl floors. I warmed them in a tub of hot water. I read more tales about the highland vet as my cold, cold toes thawed out in hot, hot water, only to have them chill again when I went to pick up my daughter and her friend from their Saturday morning job.

They wanted to shop. I wanted to read. I gave them a time limit, picked up the book, and read until they returned right on time.

The friend came to visit with my daughter while I read. They chatted and watched tedious Saturday afternoon TV which was absolutely no competition for a good book, especially a good book and another hot bath. I crawled out of the hot water into bed and took another nap.

At 7 p.m. I tried to watch a couple of my favorite shows. Halfway through a new episode, I realized I wasn't listening. I already knew everything that was going to happen in the next half hour. I turned it off and called all my grown children long distance. They were all out for the night.

I called it a day and went to sleep.

Monday night I called again.

"You don't sound as tired as you have lately," one of them noted.

"I'm not. All I did Saturday was sleep, read, and eat. That's the first chance I've had to relax since the holidays, our anniversary, and the science fair rush. It was great. I should do it more often."

February 17, 1997

I Snap, You Jump

I USED TO SCARE MY daughter every time I snapped my fingers. With a tremor in her teenage voice she now says, "When I was a little kid, I would jump out of my skin at the snap of death from my mom."

I wish I had that effect on my sons. With them, I no longer snap my fingers. I also keep my mouth shut.

When my first son went to college on a scholarship, I was very aware that he had to maintain a reasonable grade point average to keep that scholarship. Too low and his scholarship would disappear.

His dad and I worried more about his keeping that scholarship than he did. He would call home and tell us about the fun he was having, the parties and how late he had stayed up. The night he had an English paper to write he called and talked to us from the hall because his dorm room was overflowing with friends. Three hundred miles away my fingers were snapping at him to quit partying and start writing.

The only time he asked for my help came when his checking account was overdrawn, and he could not balance it with the bank's statement. He prefaced his request for help, "but I don't want you to ask any questions about any of the checks."

I helped him balance his account. I only raised my eyebrows over a couple of checks as I smashed my fingers into silence and bit my tongue as I had done when his grades skidded shockingly close to the college cutoff. After that he maintained his checkbook and scholarship without my help.

He says he made it to graduation because, "I mowed lawns one summer, and I knew I didn't want to do that the rest of my life." A month after graduation he nailed a job, announced his engagement, and began a forty hour work week.

His brother went three hundred miles in the other direction to college. About the second month he actually called to ask my advice about his honors calculus. After four semesters of calculus and hearing his problem, I immediately knew how he could solve his problem: "Go talk with your professor."

It wasn't so easy to sit back when the business office had a snafu with his scholarships. I wanted to march into that office and clear it up for him. I couldn't, so he made repeated trips to the financial aid office until the funding was released. I so wanted to snap my fingers just once at someone in that office.

Parenting at a distance is easy compared to having a son taking classes while living at home, as I have had this summer. Because I was a scared, nontraditional student, I think my son should have the textbook in his hand every minute of the day that he is not in class or working in the lab. No matter how many times I tell myself, "He's managed to keep his scholarship for three years without your help; he can handle one summer class," my fingers still itch to make him jump. Thank heavens by the time you read this, the class will be over, and my fingers can give it a rest or find something else to snap about.

August 13, 1998

The Doctor's Waiting Room

MANY PEOPLE GO TO THE dentist's and doctor's offices for medical reasons. I go to read the magazines I am too cheap to buy. With a twice yearly visit to the dentist's office, a yearly physical, a stop or two at the hospital lab, and a couple other professional visits, I fill my quota of short stories, tips on raising children and losing weight. Plus I enjoy a few minutes of relaxation in a living room setting with no dirty dishes on the end tables or dust sifting down from the ceiling fan.

So it was with anticipation last week that I decided I had time to go for all the visits I had put off during our spring rush to three graduations. With my calendar free at last of perpetual activity, I figured I could begin to fill my calendar with medical appointments.

On Tuesday, I wrote down a list of phone numbers I needed to call. It usually takes me about two weeks before I can make an appointment to see the dentist, a month to six weeks for a physical, and maybe a week to ten days for a consultation. So I estimated it would be mid-July before I would go to my last appointment.

Tuesday I picked up the phone and began calling. When I hung up a half hour later, I had appointments Friday morning, Monday afternoon, and Tuesday afternoon. So much for leisurely stringing the visits out over the summer, they all had openings now.

Friday morning I walked past the stack of magazines on the coffee table, promising myself a look as soon as I took care of the insurance. I was met at the desk, greeted, and escorted to the office. So much for an early morning magazine read.

Monday I left work early saying I would not return. I had to spend the rest of the day either in the waiting room or exam room.

At the office I signed my name on the ledger, found a comfortable couch, and had a whole five or ten minutes of reading before the nurse escorted me back to the examination room. Within half an hour of the time I walked in, I was back on the street minus the doctor's fee, holding a form to get blood work done.

I still had lots of afternoon left, so I drove by the medical lab to see if I could read their magazines before having my blood drawn. T h e y didn't have time to wait for me to read magazines. They showed me to a bloodletting room, pricked a hole in my arm, and filled a test tube. I gave up on having the rest of the afternoon off and went back to work like a responsible, healthy citizen.

Tuesday I planned on taking a long, late lunch break to peruse the very up-to-date magazines at my dentist's office. I never had a chance to even sit, let alone read. The assistant escorted me from the door to the examination chair.

The dentist poked, scraped, and pronounced me cavity free for now. His assistant polished my teeth, and I was back on the street with a half hour left of my lunch hour.

If this week's rate of medical efficiency continues, I might just have to buy my own magazines to read.

June 21, 1999

Putting Family First

THE UPWARDLY BOUND CAREER WOMAN had it all: career, handsome and successful husband, two healthy sons, two new vehicles, and a large beautiful, two-story, four-bedroom home on the edge of an idyllic golf course overlooking the water. The house was filled with top-of-the-line new furniture. The garage overflowed with yard toys and tools. Boxes of prepared foods and snacks crowded the freezer and pantry shelves.

Her husband was off working somewhere as she told me about her long hours spent at two jobs building her professional career, earning money to pay two mortgages, two car notes, buy more stuff, and the speech therapy and special preschool her youngest child needed after being traumatized by an abusive babysitter, a situation that her oldest child told her about for months before a change was instituted.

She talked incessantly.

I wanted to say, "slow down, take a deep breath, and ask yourself, 'Which is more important: family or career, house, and possessions?'" I still wonder. I watched her give the children food, videos, games, and toys. I never saw her sit down with them and listen.

It is easy to do that. I have eased in that direction more than once. The first time I had just landed a small part time job as a newspaper stringer. All I had to do was attend three or four business meetings a month and report what happened. I could do feature and community stories and take pictures, but I received no pay for my time, only so much per picture and so much per inch of copy.

I didn't care. I was being paid to sit at my Smith Corona manual typewriter and report what I saw and heard. I fell to the task enthusiastically. When my three sons, who were under seven years old, came to me with books to read, I would mutter, "Just a minute I just want to finish this."

They were fed, bathed, clothed, and put to bed, but not noticed—at least not until one son slashed our newly installed window screen, broke the neighbor's potted plants, and shredded their newspaper.

As I sat watching him clean up the mess, I did a bit of reflecting. This kid was telling me something as loudly as he could, something besides he needed a spanking.

What had changed? I had changed.

I didn't quit the job, but I did put it into perspective. Story time resumed. My budding career in journalism slowed down. I went to the meetings, wrote feature stories, and took pictures, but I also covered up the typewriter and listened to the children.

I would like to say I never made that mistake again. I can't. However, I did learn to listen to the children's actions and words and to repeatedly reconsider, "Which is more important, the job, or the family?".

I guess that is what bothers me about the young career woman I met. Both her sons communicated that there was a problem. She knew one needed extra attention, at least speech therapy, but she focused on her beautiful home and the importance of developing her career. Her sons had quit begging to be the focus of her attention. Too bad! To do so would have changed her focus. It would have meant less time at work and in town shopping but greater emotional riches now and in the future.

August 31, 2001

Six Weeks with Dr. Seuss

SIX WEEKS OF SILLY SENTENCES from *Dr. Seuss's ABC* supplied our children with more than an introduction to the alphabet. Instead of television and Sesame Street, we went down the street to the library and loaded up every week on books. "Mom the Magnificent Reading Machine" preferred to have a fresh set of books on hand when a child said, "Read to me."

As the new mother of a ready-made family, I quickly discovered the wonders of children's literature for my four-year-old, especially Dr. Seuss's *ABC Book*.

As many times as I have read it since then, I should have purchased a copy of the book with my first couch student. Instead, I checked and rechecked it out of the library every time I decided it was time to teach one of the children to recognize the letters in the alphabet.

It took a few readings to realize just how many things I could teach with that one book. Of course I pointed out the big and the little letters, but we also worked on numbers as we counted David Donald's dozen doughnuts, four fluffy feathers on a Fiffer-feffer-feff, ten tired turtles on a Tuttle-tuttle tree, nine new neckties, and a nose. The alliterations also included a lesson in colors with an orange owl, red rhinoceros, pink pajamas, and a yellow yak. For 'L,' I touched his left leg and read, "left leg" usually followed with my added, "right leg," and tap on his other leg.

As Seuss progresses through the alphabet, he provides periodic reviews of previous letters that parallel the traditional ABC song. By the time my first couch student could recognize his letters, he had pretty well conquered the song as well.

Oh, the wonderful things I could do with Dr. Seuss' letters, numbers, colors, phonics, spatial differences, and the alphabet song!

And all it took was six weeks of reading the same book every day to the same child along with a couple of other fun books.

Before the six weeks were up, "Mom the Magnificent Reading Machine" muttered in her pillow, "Many mumbling mice are making midnight music in the moonlight...mighty nice."

The book became a standard in our home for teaching children their letters. The learning time varied with each child. One child, in particular, left me wondering how much he had learned. Then a friend stopped over to chat one day, and my current couch scholar showed her our book of the month.

She smiled, opened to the back of the book where all the letters are arranged, pointed at them one by one, and asked him to identify each symbol. He eagerly played "the letter" game as I stood back and watched. I held my breath and shook my head slightly when she pointed to R. I knew he did not know that one yet.

Without hesitation, he answered, "R." Thanks to a daily dose of Dr. Seuss, he had nailed the alphabet.

Having read the book for forty days with so many, I can recite it without the book in hand. I only discovered how completely the memorization had taken root when my grandchildren reached ABC learning time. My son and I swapped Dr. Seuss quotes, relishing shared knowledge and the experience of teaching a child.

I knew the circle had come full round when we finished, "Big Z, little z, what begins with Z?..... I do, I'm a Zizzer, Zazzer, Zuzz as you can plainly see."

March 21, 2005

Copycats

I ENJOY VISITING GRANDCHILDREN MORE when I invite them to join me in my activities.

"Come break a couple of eggs for tonight's cake and help set the table," I urge them. They also seek to join me in my activities.

When I picked up my cross stitch to while away the hours during a trip last summer, they all wanted to try the skill. Fortunately, I had three extra needles and easy to stitch six-count cross stitch material.

From that point on I did little on my project. They kept me busy untangling their threads, threading their needles, and drawing designs for them to stitch.

I should have remembered all that when I picked up a basket of note cards and bid the oldest visiting granddaughter to come with me to write a note recently.

She sorted through my selection of note cards with beautiful flowers, magnificent scenery, boats, and cute puppies and kittens.

"Cats! I love cats. Cats are my favorite!" she exclaimed as she took one with a picture of kittens and began writing.

I chose scenery and had settled down to write, when her two younger sisters trailed in to see what we were doing.

"Writing cards to your cousins and aunt."

"I want to write a card," the bespectacled middle child insisted. She climbed up on the bed. I handed her a book and offered her the pen and pencil holder. She took a pen and began wading her way through the cards.

"Puppies! I love dogs. They are my favorite." She began grabbing all of the cards with pictures of dogs on them.

"Just take one. Then, if you want to do another card choose another one," I told her.

She wrote a couple words in ink, made a mistake, and reached for another card to start in again.

"No, just cross out the mistake and continue writing. Would you like a pencil instead? That way you can erase your mistakes."

She took the pencil.

Littlest sister quietly slid up on the bed with us. She wanted to write a thank you card. She chose cards with puppies and kitties without any declaration of favoritism. We all settled down to write.

I was scrambling for ideas to write when the littlest asked, "How do you spell thank you?"

I started to spell it out, watched her laborious, six-year-old printing, and decided it would be simpler if I jotted the word down on a piece of lined paper. Before she finished that evening, I had spelled out several words on the edge of the paper for her to copy.

Three little, towheaded girls scribbled away at their cards, thanking their aunt for a gift, telling their cousins they had had a birthday or would be having one, and mentioning other significant childhood news. Between helping them spell words, select cards, and address envelopes, I completed only a few sentences on my cards addressed to grandchildren.

When the oldest finished her first card, filled in her name with our return address, and asked how to address the envelope, I gave her my best guess without checking the family address list because I planned to slide all the cards into a larger envelope to mail.

It was not what I had planned for the evening's activities. It was not something I thought they all should do, but they asked to join the card writing party, demonstrating yet again that children enjoy learning and doing simple, every day activities with the adults in their lives.

October 5, 2005

Learning Something New

MANY MONTHS HAD PASSED BETWEEN my purchase of the large book on the history of trains and my pulling it out to give to my grandson, so I asked him if he was still interested in trains.

"Well, not so much," he admitted, but his face lit up as he reached for the book, "but I do like to learn about new things."

That is my favorite aspect of interacting with children—that look on their faces when they learn something.

The eager celebration of new information glowed from the face of another, first grader's face as she walked over to join me at the computer.

"Today my teacher told us how vegetables are different from fruits," she announced, a very satisfied, proud look on her face.

"Oh, and what is that?" I asked.

"Fruits have seeds and vegetables don't."

She reviewed the entire lesson and talked about the different foods that she knew were fruits because they had seeds. Then she looked at the bananas hanging on the handle of the can opener. "Do bananas have seeds?" she asked.

"Yes, but they are not very big. Banana plants actually come from part of another banana plant." She wandered off to absorb this new information.

The next morning, her older sister, up earlier than the rest, wanted to write a story. After a brief search for note paper, she sat on the couch, laboriously writing line after line.

"Grandma, listen. I wrote a story." She began reading, "I like hot dogs. I like cats. I like school. I like my sisters...." Her list went on and on.

"Honey, that is not a story," I said. "That is just a list of things you like."

"How do I write a story?"

I had to think quickly to cobble together a simple explanation of what makes up a story. "You have to say that you did something."

She sat thinking for a few minutes and began writing. After a while, she looked up and read, "I jump. I run. I like to write."

"That's better, you are doing something, but something has to happen. For instance, before you started writing you asked me for a piece of paper. You looked on the shelf, you could not find it at first, but you kept looking until you found one."

"Wait, tell me again so I can write it down," she said.

I went over the brief story of wanting, searching for, and finding a piece of paper. "Now, you write down what you did."

She wrote for a while.

"I found a piece of paper," she read.

"Almost, you need to have a problem that you solve. Like this, you needed a piece of paper for writing. Then write down what you did to get a piece of paper. Then write what you did with the paper. That would be a simple story."

She tried it again and came up with a simple story with a simple problem. Needing a piece of paper, looking for paper, asking for a sheet, finding it, taking it back to the couch, and sitting down to write a story.

For the next twenty minutes we alternately talked and she wrote until she had three vignettes that she could legitimately call stories. Nothing was close to a best seller, but each had a problem and a solution.

Tiring of our spontaneous literature lesson, she abandoned her pencil and paper, pulled out a math game, and asked her grandfather to play with her. Within minutes I overheard the two of them deep in a discussion on figuring out a simple math problem, and the learning continued.

February 6, 2006

No More Name Tags

THREE YEARS AGO, I GAVE my daughter a permanent magic marker to label everything she was taking on a mission trip to San Salvador. Last fall she left for college bearing only a driver's license with her name and address on it. It has taken years, but I have learned to let her go without excessive identification.

I began my lessons in letting go when she was barely old enough to tell people her name, let alone her address or phone number. That was the spring her church teacher decided to take a field trip to the zoo.

My sons had all been older when they went on their first field trip. My wiggle worm of a daughter with a bent to wander was pre-school aged. Until then I had only left her in the care of others in a controlled classroom setting or with a stay-at-home sitter.

The teacher planned to drive a couple of hours away to a large zoo with meandering paths and scattered buildings. She had several other mothers to help chaperone.

The trip was well planned. All I had to provide was a permission slip, a packed lunch, and my daughter.

We were up early the day she was to go. After a bath, she nibbled at her breakfast while I packed her lunch. As she dressed in an outfit suitable for the weather, I vaguely remember wondering, "What if she gets lost?"

A name tag was the obvious solution, except I knew name tags can be torn off and lost. I am sure there are plenty of logical explanations for what I did next, but looking back, I really do not remember why I did what I did: I wrote her name, address, and phone number on both of her arms. I looked her over, realized the information might rub or sweat off, so I knelt down behind her, lifted up her shirt, and wrote the same information on her back.

I don't remember where else I recorded her address. I do remember being quite pleased that I had found the perfect solution for identifying a lost child.

Once I had signed, sealed, and addressed her to be returned to sender in one piece (or in parts), we got in the car, and drove to the church to meet the other preschoolers. The other, unmarked children milled around us excitedly. Adults checked names, gathered up lunches, and stacked up sweaters and jackets.

I left her to ride the church van with her class and chaperones. I went home assured I had done what I could to keep her safe and clearly identified. I did not worry about her for the rest of the day.

She returned late that afternoon, safe and sound, sunburned, happily chatting about the animals, and without one letter of her name and address on her anywhere.

I have never seen ink wear off so completely or so quickly. No one ever said anything to me about it. I was too chagrined to ask if one of the chaperones had scrubbed it off before they left.

In retrospect, I suppose that was not the best solution. It did, however, soothe my fears enough to allow her to join her class on a field trip.

With that experience and many others in the years that followed, she went on a summer mission trip to San Salvador with only her clothes tagged and left for college last fall without one name tag on her anywhere.

April 10, 2000

My Husband, the Cheater

THE SIGNS EXISTED FOR MONTHS—EVEN years. I just did not see the whole picture. Maybe I did not want to see it. It is difficult for anyone, let alone a wife of many years, to face the facts as I have had to face them the last couple of weeks.

Finally, I admitted it.

My husband is cheating on me.

First it was with the simple things that we used to enjoy together: activities we shared with our children such as traveling, reading aloud Narnia books, meals. Of course, he did not have to do these things with just me, but then he began to exclude me from the things just the two of us shared together. I shrugged it off at first. He is retired and at home. I am at work. He has a lot of time by himself at the house and on the road.

I simply do not have the time to share all the activities that he does.

I could live with that…until the afternoon I discovered him inside our van grabbing a few stolen moments when he knew I would not be there.

"You do realize it would be more comfortable in the house?" I dryly commented as he looked up at me with just the hint of a blush.

"You really do not have to stay in the van running down the battery like that." I pulled the boom box out and plunked it down on the counter where he could see it.

"Oh, yeah," he said. He at least had the decency to look a bit embarrassed.

"Well, if you want to finish listening to that John Grisham book on tape, you can do it here in the house. You don't have to hide out in the van or wait until we take another trip." I snapped open the cassette case and thrust the cassette into the tape player.

"That's okay. I don't have to listen to it now," he quickly backed away.

Sure he backed away that day, but he could not resist Grisham's writing as read by an expert dramatist. He pretends he can live without listening to a suspense book read by a skilled actor, but he can't. The next day he met me at the door talking about Grisham's novel *The Chamber* about a man making his final legal appeals as he counts down the hours to his execution.

"He got you so you were thinking, "He really doesn't deserve to go to the gas chamber," and you are hoping that somehow he will get out of it," my husband mused as I unloaded groceries. Okay, so he fell under the influence of a very skilled author. The man did not have the decency to look abashed that he had finished listening to that book without me.

I cannot believe this is the same man who for years declared his total abstinence from novels. For years he has pounded into my brain that he just does not like to read.

Well, he certainly does like to listen. I know, because Grisham is not the first author with whom he has cheated on me.

I select and save these audio books for trips we take together. He drives. I do handwork. We both listen—together.

The first time he finished a book without me, I shrugged it off. He had had to drive on alone. I had already read the book. I knew he would enjoy it.

In the last month or so, however, the man has left me behind at least three times as he finished one John Grisham book after another, not on the road but in our house. I take the time to find the audio books. I save them to share with him when we travel together. And then he turns around and takes off to hear it through to the closing chapter without me. Some thanks!

Next time I'm taking a James Herriot book. All those veterinarian vignettes about people and animals will entertain him without the attention grabbing effect of a John Grisham page turner.

October 26, 2009

Grannie's Reading Boot Camp

"BUT I DON'T LIKE TO read," my granddaughter whined when I handed her a Nancy Drew mystery book.

"Read three chapters of it anyway," I said. It was after all not the first book I had suggested.

She reluctantly sat down and began reading. "What does this word mean?" She pointed to 'glints.'

"Shiny, sparkles in the sun," I said.

"Oh," she returned to reading, finished the three chapters, verbally summarized the adventures and assured me she had enjoyed the book—but thought I had asked her to read too much.

Later that day I picked up the book and skimmed over the pages. The cliff hangers at the end of each chapter kept me reading just a little bit more in the next chapters, reminding me why I had once eagerly read any Drew book I could find.

The next day she read another three chapters, then a fourth, and fifth "Because," she said, "it's getting pretty exciting."

"I bet it is," I agreed.

That evening we added another literary endeavor to her visit and printed out copies of the Lord's Prayer and the Twenty-Third Psalm for her to memorize. I chose them because recently I realized that many children and teens simply do not know these traditional Biblical passages rich with their blessings and promises.

"Read it out loud five times," I mandated. "You don't have to memorize it today, just read it out loud every day and eventually you will remember it."

As we took an afternoon walk around the block another day, she and I talked our way through the Twenty-Third Psalm insuring she understood what the ancient writing meant to her in this century. We had to run off more copies of each passage a couple of days later when her sisters arrived.

I introduced them to the summer reading and memorization program. Again I heard the inevitable whine, "I don't want to read."

When I insisted, they went to my bookshelf filled with books written for children and teenagers and grabbed picture books. "No, I believe you are old enough to read a Nancy Drew book or one of the other chapter books," I motioned to the shelves of books. Reluctantly, the oldest picked up a Nancy Drew book and began reading. A while later she asked, "What does 'apt' mean?"

"Capable, skilled, they are able to do something." I defined off the top of my head.

While I defined the word, the first member of my summer reading program had disappeared into the bedroom with her Nancy Drew book. Calls for her to come and join the others outside went unanswered until she emerged, a satisfied glow on her face, "I read the whole book. It's a good book. I'm going to start the next book tomorrow." And she did. I no longer closely monitor that she has read her three chapters a day. Her oldest sister reported she had read an extra chapter to find out what happened next.

The third granddaughter resisted my suggestion the longest. I pointed out several other short chapter books which I thought she might enjoy. After a false start or two, she picked up one of the Nancy Drew books. Two days later, as she sat reading across the room from me, she looked up and asked, "What does this word mean?" She spelled out 'prowler.' I pronounced the word and said, "Sneaking around like a burglar." She nodded and bent over her book again.

Between supper and bedtime, we added John 14:1-6 for daily reading with the goal of memorizing the passage. It takes about a few minutes a day to read through the verses. We hope that over time the concepts will saturate into the depths of their beings. Meanwhile we promise treats and rewards if they complete the tasks.

Last week when I talked over my granddaughter's activities someone said, "Welcome to 'Granny's Boot Camp'." It's an apt expression since only the ceiling light glints off the television sitting silently in the corner and all electronics have been relegated to the back of the closet out of view of any prowlers. They can enjoy all those things elsewhere. For this month I'm hoping they discover the wonder of a reading a good book, maybe learn a few new words, and catch a glimpse of their spiritual heritage.

July 12, 2010

Parenthood, Its Many Phases

Who's That Sleeping in My Bed?

THE AIR CONDITIONER WAS NOT working when the game of musical beds began to the accompaniment of ceiling fans.

Big Bear said, "My bunk bed is too hot. I'm sleeping on the couch." He flopped under the fan for the night.

Middle Bear said, "No draft, I can't breathe," and took a mattress from Big Bear's bunk and crashed on the floor in our room under our fan.

Little Bear got scared and came to wake me up. I stepped over Middle Bear and mattress as we went to Little Bear's room to talk.

When Little Bear calmed down, I said, "I'm going across the hall to Middle Bear's bed. I will still be able to hear you," I lied. As soon as I hit the bed, I was asleep.

That is, I was until Middle Bear, pillow in hand, standing silently in the doorway, woke me.

"Want your bed? I was only keeping Little Bear company." Half-awake I made my way down the hall, stumbling over the mattress on my floor before falling onto my own bed.

In the morning my husband asked, "What time did you come to bed?"

"Oh, about two or three, we were playing musical beds."

Two nights later the air conditioner was fixed. Middle Bear said, "I can't sleep. There is too much noise from the other bears and their friends. I'm sleeping in Big Bear's bed."

The next morning I found Little Bear on a folding cot. Big Bear was in Middle Bear's bed, the overnight company was on the couch and in Little Bear's bed.

More than hot rooms and company initiate the game of musical beds. One night I went to bed leaving the three bears watching TV. At 2 a.m. I woke up because the bathroom light was shining in my face. Rubbing my eyes sleepily, I got up, turned it, and the other lights off.

At Little Bear's room, I stopped. That was a mighty big bear sleeping in that bed. I checked Big Bear's room. That was a mighty little bear sleeping in that bed. And, Middle Bear was not in his bed, he was on the couch.

In the morning, I stopped Big Bear, "Why were you sleeping in Little Bear's bed?"

"Because Little Bear had never slept in my bed, and I had never slept in Little Bear's bed."

Only Goldilocks would have understood that or Little Bear's solitary game of musical beds alternating between bed and floor. Years ago after I had purchased a new set of matching bedding and put it on the bed, I didn't expect it. At bedtime, I folded the new covers back invitingly.

Little Bear looked at the bed, "I want to sleep on the floor."

I made a major mental adjustment, wistfully took the pillow from the bed, and spread a couple blankets on the carpet. Little Bear snuggled in and sighed happily, "Thanks."

So why am I surprised that Little Bear's bed, with its carefully arranged pillows and stuffed animals, is rarely slept in? Instead Little Bear grabs a blanket from the linen closet and sleeps on top of the color coordinated sheets and quilt so the bed won't be messed up by someone sleeping in it—at least not until someone begins a game of musical beds.

June 19, 1995

A Time for Everything

HOUDINI THE HAMSTER IS GONE. So are his escape artist friends. The rest were sold after waking my daughter one night too many as they chewed, clawed, and scraped their plastic palaces to escape.

Personally, I am glad to be rid of the night walkers.

With the plastic palaces gone, the princess discovered she had more space in her bedroom. She liked it a little too much.

She began sorting through her collection of fifty-nine trolls, selling, storing, or giving away all but her favorites.

I gasped when I heard what had happened to the 'must have' gift of recent years. But I bit my tongue; she could do with her gifts as she pleased.

But it wasn't enough. She wanted room, more room.

She sorted through the collection of stuffed animals I had found at garage sales over the years. From the beginning I said, "These are mine, but you may keep them in your room." She kept them, happily, until she began her quest for space. Then stuffed animals that fell into her disfavor were relegated to the attic and garage sale pile.

When I protested, she said, "You may keep them in your room." I left them in the attic.

Then her brothers began moving on with their lives and out of our home. The youngest son graduated from high school and into a college dorm along with our outdated computer, his CD collection and favorite fish. The middle one yielded his cot in the laundry room, gave up his summer monopoly of the lounge chair with the best lighting, gathered up his clothes, computer, collection of books, and returned to college. The oldest married and took all the odds and ends of furniture we could spare.

Little sister looked around and saw space. She began spreading out. Two hours after the last brother left, she was stripping pictures, plaques, and posters from the boys' bedroom wall. Two nights later the cot was her bed.

The boys' bedroom retains half of their bunk bed as well as a lounge chair, TV, VCR, and tapes. Her bedroom is her official clothes changing area where she stores her clothes, trolls, hamster, and my stuffed animals. The living room, minus a couple of lounge chairs, end tables, and lamps, has become her afterschool catchall and piano practicing chamber.

She eats breakfast in the kitchen and supper in the dining area. The bathroom she used to share with three brothers is all hers, but she still invades my bathroom every morning to steam roll her hair after I have it steaming hot for my own use.

Even the master bedroom has been compromised: she considers our bed the best for late afternoon naps and my closet a source of variety for her already extensive wardrobe.

When I told my sons how much their sister had taken over the house, one wrote back, "Try stringing barbed wire where you don't want her to be."

Sounds like a brotherly solution! If it gets any worse, this mother might try it.

September 25, 1995

Teenage Daughter

"Mom, I am five feet, six inches tall!" my daughter announced as she entered the kitchen. She checked her height and weight frequently these past couple of years with the measuring stick on our medical scales. Recently she was puzzled at a sudden weight gain until she measured her height. She had grown to five feet, six inches. For the youngest and therefore perpetually shortest member of our family, this was a major event.

"Hey, four more inches and you will be as tall as me," I said.

She wrinkled her nose, "How tall is Dad?"

"Just a couple of inches taller than you."

She had a hopeful look as she left for school that morning.

It was only three or four years ago that she topped her grandmother. In the Hershberger clan, children measure their entrance into the adult world by comparing their heights to their shrinking, under five feet tall grandmother. Every grandchild is delighted when they finally tower over their oldest relative.

As our children have grown, we have seen eyeball to eyeball with fewer and fewer of them. All five sons have outsized my husband, but they flaunt it in my face when they tower over me.

My daughter may not want to look down on me, but she enjoyed looking me right in the eye the other day when she was wearing the fashionably thick soled shoes, and I was barefoot.

Thank goodness my feet are still longer than hers, or I would be barefoot more often. She likes to borrow anything of mine that fits her. She wishes I were as svelte as a teenager so she could wear any or all of my clothes, as if she didn't already help herself. Recently I was admiring the blue shirt she was wearing to school that one morning when I realized, "Hey! That's my shirt! And she looks better in it than I do."

That's the difference between a daughter and a son. My daughter borrows rather freely from my wardrobe: jewelry, shirts, socks, but no shoes, yet. After twenty-plus years with five boys, it is so unexpected.

With sons, I never had to even think about them borrowing my T-shirts. I might borrow one of theirs, but they would never touch mine.

Granted, they did make a weekly pilgrimage to their dad's sock drawer for black socks to wear to church. On rare occasions they actually borrowed one of his ties, but it is not the same. They never even bothered to think about wearing his shirts, suits, shoes, or jeans, not even when they were close to the same size.

Having a teenage daughter caught me off guard at the closet door even having seen years ago that she would be like this. When she was three, I wore a full-length skirt with pictures along the hem. She stopped, stared at my skirt, and asked, "Can I have that to wear when I grow up?"

I was surprised as I looked down at this child who was then shorter than my skirt. "Yes, if you still want it," I promised. I gave the skirt away years ago, but she has more than made up for it, believe me.

March 25, 1996

Becoming Someone

"Someone, come help me tie my shoes," the four-year-old whined plaintively at the top of the stairs.

I looked around the dining room where I sat working at the sewing machine.

There was no one else in the house but the two of us. There had not been anyone but us for the past several hours.

That was the day I realized I finally was Someone.

After the wonder of each new baby passed, after all the company went home, Someone still had to change the diapers, soothe the tears, and wake up at 2 a.m. to nurse the infant. Only one person fit that description at our house.

After a day with three preschoolers, there were nights I wasn't too sure I wanted to be Someone, especially when I was too tired to even clear an emergency path through the clutter of toys and diapers before going to bed.

Nor was I thrilled to be Someone who loaded trash into the car to haul off to the dumpster. As soon as my babies were old enough to drive, I let them be that Someone special.

In fact over the years, as we added children, I had plenty of others with whom to share the privilege of being Someone. I became the Someone who delegated the jobs.

"Someone, open the door for the cat," I commanded from the lounge chair where I was keeping the fish from breaking down the glass walls of their aquarium.

"Someone, stir the stew on the stove," I holed from the depths of my bedroom where I researched current literature, word by word, book by book.

I rarely had to say, "Someone get the phone." Everyone raced to be the first.

I did not even have to ask for Someone to get the mail. All I had to do was open the door, look at the mailbox, and Someone would push me aside and race down the drive to the box.

Recently Someone has had to drive them to and from college until they earn enough money for their own car. I like being that Someone. With no interruptions all the way there, we talk and both become Someone special.

With all but one gone, I am astounded to discover that once again I have become the Someone who picks up the mail, stirs the stew, and lets the cat out.

As long as my daughter is home, though, I will never have to answer the phone. I refuse to race against Someone who is a third my age. She never lets me win.

I like being the Someone at a parent-teacher conference when the teacher begins, "What a pleasure to work with your child." But I wish Someone else had the privilege when the conference begins, "We have a little problem."

I like being Someone when my child's name and picture are in the newspaper for winning an award, graduating, or getting married. And, I wish I had not been Someone supervising when they threw forks in the restaurant, annoyed the neighbors, or managed to embarrass the family name once again.

Mostly though, whatever the age or stage my children are in, I like being Someone.

April 9, 1996

Okay So I was Wrong

OKAY, I ADMIT IT. I've been wrong a couple of times—like the time I wrote that years of living with hamsters taught our cats to roundup but not eat furry little critters.

So, of course, our tom cat brought the mole it caught in the yard into the house. My daughter decided she wanted that mole for a pet. She filled our car top carrier with dirt and watched the dirt digger tunnel to safety under the dirt.

The salivating cats joined her. They moved in close, and my daughter sharply tapped their curious cat noses. The cats backed off until she went to bed. Then the tom cat stalked the cage, found an opening, and had a mighty fine mole meal. I was wrong about the cat. I can live with one less mole on the property.

I would prefer, however, to have been right the day I told a friend I was not allergic to poison ivy. I dropped by to see her before we left on a family trip to visit relatives in Indiana. She was outside pulling poison ivy off a tree stump. As we talked, I helped her pull out the vines. We both thought we were immune to poison ivy.

We both were wrong.

I had washed my hands and arms. They were rash free. Where I pulled my hair back as I worked, though, was another story. Red welts flared everywhere my hands had touched.

Vanity and makeup went out the window. All the pictures of me from that visit to Indiana are of one red-faced momma.

So, I had developed an allergy to poison ivy. I tried to stay away from it, including the day I took the children for a nature walk around the church. I did not see any poison ivy. I did not touch any plants. I did push my hair back, just once. Two days later as I was packing for a women's retreat, my face broke out.

I pinned my hair away from my face and went to the retreat. I tried not to itch as the missionary from Israel gave her glowing report. I lacked her glow, but I was the center of attention. Every woman with a cream, ointment or other magic formula for treating poison ivy wanted to help me. I tried them all, including our family favorite: a solution with tannic acid that dries the skin. Too bad they didn't give out prizes for the ugliest person to attend that weekend. Ole Prune Face would have won easily.

So I was wrong; I'm not only allergic to poison ivy, I am very allergic. I have adjusted. When I was invited to join the students on a nature walk the weekend of the Science Symposium in Russellville, I went to the gift shop instead. The weekend my husband discovered poison ivy in the yard and on the neighbors' adjoining fences, I let him work alone pulling it to protect me from potential peril. After all, he was immune to the stuff.

He scrubbed up afterwards and doused his arms in alcohol. I gave him a hug to thank him for protecting me.

Two days later, we both broke out.

Okay, I am wrong; we both are allergic. Too bad the cat can't make a meal out of poison ivy like he did the mole. If the cat could, we would be weed free.

May 5, 1997

Today My Son is a Man

MY SON DECIDED TO VACUUM and wash his small family station wagon before he drove back home to New Orleans. Next thing I knew, my husband was out there with him with the car jacked up and the two underneath.

When they slid out and stood up, father passed the torch of car repair to his son: a car repair manual written specifically for any problem possible with that car's year and model. I did not know why he bothered; car repair has never interested that son.

The car work took longer than anticipated. Washing up afterward ensured a late start back home. The only good thing was that the baby was asleep and not fighting to be released from her car seat.

It was the wee hours of the morning before they crossed the bridge into New Orleans. As they rounded the corner onto the street to their apartment, something snapped loudly. The clutch did not respond. They drove the last half mile home in second gear, parked, and collapsed into bed. The car problem could wait. They had lived fifteen months without a car; a couple of more days without one was not a problem.

When they called to talk about it, his wife said repair shops were estimating it would cost them 120 dollars to repair the cable to the clutch.

Still in the early years of poverty, a 120 dollar car repair did not fit into their budget. My son decided to follow the instruction in the car manual and fix it himself.

I envisioned nuts, bolts, mysterious engine parts, and tools strewn haphazardly on the ground. I bit my tongue until my vision reduced to, "Well if you can't repair it yourself, I guess you can take it to a shop to be repaired." Just what every mechanic dreads getting a car with half its guts hanging out after an amateur tries to fix it.

The next night my son's wife called, "He couldn't fix it. The problem was more than putting in a sixty dollar part. We have decided to leave it alone and walk for a few months until we can afford to get it fixed."

I sighed, thinking about a perfectly good car just sitting for months. I imagined them taking a box of car parts to the mechanic.

I envisioned her struggling to carry an energetic thirteen month-old and sacks of groceries. I was quite emphatic, "Get it fixed."

"I was just teasing. He already fixed it in three hours all by himself."

My son took the phone from her, "I spent an hour trying to figure out which parts to disconnect. It took an hour to replace it once I figured that out and another hour to put it all together again."

His wife burst in, excited, and proud of her husband, "Popsie's giving us that book was providential. He did what the book said and fixed our car."

The next couple of days, his feet barely touched the earth as he reveled in his accomplishment. I should have had more faith—but, he had never fixed anything more complicated than the gears on his street bikes.

That day, my son entered another phase of manhood: repairer of his family car, sacrificing and working to ensure his wife and child rode in a car while he rode his bike to work.

April 27, 1998

Old Calendar Holds Memories

MY NOTATIONS ON THE HANDMADE calendar are twenty-two years old. I cannot remember the significance of "Bible Institute," a Saturday shopping trip with my husband, or a terse "relaxed. No rush to swimming" in June. When I came across it recently, I was ready to trash the ragged old thing.

My hand drawn calendar was obviously a New Year's resolution. Every day in January is filled with extensive notes on visiting friends, the cost of kids' boots, and after Christmas purchases. As the year wore out, so did my enthusiasm for recording family activities. By December half the days are empty. I only noted appointments and weekly activities: "Cub Scouts, caroling, company dinner."

Then April 4 caught my eye, "Grandma Waight's funeral." I turned back a page to March 29: "Grandma Waight in a coma" followed by March 31 "Grandma Waight died."

I knew that was the year she died, but I would have been hard pressed to give the dates. I had forgotten. The calendar had not.

After her funeral in New York, my Arizona sister and I stayed with our babies to visit Mom and help close up Grandma's house. Wednesday evening our little sister came home from college on her first date with her future husband. On Friday, my nephew went to the medical clinic to treat a cold. Early Saturday he went to the hospital where he recovered from pneumonia and fever induced convulsions.

A couple of weeks after I got home, I stepped on a nail. I only mention it here because it resulted in the only house call we ever had! I fainted from the pain of the puncture wound and scared my husband. He called the doctor. After reassuring my husband, the doctor stopped by our house on his way to the clinic to check on me.

In May I wrote, "Car shopping; chose one." Such a small note for a car we ultimately drove eleven years and nearly 200,000 miles!

June was busy with Bible School, swimming, company, the annual Cub Scout Father and Son campout, and canning. June 28 I picked and canned twenty quarts of cherries for pies, made four quarts of jelly and four quarts of jam, and my three-year-old cut his head while swimming.

Two weeks later I missed my little sister's New York wedding because

I was sitting in the pediatric intensive care unit waiting for that same three-year-old to rouse out of a coma induced after he ran in front of a moving car. The following days are filled with notes of his recovery and my mom's arrival. She cleaned up after my sister's wedding, packed her bags, took two weeks off from work, and came to help with the other children while I went to the hospital every day.

In the fall my husband built a kids' fort over a tool shed.

By late fall, my interest in maintaining a daily journal waned. Half the days are devoid of anything other than a date. Even though part of the year is missing, I'm keeping the tattered old calendar: It's still very full of memories.

October 26, 1998

That Girl is My Daughter?

MY DAUGHTER STOPPED BY THE office on her way to her first job interview. She didn't need encouragement; she wanted me to run an errand she was supposed to do. Having spent my lunch time running my own errands, I did not have time to take care of hers. I gave it back to her, walked out to the car with her, wished her well, and sent her off to the job interview. Before she left, she reached over and adjusted my shirt.

Twenty minutes later she was back, glowing, excited, barely containing herself, "I got the job. I start tomorrow."

I glowed for a couple of seconds myself. My daughter: the wage earner, less for me to pay, and more for her to save. All right!

After she left, one of the reporters said, "It's Joan talking to Joan. Looks like you, acts like you, talks like you," the reporter noted.

What? She and I look alike?

It wasn't the first time I've heard that, but it still astonishes me. From my perspective, my daughter and I are quite different. She's blonde, thirty years younger, shorter, and many years from having to worry about retaining her girlish figure.

We are similar in a couple of respects: we like the same sort of clothes and both stretch our clothing budgets by shopping the sales racks. The similarities end there. Everything she wears looks fantastic. I realize halfway through the day that my skirt is on backwards.

She regularly despairs of my clothing choices. She lets me know how I should dress as she frowns at the length of my slacks, tells me I am wearing the absolutely most awful socks, and hands me the correct pair to wear.

How will I ever manage when she leaves for college? I will have no one to stop me as I leave for work and moan, "Mom. Not that blouse!"

Nor will I have my in-house makeup artist. It didn't take long after I gave my teenager permission to wear makeup before she began telling me what was wrong with mine. The one advantage to having a flawless daughter is that when we travel I can count on her to remember every item I forgot to take off the shelf at home.

We may have many similar mannerisms, but it will take her a few years before she gets the same comments I did on a recent trip to Indiana. I went into a fast food place for a hamburger. The young woman wrote down my order, looked up, and hesitantly asked, "Are you a teacher?"

I had never seen the clerk before. She had done nothing wrong. Yet one look at my face and she was ready to toe the line before I made her write one hundred times, "I will take orders accurately."

The Look came as part of my facade for dealing with misbehaving children. Once I told a rowdy kid whom I had never seen before that it was time he went home. He gathered up his stuff, walked away, turned, and asked, "Are you a teacher or something?" I guess teachers have The Look.

My teenager lacks one. However, there is hope for her to develop The Look this fall when she goes off to college to study to be a teacher.

March 29, 1999

The Empty Nest

A LOT OF PEOPLE ASKED me this summer: "What will you do when your daughter goes off to college this fall? All of your children will be gone."

My answer was always, "My daughter has been preparing us for her departure since March when she began working after school. All this summer, she has worked all day and has been gone almost every evening. It won't be a lot different once she goes to college."

My son and his family came the weekend she was finally to leave for college. The dishwasher, sink, and counters overflowed with dishes. The house overflowed with toys, clothes, and people. Saturday and Sunday overflowed with activities as people went this way and that.

The overflow included a couple of disemboweled, used computers the guys were frantically working over to ensure she had one to take to college. Early, very early Saturday morning, the computer was finally fixed. Late in the afternoon we tucked it and her luggage in the car. My daughter gave me a long, tearful hug goodbye and left with her father for the University of the Ozarks in Clarksville.

The young parents gathered up their babies, bottles, and toys, and left me alone in a quiet house. In the silence that followed, I walked through the house gathering up dirty dishes, stray towels, toys, and pillows. I stacked dishes in the dishwasher, swept the floors, straightened pillows, and set aside the items each had left behind. It was all clean. It has stayed that way.

On Tuesday a friend whose last child also had gone away said her husband looked at her one day and said "Well, they are all gone now." She said, "I was doing just fine until he said that. When he said that, we looked at each other, and we both began crying."

On Saturday my husband spent the day working his way through a tedious pile of paperwork. No one interrupted a thing I did. I spent half the day preparing unnecessarily huge quantities of food for our Sunday afternoon guests.

By Saturday evening I decided an empty nest is downright boring. I had too much time to clean cupboards, catch up on the paperwork without anyone around to take my pen and scribble on important papers, demand equal time on the computer, or leave peanut butter on the counter, and spill Kool-Aid on the floor.

At church Sunday I heard tales of abject maternal misery as other college freshmen took off for their first semester. I said again we had been eased into the empty nest over the summer.

I was sure I was beyond the "parting is such sweet sorrow" stage, until I sat down to write this column, and caught myself fighting back tears. My stiff upper lip crumbles every time I proofread this page. I must maintain this professional demeanor so I'm going to quit writing now and go have myself a good cry.

After twenty-seven years of children, our house is finally clean, quiet, and very empty. I embrace the wonder of their adulthood, but I surely do miss having them around.

September 6, 1999

Becoming Middle-aged

WHEN I WASN'T LOOKING, I became middle-aged. I first noticed I was middle-aged in a picture taken of my backside as my granddaughter toddled beside me in her new Sunday dress. I recognized those legs and the hang of the skirt: They were my grandmother's.

I brushed it off and determined to never wear those shoes and that skirt again. They were definitely not me. I was not a middle-aged grandmother.

The next time I noticed I was middle aged was at the reunion with my brother and sisters. Something about the five of us, walking across the parking lot reminded me of a small family reunion I had attended with my mother. I did not walk with my mother from the car to the church. Like any teenager, I walked behind her as she plodded up the hill to the little country church with its crumbling cemetery.

At the reunion with my brothers and sisters, we were not plodding up a hill to a late afternoon reunion. We were climbing out of cars and walking across a flat parking lot to a family restaurant, but I still noticed we had all slowed down in the past thirty years. We were not yet as slow as those people at my mother's reunion but none of us were teenyboppers anymore, either.

The reality of my years hit me again last week when I had to pose for a picture at the *News-Times*.

I did not look like a teenager. I looked middle-aged. The photographer did not understand my protest that the picture did not do me justice.

How could it? In that picture I looked more like the older folks at that reunion than myself as a teenager.

Although that still startles me, it shouldn't be such a surprise. As a ten-year-old I realized that by the time the year 2000 came around, I would be nearly as old as my youngest grandmother.

I was ten in the early 1960s. As a child my primary concern with 2000 A.D. was, "How old will my brothers and sisters and I be when all the numbers on the calendar roll over?"

With four of the five of us officially becoming a year older within a couple of weeks of the New Year, each calendar change means we all are a year older. At ten, I was fascinated with the incomprehensible fact that we would all be in our forties: forty-nine, forty-eight, forty-seven, forty-five and halfway to forty-four when the calendar rolled over to 2000. Looking ahead to 2000 A.D. from the perspective of the 1960's, that seemed impossible. My mother was thirty and my father thirty-one. How could I ever become forty-eight when my parents weren't even that old?

The years have passed and as I write this, the year 2000 is a mere sixty-seven days away. My forty-eighth birthday follows shortly after. From the perspective of 1999, that doesn't sound so old anymore.

I still feel like that teenager following Mom up the hill to the reunion. My pictures say my feelings lie. I don't like that. But, considering my only other option, I'll take being almost forty-eight as the year 2000 finally arrives.

October 25, 1999

Just a Phase or Parental Failure

ONCE A WEEK FOR THE past twenty-eight years of parenting, I have been convinced that I was a total failure as a mother. Only talking with other parents has convinced me otherwise.

I married a man with two young sons for whom I was the primary caregiver. All my ideas for raising children were quickly revised under the reality of experience. Like every mother, I had to learn the hard way the truth of an observation my mother made about her concerns for her five children: "About the time I realized they were just going through a phase, they were into another one."

I wish the phases were labeled and a lot shorter, especially one child's phase of protesting against buying new shoes. That phase came and stayed way too long.

The child did not like changes. He wanted everything to always be the same, especially shoes. He hated new shoes. Every time we took him shopping for new shoes, his protests alerted everyone in the store what he thought about new shoes. It was downright embarrassing. I dreaded the day we realized his shoes were worn out. We avoided buying him shoes until he had either outgrown his old ones, or they were totally worn out.

Then in spite of his insistence that he did not need or want new shoes, we loaded him in the car and took him to the store. He sat, had his foot sized, began crying, slid off the seat to hide under it, and tearfully protested everything about getting new shoes for his growing feet. We scolded, disciplined, shoved shoes on his feet, and wasted a lot of breath trying to reason with him. He still absolutely, passionately hated letting go of an old pair of shoes.

Once a pair was selected we left the store red faced with him still insistently saying, "I will not wear those new shoes. I don't want them. I hate them." Of course, he always wore the new shoes, usually the next day. But he also always made sure everyone around heard how much he hated getting them in the first place. The whole ordeal from the beginning to the end was humiliating. Trying to understand his problem, I attributed the source of his protest to all the changes he had had to deal with during his young life. Thankfully as he grew older and life settled into a routine, his protest waned.

I signed him up to take evening swimming classes. As the children splashed behind Styrofoam boards, we mothers chatted. One evening the topic of discussion was shopping for children's clothes.

I didn't say a word. I faded into the background and only listened until one mother said her son protested everything new: larger bikes, clothes, new shoes, or whatever.

So much for my rationalizations; her son had not had a lot of changes. Only then did I dare talk about our miserable years of shoe shopping with one son. Because we talked, our shared misery was halved, and our eternal maternal guilt faded.

Both sons grew up and out of their phase of protesting changes. Our son actually developed an intense interest in shopping for the right kind of sneaker, proving, yet again, my mother's insight, "About the time I realized it was just a phase, he was into another one."

March 27, 2000

The Perfect Gift

I DISCOVERED THE WAY TO give grandchildren exactly what they want: Take them shopping as I did just before Christmas. They held and studied several toys, lost interest and allowed me to re-shelve them.

I said we couldn't buy everything, they had to choose. My daughter had the almost three-year-old grandson with her. I had my four-and-a-half-year-old granddaughter. We looked at dolls, crafts and gadget toys, but nothing interested her.

We were doing pretty well not finding anything until we reached the craft aisle with several intriguing projects that we selected. She was pointing out a couple that interested her when she saw the package of rainbow colored clay with tiny animal shaped cookie cutters and four colored molds. Her interest soared. It was a great hands-on project for a little cash.

"We can't buy everything," I reminded her. "We will have to put some of the other things back." She didn't care. She held tightly onto her package of clay.

We found her little brother and my daughter exploring in the aisles of action toys. My grandson had found a display of small emergency vehicles that rolled forward, whistled or rang when a string was pulled or a lever pressed.

He picked out three and pushed them into his aunt's hand. "These are for you." He was so earnest. "When I come to you house I can play with them."

"Why, thank you. You think I really would like these?"

"Yes, I am going to give them to you."

"Which one do you think I would like the best?"

He studied the three packages and picked out the ambulance and the fire truck that he would get for her.

"Of these two which ONE do you think is the best?"

He studied them again and selected the fire truck with the button that activated the wheels, a siren and moved the ladder up and down.

"You want to give me this?"

"Yeah," He looked longingly at the little fire truck.

"That would be very nice wouldn't it?"

He nodded his head.

My daughter and I smiled at each other. She put all of the little vehicles back on the shelf and pushed their cart away. I picked up a fire truck and hid it beneath a couple other packages and whispered to his big sister. "Don't tell. It's a surprise."

Her eyes gleamed with the secret.

At the checkout, she leaned over towards her brother and whispered, "We have a secret for you."

"Shh, don't tell," I reminded her.

Fortunately he didn't hear us.

Right after Christmas we celebrated his third birthday. After he blew out his candles, we handed him the fire truck.

He danced around impatiently as grandpa cut the wires and plastic that bound the fire truck to its box. He ignored the rest of his gifts, placed it on the floor and pressed the lever. The little siren whined, the wheels turned and the ladder moved up and down.

"Thanks! This is the neatest present ever!" he yelled. But of course it was. We had, after all, gotten him exactly what he wanted—even if he said he wanted to give it to his aunt.

January 7, 2002

Role Reversal

MY LIFE IS NOT THE way that it used to be. It isn't even the way I thought it should and would be.

As a young bride, I knew my hard-working husband left for work in the wee hours of the morning, while I slept until I needed to wake up and see the children off to school. I did not worry about medical bills. One of the benefits at my dearly beloved's company was excellent insurance coverage for any doctor we chose and a company employed liaison who took care of filing medical reports.

My days were filled with reading books to children; doing the family's laundry; baking bread, cookies, pies, and cakes; sewing new clothes for the children and myself; gardening; canning; and cleaning house when absolutely necessary.

With our one car needed to get my husband to work every day, I used a big wooden wagon for hauling children, library books, and anything I purchased in the town about a half a mile away. It was an idyllic life the way things were supposed to be. I even said so in a letter to my sister.

That was then. This is now.

This morning I came to work while the birds were still singing their early morning songs, and my husband and kids were sound asleep. I will put in my eight hours at *The News-Times* developing ideas for columns and thinking ahead to stories I need to write for the next special section.

Before I ever see my paycheck on Friday, a significant hunk of it will disappear into the coffers of an insurance company that wants pre-verification before treatment with a medical provider, preferably one of their choosing.

While I am gone, my husband will check his email for responses from companies and institutions interested in contracting his work for them. He will work with my daughter on building a desk. My daughter will also get her hair done, do a bit of shopping, and maybe fix supper. My son will read, go to work, study, and wash his own clothes. While they are all at home, I am at work earning enough money to pay for the insurance, automobile upkeep, and groceries.

Our lives have changed. My husband, not me, has made most of the family related phone calls regarding our daughter's upcoming wedding. Since his plant closed last winter, he has spent three or four weeks with the youngest grandchildren while I stayed in town and went to work.

The tables have definitely been turned around here. The traditional mother of the bride at home fussing over things with the bride, while Dad is off at work, has become a working mom gone to the office while the father of the bride and the bride are off shopping. When I came home one evening, he was having a jolly good time assembling odds and ends he had purchased as favors for the guests. Not wanting to miss anything, I stayed up late in order to be involved.

As a housewife, I was never bored. My list of "things to do, to make, and places to go" continually replenished itself. Last week my husband echoed that sentiment when he said, "I have so many projects to do right now that it will take me at least another six months to a year to finish them."

The only thing that has not changed is the immortal question, "What's for supper?" proving yet again, that the more things change, the more they stay the same.

June 17, 2002

Change is Good, I Guess

EVERYWHERE I TURNED THAT WEEK, the message was the same, "Change is good; it provides growth, insight, experience, and opportunities to try out new things."

I knew all that, but I really did not want to be reminded right when we were considering a major change in our lives: a new job for my husband in a new community. I really hated to move on. I was comfortable where we were, but there we were, visiting a new community with my husband sitting down for his final job interview.

While he interviewed, I visited the real estate offices, the schools, and the shopping centers. Driving around to assess the housing situation, I switched on the radio and heard some dude chattering about the benefits of new experiences. Back at the hotel I clicked on the TV only to hear the radio talk show host spouting the same axiom. I switched off that banal chatter and picked up a newspaper. The column I scanned embraced the same Pollyanna outlook on life.

I wanted to be negative and miserable. I did not want anyone suggesting that the prospective move could possibly be beneficial. However, even the book I had brought to read on the plane ride home echoed the thought. I could not escape it.

Back home again, I chatted with friends about the visit and our upcoming weekend retreat. Reviewing the week's visit to schools, realtors, and shopping centers, I mentioned the irony of hearing and reading so much about change.

"And here we are preparing to go to this weekend retreat. I know what the guy will talk about. It is inevitable he will find some way to say 'change is good for you.' I really don't want to hear it again," I said.

At the retreat we were barely into the first evening's message when one of the women I had talked with that day turned, winked at me, and grinned. The speaker had just finished outlining the weekend's messages. Each one would deal with the blessings and lessons he had received through circumstances that had forced him or his family into one change or another.

I grinned back at her, shook my head, and shrugged. What could I say? Obviously, until I accepted the axiom, I would continue to encounter the paradox that however disturbing and upsetting new circumstances might be they do provide opportunities for growth and insight.

I listened, took notes, and begrudgingly learned the concept. We did not actually end up moving at the time, but neither did we escape experiencing change. The onslaught of the message and events at the time forced me to begin reconsidering how I reacted to life's little and big upsets and how I dealt with expected times of rejoicing and unexpected times of sorrow.

I love the philosophy that life is a process of letting go of what we have so we may freely embrace what awaits us. I just hate having to live it.

Letting go of what I have is no fun. The past three years I happily spent weeks and months preparing and celebrating each new family member gained through marriage. Afterwards, each time I slumped into post wedding blues.

The party was over and their success in marriage meant it was time for me to grow again as I let go of each child and embraced the insight, experience, and opportunities to interact with the new Hershberger. I love the new folks, but I hate stepping back. I keep reminding myself change is good.

Given a couple of years, I might actually believe it.

September 1, 2003

My Daughter the Woman

SURELY IT WAS ONLY YESTERDAY that our daughter sat front and center on the stage as a preschooler singing the *Wiggle Worm* song.

But, that would be impossible because last week she stood front and center in her church choir energetically singing a worship song. As I stared at her, I suddenly understood why, in the musical *Fiddler on the Roof,* Tevye sings "I don't remember growing older. When did they?"

She entered our lives as our only cheerleader for her basketball team of older brothers. She provided the energy, the enthusiasm and the sassy attitude they needed to keep them in line.

Since she was my four-year-old, I made sure her face was scrubbed and her dress was clean. I pulled up her socks, buckled her shoes neatly and hoped she would stay neat long enough for the program. Now she moans in despair when I shrug off not having changed my brown loafers for my black sandals before I leave the house.

The toddler I closely guarded from all sorts of dangers grew up, went off to college, and reported the creep who thought he could get away with sexual harassment. Her experience prepared her to be a teacher at one of the state's largest high schools where she works with boisterous, bold, mouthy teen-agers. It took little time for her to realize she had to make it very clear to them that she might look young, but she is their teacher.

I remember the tomboy holding out a caterpillar for me to pet and the child who ran to me for Band-Aids for her boo-boos. Last year after she fainted a couple of times, she made her own appointments, talked with doctors whom I have never met, picked up a prescription, and called me afterwards with the doctor's diagnosis.

Tevye wonders, "Is this the little girl I carried?" I ask, "Is this the little girl I washed off after she played in the red clay mud in the backyard?"

Twenty years ago, she tracked mud in my house. Now she scrubs and cleans her house so thoroughly that I am not sure that the muddy little kid of yore would be allowed inside her back door.

Our tomboy has become a beautiful young woman who wears cute outfits, heels, and carefully applied makeup, and has her own tool box with wrenches, tape measure, screwdrivers, and a hammer.

We did her hair until the summer she insisted we pay for a swinging teenager haircut and replace her Coke bottle glasses with contacts. Even good friends did not recognize her when she walked into class the next fall.

I made the white dress the school insisted she wear under her high school graduation gown, bought the flowers to hand to her when she left the podium with her college diploma in hand, and wrote the check for her wedding gown. Last week she planned a surprise party for her husband and told me what I needed to wear that night.

I helped her pick out her college. Last year she enrolled in graduate school. I still am not sure which university she attends.

I needlessly hum and echo Tevye's question, "What words of wisdom can I give them? How can I help to ease their way?" Last month she and her husband picked out and bought their first home, chose the paint for the walls, ceramic tile for the floors, light fixtures, and their own appliances. She didn't need or want our input. She chose colors and styles I would never consider and declared them perfect.

Car repairs, new jobs, house repairs, and phone conversations long ago forced me to realize that her team of brothers had become men. But it took seeing her front and center on stage twenty years after the *Wiggle Worm* song to realize she too had grown up and become a woman.

May 30, 2005

Learning to Ride a Bike

A CHILD'S FIRST TWO-WHEELED BIKE ride captures the angst, the joy, and the exhilaration of growing up. Our first did not get the option of training wheels. His dad held the bike steady as the child climbed up on the seat and grabbed the bicycle handle bars with a death grip begging, "Don't let go, Daddy!"

Daddy did not let go. Day after day he trotted alongside the bike, keeping it from falling as the two made their way down the street. That child provided his father several afternoons of exercise before he rode away alone.

His brother followed exactly the opposite path and not only insisted on the security of training wheels but refused to consider riding without them. We could see him balancing the bike, but the thought of falling off the bike terrified him beyond his ability to trust us that he could ride without falling.

We left the training wheels on until they were thread bare. Finally, under the duress of keeping up with the other kids, a training wheel broke.

I refused to buy another one.

"I know you can ride without it," I insisted.

He argued with me, certain that he needed the trainers.

I promised to run alongside and hold the seat of the bike while he tested his ability to balance and pedal. Grumbling, complaining, making sure that I knew he thought I was the absolutely worst parent in the world, he swung onto the bike and began pedaling. He did not fall; he pedaled just as strongly as he had for weeks and quickly left me far behind. At the corner, he stopped, turned around, and came back, his face glowing.

He loved it. He could not believe how great it was to not have the training wheels. For the rest of that day and the next, he pedaled all around the neighborhood reveling in his freedom from the drag of training wheels and a protective parent's touch.

When it was his younger brother's turn, he shrugged away the idea of training wheels. He asked his Dad to help him get started down the road.

He didn't want or need much help. Sure he fell a couple of times, but in short order he retired his father and joined the other bikers.

Recently, my son became the daddy holding the bike and wrote the following on his weblog:

"We went to the Mt. Gretna Rail Trail today. Ginger and Basil brought their bikes. The rest of us walked.

"At some point, Ginger was off her bike. I asked Violet if she wanted to try to ride. She hopped on. Ever the mother, Alexis reminded me to make sure she wouldn't fall.

"I held on to the bike and Violet for a little bit, then just the bike. Then, I just put my hand beside her shoulder. Finally, I let go completely. Bam! Down she fell.

" 'Want to try again?' And she was back on. This time she stayed on. A couple of other mothers who happened to be riding past at that moment cheered.

"Violet was ecstatic. 'Can we take the training wheels off my bike now?'

"Violet knew she was ready to go solo. Everyone who saw agreed and celebrated with her."

We all celebrate whenever a loved one, wobbly as they may be, hops up and rides off alone without our help.

January 30, 2006

Phases of Life

As a young bride-to-be, I listened with wide eyes as the older ladies at the sewing factory where we made cheerleader uniforms chatted around me. The young married women talked about adapting recipes, preparing meals, and finding babysitters. The older women's conversations focused on grandchildren, community projects, and activities. Each reflected a different phase of married life.

The first few years of marriage I focused on setting up housekeeping, figuring out what we like to eat, buy, and do together. My own preoccupation with finding, discovering, and trying out rich, calorie laden desserts has been replaced with research for variations of heart healthy salads.

The early years of parenting I spent long hours reading books, playing games, and teaching children. All too soon the children began reading their own books, finding other game partners, and pushing away my help saying, "I can do it by myself."

The mom's taxi phase lasted until the youngest child went off to college and left the debris of childhood behind.

My husband and I went through our empty nest phase, carefully tucking aside everything they once used. But of late, we have been shifting into the retirement phase and cleaning house. My husband emptied our attic of everything, added lighting, and organized storage space for our stuff. I joined him in revamping the house, sorting out the accumulated clutter, and encouraging our children, who now each have their own homes, to take their collection of toys, books, college texts, and old favorite things.

With each box sorted, we remembered the phases of their childhood: The years when the boys became building engineers with Legos and Tinker Toys the too short time when my daughter collected dwarf dolls, years when stuffed animals held a high priority; and the baseball card collecting years which consumed their spending money and conversations.

My own interests have shifted. The empty house and empty evening hours provide me with plenty of time to work on cross stitch and quilting projects. Similarly, my sisters have plunged into quilting, knitting, or crocheting projects. None of us leave the house without hauling along a bag holding our current needlework project.

And the circle has come full round. This year my daughter entered a new stage of life with her first pregnancy. She quizzes me over and over about labor, delivery, and demand versus timed feeding schedules. Should she let the baby cry? Surely forty-five minutes is too long, but how about five minutes?

She does not know what to expect. I promise her she will do fine and will, in time, develop her own style.

And inwardly I am gloating that her teenage, know-it-all years have ended! I have entered the stage of being the older, wiser woman, the one sought for advice. I intend to fully enjoy this phase until she starts telling me how to burp a baby.

October 9, 2006

Assembly Line

NOTHING LIKE SPENDING EIGHT YEARS in college and post-graduate studies to learn you qualify to work on an assembly line.

The irony is rich. At twenty, my youngest son took a temporary job working on the production line at the chicken processing plant to earn cash for college. On his twenty-first birthday he had no big party celebrating the milestone, only another day of moving trays of frozen chicken and hours spent in a classroom studying books, pursuing a degree in biology.

That degree took him into one of the labs of the human genome project where, shortly before his twenty-sixth birthday, he and thousands of others celebrated the completion of mapping a rough draft of the human genome. Although more research followed, he returned to the classroom to study pharmacy.

Four years later, he accepted his doctorate in pharmacy and a job filling pill bottles. He settled behind the counter until circumstances led him to look elsewhere for employment.

That's when he entered the world of mail-order prescriptions. It is big business, with lots of pharmacists working at tasks few folks realize a pharmacist does. He really liked his desk job in pharmacy; he could even do some of it at home from his computer. The company mandated overtime. He called customers and chatted a bit with them about their medications: when and how they took them, any activity or product they might be using that might be helpful or contraindicated with the medication and then he wrote a report.

After the swing shifts of the grocery store pharmacy, he welcomed the regular nine-to-five hours of office work. But the mail order company had other plans for his desk job. Within months, they outsourced it hundreds of miles away and left him with three weeks to find another job within the company or otherwise.

He returned to the last place he expected to be.

He landed on a production line, working the night shift five to six days a week with mandatory overtime some weeks. He landed on a production line that employed only licensed pharmacists who verified the output of robot pill dispensers.

Pharmacy technicians dump bar coded boxes of pills into the machines that electronically count out pills to fill prescriptions. The robots do a good job, but no prescription leaves the pill popping plant until a pharmacist manually inspects and approves that the robot has correctly filled the prescription. If something looks even a bit odd, the pharmacists pull the prescription off the line to be scrutinized and fixed before it is shipped for home delivery.

In this wave-of-the-future pharmacy, my son works with twenty pharmacists on one of the two ten-hour shifts checking prescriptions at a state-of-the-art factory line with machinery designed for accuracy and cleanliness. For each pharmacist there are two to four pharmaceutical technicians at work. Filling medications is big business.

At this plant potential customers tour a couple of times a week seeking the best source for their employees' mail order medications. The pharmacy company works hard to welcome and impress prospective customers including mandating that staff wear a pharmaceutical smock on visitor day.

"White coats for pharmacists and blue for techs, but they don't call them that," my son sighed. On visitor day, everyone wears a coat or smock including those who only work at computers.

"At school, we were told that a grocery store pharmacy would feel pretty good if they filled two hundred prescriptions in a day," my son said. "At this plant our goal is to fill 70,000 prescriptions in a day."

Medicine is big business these days and requires highly trained persons to perform the same crucial medical procedures over and over.

So, after eight years of post-high school education, my son, who just needed a job to support his family, returned to the assembly line as a pharmacist.

February 7, 2011

Blizzard of 1978

EVEN WITH SNOW PLOWS AND trucks designed to salt and sand the roads, everything shut down for a day or two after the blizzard of 1978.

The wind whipped up huge mounds of snow and the clouds dumped so much snow that the snow plows could not keep the roads clear. We literally could not drive down the street until the city's large pay loader came in, scooped up huge mounds of snow, and cleared a path. After it left, my husband and sons had to dig out a path for the car to reach the road, but at least they did not have to shovel the entire street.

My husband and I recalled that winter as we converted photographic slides to digital pictures last month and saw pictures of our family bundled up in winter coats, mittens, scarves, boots, and mufflers standing in a row with a wall of snow behind us.

For me it was the best of times. My husband could not get to work. The silent lumber yard kept him from starting yet another house remodeling project. The boys could not go to school. The snow prohibited the newspaper carrier from bringing the usual bundles of newspapers to our house to challenge the older boys to tackle the snowy streets on their paper route.

And, I did not have to go to the grocery store. I made our bread during those years and always kept a minimum of twenty-five pounds of flour and a huge can of yeast on hand. Our basement shelves held rows and rows of colorful jars of fruits, vegetables, and jams that I had canned the previous summer. With meat in the freezer and gallons of farm fresh milk in the refrigerator, we could hunker down and wait it out.

Only we never hunkered down to wait out anything. Not on your life! We could not do what many did; we could not watch television. We did not own one. We had too many things to do even when a blizzard kept us house bound.

We did the obvious: made popcorn, pulled out books to read, games to play, and ingredients for baking and cooking. The older boys, fourteen and eleven, did the unusual. They bundled up and spent the entire day outside building an igloo that kept out the wind.

They made blocks and stacked them in increasingly smaller circles until they only had a small hole in the top to let out the smoke from the cozy fire they built inside the fort. It took them all day long to gather the snow, mound it together, and build it.

From the warmth of the kitchen I watched bemused. If I had told them to go out in that weather on their paper route, they would have moaned and groaned, but with no mandate to bundle up and go out, they had spent all but meal times outside and immersed themselves into the snow drifts.

Once they finished, my husband snapped pictures of them wearing hooded winter coats and mittens, sitting inside the igloo at a fire. They had conquered the elements, found shelter, and a whole lot of fun on a cold, snowy day at home.

February 14, 2011

Electronics Erase the Simple Life

BIT BY BIT THE ELECTRONIC age sidled up alongside me, promising great and wonderful things if I would just make one little exception to my lifelong refusal to allow it to dominate my home.

My first thirty-five years while everyone else chatted about their favorite program I lived without a television, content with a modest radio and record player.

Then I bought one small, handheld Pac Man game for one child's birthday, and it's been all downhill from there. A few months later I found a secondhand Atari console with several game cartridges. A great buy, except without a television we could not use it—at least not until I found an old black-and-white set at a yard sale.

All it took was one semester of Introduction to Computers and I wanted one. We did not need a computer. Not with the perfectly good manual typewriter I had received in high school and used through college for writing papers and my weekly letters to loved ones. I still insisted we needed to buy a computer.

My husband found a portable computer. We invested more money in that computer than we have since in television sets, VCRs, DVD player, cassette players, record players or radios combined. Although it was termed portable, it was nowhere near as thin as the laptop I now own. We used five-inch floppy disks to save our programs and letters. My son, the computer geek, cut his computing teeth on that machine, taught himself his first couple of computer languages, and wrote a program that he sold for half the cost of the computer.

As a child, I missed every episode of *Bewitched*. Now I watch re-runs on *Hulu.com* as I use my exercise machine. My grandparents, the farmers, did not need an exercise machine to clock the miles they walked and calories they burned. The cattle and crops took care of burning off all their excess calories.

The farming grandparents somehow managed to survive, even thrive without cell phones, computers, Internet or electronic games, and gadgets. I thought I could, too. But according to our children, we can't. They insisted we needed a cell phone, gave us one a few years ago, and told us to use it.

Six, seven years later, we still have the same cell phone. My husband still fumbles to pull it out of his pocket and connect to the caller before it goes to voice mail. But I don't, at least not with my cell phone. I pulled it out this morning to call the computer at work and clocked-in for the day on my way to an assignment.

My ancestors wondered why they needed a crank phone wired into their home. I use my wireless phone to take pictures, log my phone calls, retain contact information, and to send post cards which we now call text messages. And, if I ever figure it out and decide to use it, I could also connect with the worldwide web and do much, much more.

In some respects, I do the exact same thing that my parents and grandparents did to stay connected with family and friends. They wrote letters, read the newspapers and found interesting articles and obituaries to clip and send to my folks along with their weekly letters. I forward links to articles or videos I find interesting. Each December, my mother shared family news with friends. Today we keep a Facebook page: a weblog of family events, where we send out our thoughts, rants, and raves before we can change our minds about what we wrote.

My aunts took pictures, had the film developed, and sent us a copy along with a letter in an envelope. But today I can take hundreds of pictures with no thought for the cost of developing the film, post them to my picture website, and show them to family hundreds of miles away shortly after shooting the last frame.

Last month we realized that those thousands of family pictures on slides stored in slide trays and in picture albums could all be digitized and stored on a high density postage stamp-sized, photo cards that slide into a camera smaller than a bar of soap.

I may not have Blu-ray, innumerable applications on cell phones, or voice activated anything, but from living the first half of my life without a television, I definitely have entered the electronic age.

February 21, 2011

Entering My Sixties

BIRTHDAYS PROVIDE CONVENIENT MARKERS OF progress and changes in life, so I give you a few reflections on the eve of leaving middle age.

At ten, kindly adults would enter conversations with me by asking, "What are you going to be when you grow up?" At sixty, folks wonder, "When are you going to retire?"

At sixteen, my parents had to ride with me when I drove. At sixty, my family offers to drive for me.

At twenty, I wanted to have a dozen kids. At thirty, I had half that and said enough. At sixty, I am happy to have more than that many grandchildren.

At ten, my grandparents were so old. At sixty, my middle-aged sons are so young.

At twenty, I really liked our fixer upper first house. At sixty, just looking at a fixer upper leaves me shuddering.

Before I turned ten, I proudly anticipated the decade. Before I turned sixty, I dreaded the decade and reminded myself frequently of its advent.

At twenty, friends wondered how many children my husband and I wanted to have. At thirty, they wondered when we would quit having children. At fifty, they were surprised that I had grandchildren! At sixty, they are astounded that we have so many grandchildren.

At twenty, I dropped out of college to marry. At thirty, I wanted to return to college to finish my degree. At sixty, I rarely use any of the skills or classroom information I studied for my degree.

At fifty, I was insulted to receive an invitation to join the AARP. At sixty, I ask if I qualify for the senior discount.

At thirty, I quickly lost twenty pounds after the baby's birth. At sixty, the twenty pounds, and more, have returned time and again.

At twenty, I sat and listened politely when older folks talked. At sixty, I work hard to sit and listen politely when younger folks talk.

At twenty, I blithely promised my husband for better or for worse, in sickness and in health. At sixty, I remember the effort it took some days, even some years, to keep that promise.

At twenty, I figured I was more than ready for marriage and a family. At sixty, I realize how little I knew then and how much I have yet to learn.

At twenty, I had no clue just how much money it took to feed a family, keep them healthy and in a warm house with clean clothes. At thirty, I knew how to can fruits and vegetables, how to sew a three-piece suit and how to stretch a dollar ten different ways. At forty, I suffered sticker shock at the price of college for my children. At fifty, I looked in astonishment at the ways God provided for their college. At sixty, I thank the Lord we can still afford to travel to visit our far-flung family.

At thirty, I smugly said "I don't need glasses." At forty, I admitted readers made it easier. At fifty, I began yearly visits to the eye doctor. At sixty, I reach for my bifocals and wear them every day.

At ten, I figured I would live forever. At twenty, I saw my grandparents' health fail. At thirty, my parents became the oldest living generation. At forty, my mother passed. At fifty, my family began arranging a home for my father. At sixty, my husband and I talk about final arrangements.

At ten, I asked my grandmother to teach me how to knit. At sixty, I ask my granddaughters if they want me to teach them how to knit.

At sixteen, I moved across the country and wrote dozens of letters every month to keep in touch. By sixty, my children had moved across the country and keep in touch with Facebook, email or Twitter, and rarely send me a letter.

At ten, I proudly celebrated when I blew out all the candles. At sixty, I wonder, who has that much breath?

January 11, 2012

Do You Do Windows?

Truck Party in the Yard

WE HAD A PARTY AT our house. I invited the guests, paid for the entertainment, but I was not included in the fun. It wasn't my type of party anyway, just a bunch of men in trucks.

We don't own a truck. My husband prefers little sports cars. That morning his sports car was ailing from too many sporting runs across the country (or something like that). I took him to work in the minivan.

The truck party had already started when I came home. A truck and trailer were parked in the driveway. Men were in the yard having a tree climbing contest as they trimmed the dead wood and damage left from last winter's ice storm.

"Thought I'd never come, didn't you?" the boss man yelled.

"You're right on time," I said as another truck pulled in.

I walked with that driver around back where we had an air conditioning unit. He had to play a game of pin the tail on the problem. He had come the day before, found one problem, and assured me that even if the house cooled, we would soon need to replace the unit.

The house had not cooled. We needed a new unit. I decided he was a rather expensive guest but agreed with him. In August, it is no fun having a party without an air conditioner.

While we stood talking about the new air conditioner, the tree climbers were filling the trailer with pine boughs. When it was heaped to overflowing, they left followed shortly after by the air conditioner man.

The tree climbers returned and hauled off more limbs and a tree trunk. After another trip they were ready to tackle the back yard.

Then the new air conditioner arrived, riding proudly on the back of yet another truck. That driver came to the side door. I showed him where to go and turned to answer a question at the back door from the guy with the chain saw. I resolved that problem, and the front doorbell rang.

I looked out the window. Another truck was in our drive.

I knew I had invited the other two trucks already in the yard, but I could not remember having invited anyone else to my truck party. I went to the front door.

"Hello, ma'am, I'm here to pick up for the Habitat for Humanity garage sale." The smiling man in a red shirt reminded me I had invited one other truck to stop by sometime. I indicated the bags of clothes, knick knacks, and household goods waiting off to the side.

My party was in full swing: one truck in the drive, one at the side yard, and one in the back. Men were all around the house taking away our old limbs, the old air conditioner, and old clothes. Out with all the old stuff (including that extra cash cluttering our savings account) and in with the new (as my list of bills to pay grew).

It was a great party, but it did not end there. One of the trucks got stuck in the backyard with a dead battery. I invited one of my neighbors with a sturdy looking truck to thread his way between the fence, house, and shrubs to the backyard where the party was winding down.

Strangest party! No one could come inside to cool off. The inside of the house was hotter than the outside. By the time the air conditioner had done its job, the trucks were gone. It was a great party even if a bit expensive.

I hope I never again have to have another one like it.

September 12, 1994

Better Than Boredom

"You never have a dull moment at your house, do you?" someone asked me after reading about our truck party. Well, no. When things start to get dull, we make some excitement—like the time we watched the ice maker dump the ice.

It was our first automatic ice maker. For days we startled when it clicked, hummed, and filled with water. I decided to see what had replaced the plastic trays, the balancing act, and quick twist of the wrist once necessary to produce ice cubes for our cool summer drinks.

The next time I heard the faint click that preceded the dumping of the ice, I called the boys to come and watch. We all crowded round the open freezer door. Breathlessly we watched while the plastic paddles rose up, slowly made a half circle turn, carefully lifted the ice up, and shoved it with a clatter into the plastic tray beneath. As we closed the door, we could hear the surge of water entering the hidden ice chamber ready for the next batch of ice.

It was a most satisfying experience.

I thought about that recently. My daughter assured me that life was B-O-R-I-N-G around our place. I looked at her astounded. Out of the twelve weeks of summer vacation, she was gone six or seven weeks on trips, to camp, or visiting friends. With all that traveling around, packing, unpacking, and clothes to wash and sort, when did she have time to be bored?

I suggested she wash a few dishes and vacuum her bedroom to break her boredom.

She rolled her eyes at me and told me that was not high on her list of exciting things to do.

When she finished the work, I offered to take her swimming. She suggested going shopping. I rolled my eyes at her and asked "Who's buying?" Her eyes twinkled knowingly as she smiled and looked at my checkbook.

We went to the library. I introduced her to some interesting books, which she checked out. It took her several hours to read them and took absolutely nothing from my checkbook.

But recently my child who sings, "I'm Bored," informed me that she had had the most exciting afternoon watching the washing machine wash the clothes.

I raised my eyebrows and asked, "You did what?"

"I opened the lid and watched the clothes go through all the wash cycles. I had to close it during the spin cycle though. The water was flying out on me." She looked rather pleased with herself.

I thought she was kidding me. I didn't think the machine would run with the lid open. But the next time I had a load in, she showed me exactly how to do it by carefully balancing the lid away from the switches.

I might have realized watching the clothes wash would intrigue her. When we were at an appliance store recently, she wished we owned the demonstrator dishwasher with its glass front. She thought it was fun to watch it wash dishes.

Watching clothes wash one time was not enough. She had to share the fun. She invited her brother to come watch. They had so much fun maybe next week we'll paint the fence just to watch it dry.

Like I said, we never have a dull moment at our house. If it even hints of boredom around here, we find some way to entertain ourselves.

September 19, 1994

There's No Vaccine for It

THE CLEANING BUG HITS AND there's no vaccine against it.

Saturday I planned to work on the family finances. I went to look for the canceled checks among the boxes on the closet shelf. I knew they had to be in one of three boxes, but the boxes were blocked by a very wobbly pile of slide trays and college books.

"We don't use all these books," I said.

Books plunked to the floor. Behind the books were the tennis rackets we had looked for in the summer.

Clearing off the rest of the shelf, I told my son to take the box of train cars to the attic, moved the three-year supply of Christmas wrapping paper, and found a Russian Bible Story book we had looked for last winter.

Out went the junk, anything not used in the past couple of years, the clothes and shoes no longer worn. Boxes and sacks of miscellaneous item went to the garage for storage, to a pile for our next garage sale, or straight to the dumpster. I actually vacuumed the carpet all the way to the back wall of the closet. The rearranged boxes of slides no longer threatened to topple on my head. I even found the checks.

Finding the checks led to sorting through all the important papers in the desk and its ten drawers. Between toting out garbage bags and moving things to the attic for me, my teens had a plastic card cooking party with credit cards, ATM cards, and phone cards we no longer use.

About 1 p.m. I remembered I had made tentative plans to meet with a friend that afternoon. I promised myself I would call as soon as I finished cleaning out the last desk drawer and took care of the stuff on my bed.

At 2 p.m. she called, "Are we going to get together today?" I looked around at the stuff still waiting to be sorted on my bed. I told her that the closet had lots of space, the back of the bookshelf had lost twelve years' worth of dust, and the desk was totally organized. "I have a few more things to take care of, and then I can take it easy."

She laughed, "You sound like you are in a cleaning mood. We'll get together another day. That mood might not return for a long time."

I didn't believe her, but when I went to vacuum the hall closet, the clutter of cold weather clothes and swimming goggles annoyed me.

Coats, hats, and gloves went flying.

At 10 p.m. both hall closets and the utility cupboard were neat, the desk was organized, and the bookshelf dusted. I decided to go to bed and read a good book. I went to the kitchen for a dish of ice cream to eat while reading. The ice cream sat melting on the counter while I relined two shelves with clean paper. Unable to concentrate on my book, I decided to brush my teeth and go to bed. As I was brushing my teeth, the jumbled bathroom drawers demanded my attention.

By 11:30 p.m. after unscrambling the drawers in both bathrooms, I turned out the light so I couldn't see anything else and collapsed into bed. May the cleaning bug hit me next time on a day when I am far, far away!

January 23, 1995

Clean Refrigerator Day

I MISSED IT: WHIRLPOOL CORPORATION'S "Clean out Your Refrigerator Day." The idea was to ensure a clean appliance for the holidays, but I did not have time to clean out last week's leftovers and unidentified shriveling objects (USO's) from my refrigerator before the holidays hit. I was busy preparing for my first holiday feast, a carry-in supper.

The whole idea was to remind folks to do the job before the refrigerator fills up with holiday foods. I heard about the official day too late to prepare the refrigerator for the holidays. I already had spent a month stockpiling holiday foods.

As soon as the grocery stores started advertising holiday foods at sale prices, I began stocking up. Why wait to pay more? If I can, I stock up now and avoid the shock of paying for it all at once. Plus, I keep thinking of more items I need to buy for special foods to fix for my poor, starving college kids.

I'm not worried that I missed the official day to clean out the refrigerator. I already am doing better than the 3 percent of the population (according to statistics) who never wash out their ice box. I even clean it more often than 18 percent who only clean it twice a year.

When they were younger, cleaning the refrigerator was easy. "You two with nothing better to do than tease each other. go clean out the refrigerator and wash the kitchen floor." That stopped the teasing every time.

It is becoming harder to keep the clutter cleared out. We don't have as many at home. Fortunately the college-aged sons and their friends are home often enough to put a dent in the refrigerator clutter. They vacuum up food from the refrigerator, cupboard, and freezer—sometimes even before it's carried into the house from the car. I do still have my teenager here to ensure the fridge is cleared of clutter. If I happen to slip and forget to toss out something, one of them will remind me: "Hey, Ma, have we kept this jam with the moss on top of it long enough?"

I still do have the pre-payday opportunity for cleaning: family food funds are low, so I don't go grocery shopping. Leftover goulash and broccoli join forces to become once-in-a-lifetime dishes. Odds and ends of vegetables are consumed, milk cartons emptied, and, before payday comes, the USOs hiding in shame in a back corner are exposed.

Even with the overload of Thanksgiving I can guarantee the fridge will be cleared of clutter. After a hectic day of supervising everyone else cooking and serving a meal, I will flop into the nearest chair and tell them to keep from starving the rest of the day by nibbling leftovers.

Did I say leftovers? Not for long! After a couple of days, we will know it is time for them to be heading back to the campus by the way their voices echo when they open the refrigerator door and ask, "Is there anything to eat?"

If the only answer is USOs, then we can be thankful that we have so much food that some goes to waste.

November 25, 1996

An Empty House Stays Tidy

WARNING BELLS SHOULD HAVE GONE off when my son said he was coming home with his wife and baby to see how much his childhood home had changed after our remodeling project. But, no warning bell sounded as I dusted the bookshelves, urged my husband to clear away as much of the remodeling debris as he could, and we rearranged the furniture.

I made up the bed in a room that used to be my son's and laid out toys, books, stuffed animals, and stacks of my latest garage sale finds in baby clothing. Thursday night I sighed happily. The house was perfect: counters cleared of dishes and food, floors swept and washed clean, and the dining room table free of the daily clutter of opening mail.

I don't know why I bothered.

They came, marveled at the new, open look in the living room, told us it all looked fantastic and began to unload their car. They hauled in luggage, baby toys, baby food, oriental vegetables, and trash from traveling. Snacks and drinks cluttered the counter and table. Suitcases and baskets of clothes lined the walls of the guest room. Shoes, socks, and diapers quickly decorated the living room.

Then my youngest son came home from college with an overflowing laundry bag labeled 'Hi, Mom, I'm home,' a backpack with notebooks spilling out, his camera, case, film, and albums of the photos. He was assigned to sleep in the living room so his gear landed in the corner behind the lounge chair. I have grown accustomed to college clutter and welcome the suitcases and snacks of the visiting sons and their wives. I had forgotten, however, just how much babies add to the confusion of living, especially after they begin to walk.

Just like all my children, the grandbaby picked up keys, books, and important pieces of paper that she left any place except where she found the stuff. She pulled picture books off the bottom bookshelf for me to read to her and put none of them back. Finger food went into her mouth, down her shirt, on her chair, and to the floor beneath her chair. When the baby saw the toys I had laid out for her, she picked them up one by one, cooed an excited baby "Wow!" and casually dropped each one as she reached for something else.

She continually reminded me how many things are not childproof: the framed family pictures my daughter and I arranged on the end tables, the breakable dishes I had moved to lower cupboards after I no longer had toddlers around, and my basket of cross stitch projects.

And I loved every minute of it. I talked, shopped, cooked, and played with the baby. After the last one left, it took less than an hour to pick up, wash the floor, and put away the dishes.

That done, I sat down and remembered what older women had told me years ago, "Don't worry about the house when your children are young. Enjoy them while you can. You will have plenty of years when they are gone to clean the house."

How right they were!

April 20, 1998

Keys to a Happy Home

WE WERE RUSHING AROUND ONE Sunday early in our marriage, preparing for a morning of worship. I was peeling potatoes for dinner, tossing necessary items in the baby's diaper bag, and yelling up the stairs at the boys to quit fighting and get dressed. In between all that, I threw a tablecloth over the table and slapped the dishes and silverware in place so we would not have to wait for dinner after we came home.

Finally we were ready. All the bambinos were dressed in their best bibs and tucker, hair plastered in place. Their breakfast of cereal and peanut butter and jam toast washed off.

My husband reached into his pocket for his car keys. They were gone. He was sure he had had them earlier that morning. The kids stood at the door watching us play "find the keys."

We only had one key and neither of us could find it. The Sunday School hour went by, the church hour began. No keys.

I gave up and put the finishing touches on dinner. We ate. The kids and my husband gathered up the dishes and pulled the tablecloth off the table. Keys jangled to the floor. In my Sunday morning rush, I had tossed the tablecloth and dishes on top of the car keys and never noticed them.

The next day my husband came home with four sets of keys and key rings. I hooked them on the Spanish wrought iron chandelier over the dining room table out of the reach of eager little fingers.

A few weeks later I could not find the scissors the children used in a craft project. I went to town, bought more scissors and hung them on the Spanish chandelier along with the keys and any scissors I subsequently found. That chandelier had a lot of handy hooks. I used every one of them in our quest to keep track of things.

One evening we had a family that had three daughters come to dinner. As we ate, the husband looked up at the chandelier, keys, and scissors hanging over his head. A pair of scissors aimed at his eye.

"You lose a lot of scissors and keys?"

I followed his gaze and realized how odd it must appear to have scissors and keys decorating the chandelier.

"Not since we began hanging them up here," I said, reaching up and unhooking all the scissors. I carried them to the kitchen and promptly lost them in the junk drawer.

Through the years we added more little fingers to grab the keys adults carelessly laid down on tables, assuming they would be there when they returned. We also lost keys in coat jackets, purses, and behind the furniture, but thanks to the chandelier and the extra keys, we could always drive to town and get more.

When we moved to our next house, the dining room chandelier lacked the hooks and curves of its wrought iron counterpart. I bought a key rack and stuck our scissors in the junk drawer. We lost our decorated chandelier but kept track of our keys.

Well, we do most of the time. My list of "Things to do today" includes "copy the keys." We are down to three sets—again.

June 15, 1998

Such a Good Son

MY SON'S THREE-WEEK-OLD SON IS a good baby, but he is still an infant with a twenty-two month-old sister. Momma is overwhelmed with two babies, housekeeping, and meal preparations.

Recently she said my son asked her, "Why don't you keep this house clean? My mom kept the house clean all the time." His memory is a bit faulty.

His father wearied of the children's clutter just as much as my son does now. Occasionally on Sunday afternoon hubby would take a broom upstairs to the back bedroom and start sweeping. Toys, clothes, sneakers, game pieces, homework assignments whirled before him. By the time he started sweeping down the stairs, he was pushing trash and dirt. Everything else had been put away.

Downstairs my husband swept the dining room, kitchen, and bathroom. Once everything was restored to order, he sighed happily, went to the kitchen, and popped a couple gallons of popcorn to begin a new mess.

I told my son about the week I stayed home from Bible Study because, "The house is a mess. I have to get it cleaned up."

When he was eight, our last child and only daughter was born. It was the very beginning of the gardening and canning season; school was out and all her brothers were home. I had my hands full just making it through each day. I didn't realize how poorly I was doing until my husband said, "The family reunion is Sunday. We're going. I want something to eat besides scrambled eggs." We went to the reunion. He ate pot roast, ham, meat loaf, and tuna surprise. I showed off the new baby and quit making eggs for supper.

When the baby was three weeks old, we were expecting company early one evening. My husband looked around and said, "We need to clean up before they get here. There are diapers everywhere."

I guess my son, the new father, was too young to remember those days, but he should have remembered our house cleaning routine when he was in grade school. Beginning with the oldest child and going down, I would say, "Okay, time to clean up. You pick up seventy-five things; you take care of sixty, and you fifty, and putting away the building blocks only counts for five things." (I added that clause after my second son counted each piece as he dropped Tinker Toys back into the can while the rest of us took dishes to the kitchen and pulled out shoes and socks from under the couch.) The young father had forgotten.

"Aw, come on," I said, "surely you remember coming home from college and veg'ing out with your brother over Christmas break, watching one movie after another while you ate everything in sight."

After several movies the room was a wreck. They wanted more movies. I told them, "Sure, when this place is cleaned up." They moved for the first time that day, shaking crumbs out of the blankets and pillows, gathering up their trash, vacuuming, and returning dishes to the kitchen.

Nope, he didn't remember that, but he did remember that his mother kept an immaculate house. He is such a good son; now to work on that father and husband thing!

January 25, 1999

Ironing for Mom

WRESTLING THE IRONING BOARD INTO an upright position, Mom plugged in her iron, pulled the basket of rolled shirts, slacks, and dresses that had been sprinkled with water next to her, and began ironing and ironing and ironing.

As a six-year-old, I watched and asked to do it.

She didn't offer to buy me a toy iron and ironing board. She did not say, "No, you might burn yourself." She didn't say one word about waiting until I was bigger. My mom believed kids could do a lot of things very early in life.

"You can iron some handkerchiefs as soon as I get some clothes ready for church," she promised as she expertly whipped clothes from basket to board to hangers.

Lowering the board and turning the heat down on the iron, she showed me how to press the white squares my dad carried in his shirt pocket and the blue and red paisley squares he carried in his pants pocket.

"Smooth it all out flat with your hands. Now pick up the iron and iron it. Careful, don't iron in a wrinkle. Put the iron down. Now fold it in half; iron the fold. Fold that into another square, iron the fold, and then make a rectangle and iron it all flat and neat."

I suppose she said something about the iron being hot, about keeping my hand away from the heated base of the iron, but since she always said she had very smart children, she probably did not belabor the point. She expected us to use our brains and was not one to fuss and refuse to let us try things because we might get hurt.

She watched me press a handkerchief and then handed me several that needed ironing. I proudly stepped up to the board and tackled my job of ironing handkerchiefs.

In time I worked my way up to ironing skirts, slacks, and shirts with buttons. She reserved pressing my dad's suits for herself. That required a damp towel placed over each section of the coat before pressing. Pressing most anything silk or wool waited until I had matured enough to understand the expense and delicacy of the fabrics.

As a child of the 1950s, ironing was simply part of a girl's growing up and learning to take care of herself and her house. No self-respecting female would ever show up in wrinkled clothes; that would bespeak slovenly habits. No matter how much our family income fluctuated, my mom made sure her children left the house neatly dressed.

Once, just once, I tried to do less when she was around.

I had arrived at my parent's house with my family of boys and a heap of luggage. As the guys ran outside to play that first morning, I pulled a cotton sun dress out of my suitcase and slipped it over my head. I looked in the mirror and noticed a couple creases but figured it would do.

That's not how my mom figured it. She took one look and said, "My ironing board is in the bedroom if you want to use it."

I took the hint and spent a couple minutes smoothing out the travel wrinkles.

Within half an hour my grandmother drove up to see me and my family. She complimented me on the sun dress. I told her I had made it. An expert seamstress, she looked at it closely.

After she left, Mom turned to me, "Now aren't you glad you ironed that dress?"

Her remark followed me across the years and miles to this morning as I dressed, looked in the mirror, and saw wrinkles on the polo shirt I planned to wear for the day. Looking at the clock, at my already combed hair, and the still folded ironing board, I sighed, plugged in the iron, took off the shirt, and ironed it. It took all of three minutes to smooth the collar, the sleeves, the back, and front of the shirt to meet my mom's approval...and I'm sure grandma would have given me a compliment as well.

April 19, 2010

Kitchen Service

"We always knew the grocery store's special of the week. When chicken was on sale, we received a lot of chicken casseroles," observed the bemused mother of a young family. She had mostly finished a lengthy recuperation from an accident. She was not complaining. With weeks of rehabilitation, she welcomed everything anyone did to help her family through that difficult time.

Until a family crisis disrupted our quiet, empty nest, I did not understand how much she appreciated the help. My husband and I threw a few clothes into carry-on bags and flew away to assist as needed and keep tabs on the crisis. By default I took on kitchen duty and some supervision of the children.

Standing there in an unfamiliar kitchen with a confusing array of roads to unfamiliar shops and markets, I was unsure where to begin a meal. Then a woman from the church called to ask what we needed, could use, and how much storage space we had available in the freezer.

The next day a Thanksgiving dinner arrived: a gallon of gravy, a tub of mashed potatoes, a tray of sweet potatoes, one huge turkey, a heaping bowl of corn, trays of rolls, and cranberry sauce.

The kids loved it. Of course, there was no way we could eat it all in one sitting, but the leftovers staved off hunger and kept us occupied developing a variety of dishes for subsequent meals. The two rotisserie chickens that came a couple days, turkey with leftover gravy and vegetables made chicken salad, and a couple of fantastic chicken pot pies that everyone scarfed down.

As I made my way through the collage of foods that followed, I became keenly aware of the blessing of helps provided through this ministry. Some of the women I never saw. They left a frozen casserole at the church or sent one along with another person's delivery.

The meal coordinators even called and visited to gather information on what help and foods the family needed and passed the information along to others. When a grandchild answered the phone and then asked me, "Do we still need peanut butter?" I thought it was a family member in the grocery store.

"Yes," I said thinking of peanut butter and jam, one of my comfort foods and handy for quick sandwiches for kids to make and carry to activities.

Besides being free from most shopping, I also did not have to deal with stacks of dirty dishes from cooking. I could focus on the crisis and keep the children on task with their school work or sit down at the computer and update concerned folks with the latest news.

The grandkids also amazed me with their willingness to pitch in, take care of their own clothes, their own dishes, help with younger siblings, and clean up their own messes. When we worked together, I did not need to coach them through the process of making cookies, washing dishes or rearranging the refrigerator for the turkey leftovers. They knew what to do and jumped right into doing it. But the prepared meals also gave them time to make "get well" cards, focus on their daily routines, and still have time to play.

I am quite capable working in a kitchen, but in the midst of a crisis, I realized the relief of being able to focus on the crisis and the family. For all the folks who ever prepared meals for others through the years, if no one ever said, "Thank you," take this as your personal note. Your contribution is, and was, greatly appreciated.

October 11, 2010

Convenient Couch

THE FAMILY COUCH SERVES MANY purposes: extra seating, spare bed, conversation corner, landing spot for jumping kids, hospital corner for the sick, raw resources for a fort, and physical therapy.

Our first couch came with the fixer-upper house we bought. Its dusty rose cloth upholstery matched the overstuffed chair from the 1940's.

Every couple of years I sat on the couch for family pictures as we welcomed each new baby. We have pictures of a big brother bringing his favorite comforter to the crying baby, big brothers crowding around to welcome the newborn, and pictures of the infant propped against pillows in the corner of the couch.

Preschoolers loved to stand on the couch arm and jump into its cushions. They thrilled with their brief moment of flight, quite convinced that they had just performed some fantastic feat worthy of a spot in a circus. It provided a soft landing for practicing their new skills in jumping and was none the worse for wear.

For a brief time after an accident, we followed a prescribed physical therapy regime at home. I arranged the couch's cotton stuffed cushions over table leaves wedged against the couch to make an incline plane for the exercise of rolling up and down.

On rainy days couch cushions provided hours of entertainment, especially combined with the cushions from other furniture, pillows, and blankets. We had lots of cushions after we replaced the vintage couch and chair with two couches, a love seat, and another chair. Standing couch cushions on end, the children made tunnels, bridges, and hidden rooms using blankets dragged to the living room to serve as roof coverings and additional walls.

During their day of play I lost the living room to a maze of cushions and blankets stretched from wall to wall. I lost the kids as they squirmed under and through the fabric maze they had created. And yes, I lost my nomination for Home Beautiful with the mess, but I knew they were building memories, entertaining themselves, and developing self-confidence and their imaginations as they designed and built a pillow fort with designated areas for sleep, play, and eating.

In recent years, I have seen cloth play houses for children: Cute collapsible structures of light plastic frames with fabric walls that easily fold and stash behind the couch. These collapsible houses provide less mess, less wear and tear on the furniture, and more appeal than stripping the beds of blankets and furniture of cushions, but they lack the versatility of the family couch.

Imagination gives way to comfort as the couch becomes a hospital bed for teens recuperating from dental work or some minor injury.

Occasionally the couch bed provided extra sleeping space when an overflow of visitors maxed out the sleeping space in the bedrooms. Add a couple of sheets, blankets, and pillows, and the couch had an eight-hour resident—after the evening games ended, that is.

Playing UNO, Sorry, or Monopoly at the coffee table with players perched on the couch provides a spot sturdy enough to absorb the energy and excitement of players caught up in a game, bouncing on the cushions in their excitement. During late night movie times viewers piled around the couch for comfort in the scary parts.

Conversation flows down memory lane when we pull out our ancient slides, prop the projector on a chair, remove the pictures from the wall, and once again come together on the living room couch.

The versatile couch has seen toddlers hiding in its cushions, grade school students flopping down to read a book, and teens chatting with friends. It's a comfortable place to hang out, especially this week when I stayed home with a cold and needed to work on a column.

Add one laptop to the couch, and I had an instant at-home office, but what else would we expect from the versatile living room couch!

June 13, 2011

Meal Times

When the Kids Turn the Tables

MY TODDLER PLAYED AROUND MY mom's couch as I stood in my bare feet at the counter washing the morning dishes. The morning clutter cleared away, my mother and I prepared to talk. My mom tipped back her lounge chair. As I propped my bare feet on the ottoman, the toddler walked by my feet, stopped, and stared at the bottoms of my feet.

"Dirty, dirty," he tsked and went to the kitchen. He returned with a wet paper towel dripping from his hand.

Wadding the towel into a tight ball in his hand, he knelt down, and began scrubbing the soles of my feet. Mom and I stopped talking, barely breathing as he worked. We quietly smiled at each other, sharing, only with our eyes, the holiness of that moment.

He finished, dropped the towel on the floor, and went back to his toys. My mother and I quietly resumed our conversation without referring to my foot washing. Some events are demeaned with words.

He never washed my feet again, but one Sunday after a light lunch in town, we went home to collapse into sleep. I woke to scrabbling, scratching noises, whispers, and quick hushes.

As I wandered out to the kitchen to start supper, I noticed that the "elves" were up to something. The youngest was rummaging in the china cupboard. Candles were laid out on the counter.

The foot washing toddler, now a tall, teen-aged male, sported a kitchen towel draped over his arm. He was followed by a smaller female version with a towel over her arm.

Something was up.

I went to the bedroom and told my husband to prepare for our surprise.

"Is Dad ready, yet?" the waiter asked.

"Almost," I whispered.

The waiter passed the information on to the waitress and a flurry of noise ensured.

Anticipating being entertained at a fancy restaurant with our blue flowered china, matching tablecloth, and polished wood candle holders, we went to the dining room.

The red plaid terry cloth of the past two meals was still on the table. Paper plates in bamboo holders graced each setting. One white and one brown root beer bottle with mismatched candles stood behind the bottles of seasonings.

When we were seated, the waiter stood beside us, holding a pad of paper, "What would you like to eat?"

My husband and I stared at him, at a loss for words: We didn't have a menu. The waiter heard us anyway, "Ahh, an excellent choice."

The waitress pulled out the casserole I had prepared that morning.

She carefully filled the pint jars with water while he explained that the table decor was supposed to be an old, Italian restaurant.

"Very realistic," I murmured.

As we picked up our forks, the phone rang. I quickly answered, recognized the caller, and asked, "Could you call back in about half an hour? The children are serving us dinner."

It isn't often that my children do the serving. I intend to relish every moment of it that I can.

November 8, 1993

Supper on the Roof

"MOM, SOMEONE IN SCHOOL ASKED me today if we really ate supper on the roof." My child was outraged at the question.

For years, that rumor has spread. My daughter and sons have been quizzed every year by the new kids who hear the rumor.

When I taught in another school, transfer students told my students, who also asked if it were true. It is time to put the question to rest.

Yes, we did, but only years after the question began to be asked. The rumor began several years ago when my teenaged sons were coming home for lunch every day often inviting their friends. One spring day I made up sandwiches and juice to feed them and a couple of friends. However, the lunch crew that stormed through our door was twice the normal size. Counting the hands grabbing sandwiches from the plate, I grabbed mayo and bread to make more.

Waving a fistful of sandwich, one guy said, "Let's eat outside." They disappeared out the back door to the picnic table on the patio as quickly as they had barged in the front. It was a perfect warm, sunny spring day for a picnic.

Inside I hurriedly slapped together more sandwiches, stirred up another pitcher of juice, and carried it all outside. No one was there.

I could hear them, but the picnic table was empty.

"Hand'em up," the voice was above me. Sons and friends were perched on the peak of the low grade roof of our ranch style home. An extension ladder still leaned against the house from where it had been used the previous afternoon to get a Frisbee from the roof. I stood on the picnic table and handed him the plate of food. His brother scrambled down the ladder for the pitcher.

As they ate, they waved at friends driving cars past our house on their way to and from lunch. From that day on the legend of the high rise meal at the Hershberger's house began and has grown.

Sure, the Hershbergers, a couple of them, ate lunch, not supper, on the roof that day, but so did a number of their classmates. No one ever asks about them.

We had the name, so we played the game. As my daughter grew up, she included time on the roof in her list of ideas for entertaining friends. Last fall I realized how casual I had become about rooftop experiences. A concerned friend said, "I don't know if I should say anything, but last week when I was over in that area, your kid and a friend were sitting on the roof."

Puzzled, I asked, "And this is a problem?"

I went home and cross-examined my child about who, when, where and how safe was the roof.

When my son's fiancée visited us the week before her wedding she asked to do something different. The best man for the wedding arranged the ladder, my daughter laid out a picnic table cloth, I fixed a chicken supper and we initiated her into the grandeur of eating supper on the roof.

That's the only time I have ever been on the roof. So yes, we ate supper on the roof, but it was many, many years after everyone began asking if it was true.

December 2, 1996

Knock Off the Peanut Butter

OF ALL MY CHILDREN, THE oldest son loved peanut butter the most. At seven-years-old, he loved it in a sandwich, on celery, and smeared over pancakes, waffles, and French toast.

I blessed the inventor of cheap peanut butter sandwiches and quick celery snacks.

I objected loud and clear to anyone eating pancakes, waffles, and French toast with gooey peanut butter spread over them instead of sticky syrup. He was in that charming stage of childhood where the only food to eat was peanut butter. He could not see why I objected.

I was in the early stages of adulthood and exploring food from various ethnic groups with new recipes every few days. I could not see why peanut butter was all he wanted to eat.

In spite of his protests, his love for peanut butter stuck longer than with any other child I had. I bit my tongue a lot, but not enough.

I told other mothers about his obsession with peanut butter. They told me that their children loved peanut butter on apples, between parts of split banana, and with raisins. Someone, I refuse to remember who, said they actually liked a good peanut butter and banana sandwich.

One day when I was weeding our garden, my next door neighbor, Elizabeth, a grandmother, came out to pick lettuce in her garden. We visited a bit. I commented on the seven-year-old's obsession with peanut butter. She laughed. She had seen plenty of her own children, grandchildren and great-grandchildren go through the same phase.

"You know," she said, "every so often even Aaron likes to take fresh leaf lettuce from the garden, spread a slice of bread with salad dressing, another slice with peanut butter, and put leaf lettuce between."

I shook my head in disbelief. Aaron was her seventy-two-year-old husband. "I thought it was such a strange thing to eat," she continued, "but I tried it one time and was surprised that I liked it."

I looked at her incredulously: peanut butter, mayonnaise, and leaf lettuce? It did not sound very appetizing to me. But a few days later, I wanted something different to eat. I made a trip out to our garden, grabbed a handful of lettuce, washed it off, and tried her sample recipe. It actually wasn't too bad.

I sat back and reconsidered my position from the wisdom of my whole twenty-odd years. I surely had never had any major food obsessions like this. Then I remembered that as a seven-year-old I ate a lot of toast with catsup. I decided it was time for a truce.

As we approached the peanut butter lover's birthday, I went to the grocery store and bought two five-pound jars of peanut butter. One I put on the shelf for family use. The other I wrapped up and gave to him for his birthday.

"It's yours. Do with it as you please. I will say no more."

He grinned, grabbed a waffle, and smothered the thing.

After his jar was empty, I even put a jar of peanut butter on the table myself when we had pancakes, waffles or French toast for breakfast.

October 7, 1996

Get All You Can, Can All You Get

As a college student the pioneering spirit called me. I yearned for the experience of gardening and canning its produce. I married a man with a similar dream. He raked the freshly plowed garden, made furrows, planted seeds, and spent his weekend eliminating weeds.

He relished each piece of fresh produce from our garden that we ate, canned or frozen. Initially we borrowed jars from his mother's excess. Eventually I owned hundreds of jars that I filled each summer and emptied each winter. Our ten-feet-deep basement had two ceiling-to-floor sets of shelves built just for canning jars. We bought the largest freezer we could find to hold fruits and vegetables, sides of beef, and the fifty pounds of popcorn our family of five sons consumed for snacks each year.

Canning season began shortly after the school year ended with flats of fresh strawberries I transformed into quarts of jam. We spent weekdays in the garden and weekends at nearby orchards picking bushels of fruit.

The easiest day was when we picked blueberries and bagged them for the freezer. The worst day was when I cut up dozens of tiny, sweet pumpkins to puree and process through the pressure cooker. The next day my cutting arm would not move.

In our ninth and tenth summers, I kept busy canning or freezing about seven hundred quarts of fruits and vegetables. At the beginning of our eleventh summer we sold our house, garden, and canning shelves. Just before the Realtor called us, I had gotten a bushel of green beans to clean, cut, and can. I was so stunned I forgot about them. They rotted in their basket.

The moving company sent three men to pack up the house. One man wrapped and boxed canning jars. The other two packed everything else.

We left our two story house with a basement and the fertile soil of Indiana for the hardened clay of Arkansas and a cement slab house. I spent hours unwrapping canning jars. The top shelves of the kitchen and laundry room were crammed with jars. I was ready to begin canning, but I never did. Gardening wasn't the same as it had been in Indiana. And—let's face it—I was tired of my great pioneering adventure.

I coveted my kitchen shelves for other things. I stuffed boxes of canning jars in the storage space over our garage and stocked up on grocery store sales of fruits and vegetables. Through the years I sold all my canning equipment and most of the jars.

In the summer I overhear women chatting about their busy week putting up butter beans, canning peaches, or making brine for pickles. I listen with empathy. Sometimes at a pot luck dinner I get a taste of triple sweet corn from someone's garden, blanched, cut off the cob, and frozen. It tastes so good. I think wistfully of garden fresh corn until I remember those hot summer days spent fishing ears of corn out of steam baths. And that's quite enough to make grocery store corn taste mighty good. The pioneering spirit calls, but I am no longer home.

August 16, 1999

Macaroni and Cheese

KNOWLEDGE OF MY LIFELONG AFFINITY for homemade macaroni and cheese has spread across the Internet to the rural community of five hundred in Goessel, Kansas, where Terah Yoder Goerzen lives. In April she wrote, "I came to read your blog through an odd open source software and Mennonite connection that could only happen online." It makes sense to me. Hershberger is, after all, a very popular Amish/Mennonite last name.

She identified with my early training in the kitchen. "I was in fourth-grade when my mom went to work full time, leaving me with daily instructions for how to get supper going. That really is a great way to learn your way around a kitchen!" she wrote.

It was my favorite dish which caught Goerzen's eye.

"Just yesterday I was searching through recipe books for a good baked macaroni and cheese recipe. The ones I found basically said to make a white sauce, add some cheese, and bake. I want something with more pizazz (aka fattening flavor) like a great-aunt would bring to a potluck. Your story made me wonder if you might have such a recipe. If you do, would you mind sharing?" she wrote.

Her letter stumped me. One of my sons loves macaroni and cheese. His wife has asked me to give her the recipe. Since I don't have one, I've tried to tell her. I just sort of know how to make it. That evening, I made the dish and tried to capture the recipe on paper and emailed Goerzen as follows.

I am really going to have to get my recipe figured out more precisely. Basically, it is about a pound of elbow macaroni. If you want, add a bit of onion for extra flavor to the boiling water. While it boils, I grate a block of sharp cheese, one to two pounds. This really depends on how much I am making. I like LOTS of cheese. I put it in a greased bowl with a couple of eggs, salt, pepper, and maybe a squeeze or two of mustard.

Stir all the macaroni up with the cheese, eggs, and seasonings and add enough milk to fill up the dish and bake at 375 degrees.

Of late I have hurried things along by using the microwave, but then I stir it every five to ten minute to heat it through. This makes a very creamy textured dish. I like it baked in the oven because then it becomes a molded half-sphere with a browned edge.

I have varied it by adding broccoli bits, hot dogs, or bits of ham. I tried peas. I didn't like it.

The type of cheese makes a difference. My mother made it when my sister's family visited. Her husband raved about my mother's mac and cheese and miffed my sister because she knew she always followed Mom's recipe. She had. That time Mom had used a milder cheese. I've used odds and ends of all sorts of flavors of block cheese, including jalapeno cheese (nice and spicy).

Once I went to a fancy restaurant with my sister. We ordered a tantalizing sounding entree using an exotic white cheese. We took a bite and laughed; it was mom's macaroni and cheese using spaghetti.

As children we took leftover macaroni and cheese, sliced and fried it in lots of butter for breakfast. Okay, it exceeded the fat calorie limits, but it was crunchy, delicious.

In Kansas Terah received my email and tried her hand at using my loose guidelines for macaroni and cheese including recognizing the flexibility of the recipe.

"Your recipe was even a hit with my husband who claims that he doesn't like macaroni and cheese. I told him it was a 'cheese casserole.' I had a half cup of cottage cheese waiting to expire in the fridge, so I added that too. I love the thought of fried macaroni for breakfast! Definitely something from the days when fat, calories, and cholesterol didn't matter at all! Thanks, again!"

No problem, Terah. I aim to please, and good food is the shortest route to anyone's heart.

August 11, 2008

Eat It Up or Else

MY MOTHER ALWAYS ADMONISHED HER five children to "eat what is put before you, especially when you are company. Don't make any complaints." She stuck with the ordinary, standard dishes, thoroughly tested, and well liked and only served milk or water for beverages. (I know that is going to be hard for a southerner, brought up on iced tea to understand, but my father owned a dairy farm, and he believed in his product.)

As I remember my first encounter with my then husband-to-be's family, one Sunday afternoon his three brothers, sister, and their spouses were there.

His mom had prepared a feast for our eating pleasure around the kitchen table. I don't remember the meal, but I do remember the dessert. She had made her first key lime pie. She said she followed the recipe closely, except "When I make lemon pie the recipe calls for me to grate a bit of rind into the filling. So I decided to do the same with this lime pie recipe."

My guy was the first to taste his mom's pie. He chewed, grimaced, swallowed, and gasped, "Don't eat it, it's awful."

We all looked at him in shocked surprise. No one took his advice. Everyone took a piece of the key lime pie. One by one we plunged our forks through the meringue, into the filling, cut the crust, carried it to our mouths, and began chewing. It had a marvelous whipped meringue, lovely rich filling, and flaky crust.

I relaxed as I tasted that filling. I love a good lemon pie. I wondered what his problem was until I tasted one of the bitter, bitter bits of grated lime skin liberally sprinkled throughout the tangy filling.

Like something out of the Twilight Zone, we all grimaced in unison as we each finished up our pieces of pie, almost liking each bite until we got yet another one of those pieces of lime rind. Everyone said, "It's awful." But, everyone ate their whole piece of pie.

It must have been love at first bite for us. We came from kindred backgrounds with a cardinal rule: "Eat what is put before you." But at his house with his folks, while we ate the stuff, we could jokingly complain the whole time.

January 8, 1996

Family Life

Keeping Up with the Clutter

MY SON WAS HEADING OUT for a day of mowing lawns. As he walked out he turned, looked around, and frowned at what he saw. The current woodworking project with the sand paper, hammer, and glue graced one corner. Duets of shoes and dirty socks made a semi-circle around the TV. Empty popcorn dishes and plastic glasses littered the floor and end tables. Wadded blankets and pillows decorated the couches, chairs, and floor. It was a typical Monday morning mess.

"Mom, this house needs cleaning."

"Sure does, and your shoes, socks, and dirty dishes are included."

From the parents on down, once Sunday dinner is served, no one works around here on Sundays. The house always needs cleaning Monday morning.

Once the Sunday dinner dishes are loaded into the dishwasher after eating, all the snacks, supper dishes, and the huge washbasin used for popped corn waits for Monday morning. We are taking our seventh day of rest.

Once upon a time on Sunday afternoon, when the children were much younger, my husband swept up everything in his path from the bedrooms to the front of the house. The kids would rush alongside him, rescuing stray toys, clothes, and building blocks. Once the house was clean, my husband would go to the kitchen and make the biggest pan full of popcorn ever seen. Then the kids tackled the task of spreading popcorn to every corner of the house.

As the family matured, the toys were sold off at garage sales. The clean sweep routine ceased but not our traditional Sunday evening pan of popcorn. It still leaves strays on the carpet, chairs, and couches. Monday morning, I crunch over kernels on the floor in the kitchen as I clean the stove of the spattered oil and a few un-popped kernels.

By Monday morning not only does the great room and kitchen need cleaning but so does the bathroom with its mountain of dirty clothes that has accumulated since Friday.

I grabbed enough blue jeans or T-shirts to make a load for the washing machine. I assigned each child to take care of fifty things that no one admits to having left behind. Years ago, I gave up arguing about who left what where. Since no one will admit to leaving anything anywhere, everyone helps take care of everything.

Once when I mentioned, in passing, my standard, "Okay, everyone pick up fifty things apiece," the listener turned to me in relief and said, "You have that much clutter in your house, too?"

Well, sure, our four children keep pretty busy helping us make messes. I hate to admit it, but Sunday isn't the only time this house looks like we are major slobs. We do so well on Sundays because we practice so much during the week. I actually have told my four children, "You each take care of seventy-five things before you watch any TV or go out to play."

Ahhh, thank heavens, they are all so much older, more mature and capable these days, and off to college. The house stays so much cleaner this way except Monday mornings.

August 22, 1994

Hard Work Pays Off

"I GOT A C IN Phys. Ed," the thirteen-year-old son sighed. He gave me his last report card for the year.

"I had a few C's in gym myself," I said as I handed him the newspaper sack heavy with the day's papers. He shrugged, hooked the sack to his bike's handle bars, and rode off to deliver newspapers before supper. After supper he and his dad were too busy digging a hole under our house to discuss the grade.

At the time we lived in Indiana. Building foundations have to be four to six feet deep to reach below the freeze line. Many home builders go a few feet deeper to make the area into a cellar or basement.

Our house had come with enough space to store a few things underneath, but was far short of the full eight to ten feet deep basement with cement floor and block walls. Although we lacked the funds to pay for a professional to jack up the house and clear out the dirt with a small bulldozer, we could afford the couple of dirt elevators to move the dirt above the ground, a pick ax and shovels to load the elevators.

Father and sons began moving the dirt out from under the house by the shovelful. The preschoolers and I stayed out of the way, taking care of the newest baby.

As they dug deeper and farther under the house, father and sons propped up the house on eight-inch oak beams. My husband would arrange a base to secure the jack and beams used to raise our two-story home a couple of inches. The average grade Phys. Ed. student helped move, lift, and push ten-feet oak beams into place, held them steady, and eventually cranked the jack a few times to lift the house a tenth of an inch. With the floors moving slowly up and (sometimes quickly) down, I lived in my own personal, manmade, earthquake zone.

As the summer progressed, the heavy dirt elevators were moved and adjusted a couple of times to make them more accessible.

Among summer fun, paper route deliveries, and work, the men toiled at digging out the basement with some help from their friends. The women and children stayed out of the way.

I watched amused and amazed when our teenager and his dad shared glances of camaraderie during meals as they talked about the dig. Our son exuded confidence and budding manhood from every pore as the summer progressed.

They finally began moving cement blocks down into the big dirt hole under our house. As the wall of blocks rose ten feet to meet the house and oak beams, the once ninety-eight pound weakling whacked them out of place with a couple of blows of a sledge hammer.

He went back to school and Phys. Ed. class. When he received his five week progress report, that same coach gave him an A. During parent-teacher conferences my husband asked the coach about the difference in the grades.

"I have never seen such a change in a kid over one summer in my entire life," the coach said. "He can do anything." It was an amazing summer of hard work; it truly was.

March 18, 1996

Breaking the Habit

I TRY TO QUIT, BUT this twenty-five year habit of mothering is hard to break. Take this summer. My youngest is now fifteen. Everyone else is out of the home and does not need to be told to get up, go to work, and be responsible. All of them have learned to take care of themselves.

But can I stop reminding them?

No. Not me.

Not with my two college students. They both made it through a whole year of dorm living, washed their own clothes, and got to class and work on time. They studied and did their assignments well enough to make the dean's list this past semester. They did it all without my help or prodding. Nonetheless, as soon as they walk in that front door, I shift into my mother hen mode.

I really try to hold my tongue and not tell them to get up, get going, and be at work on time.

Sometimes I actually succeed.

Take last week. My son with the oddest hours for work was off visiting friends. He was having a grand time for a few hours before knuckling down and being a responsible adult.

He had a couple of hours drive to get home for work that night. I knew he needed to stop by the house to pick up a couple of things before work. My overly anxious, maternal instincts began wondering where he was five hours before he needed to be at work. It takes him less than fifteen minutes to drive to work.

My adult, non-maternal, logic kept telling me, "As long as he is home half-an-hour before work, he will have plenty of time."

Once, twice, three times, my hands started to pick up the phone and dial where he was having fun to say, "Look, you need to start home by at least 4:30 to make it to work by seven."

I didn't do it. I didn't even touch the phone, but I surely did think about it a lot. He walked in about 4:30. He had come back early enough to take care of some business at the bank. He tossed his dirty clothes in the hamper, cleared out the refrigerator, chatted for a while, and left for work with time to spare.

When he had a 7 a.m. shift, he opted the night before to watch videos and stay with a friend who is going away for several weeks. I was up at 5:30 a.m., watching the clock, and slapping my hand back from picking up the phone to call and make sure he was awake. He came in at six. He had actually slept most of the night and got up early enough to gas up the car. Pretty good, especially considering that both his parents' cars registered empty! Who needs reminding to take care of things anyway?

Okay, so even with irregular hours, he can get to work on time and take care of his life. I can quit worrying about him.

But there is always my other son who is off to college for a summer session. Heavy things those summer classes: Class every day, intense intellectual stimulation, the nightly bull sessions, and weekend expeditions to explore the big city of Chicago.

When I couldn't reach him by phone after 10:30 one night, I sent him an email asking if he was getting enough sleep.

He emailed back his sleeping schedule.

He's sleeping more than I am. I must learn to let go.

And I will, as soon as I wake up my fifteen-year-old.

June 24, 1996

House Rules

"I REALLY LIKE IT HERE," my son's friend said as they played a game of chess on the floor. "I would love to live here." He was looking for a new place to live. I overheard his comment from the corner where I sat working at the computer.

"Yeah," I said, "that's what his roommate said when he was here this spring. He wanted to come and stay for the summer until he found out what the house rules were."

Friend looked at son, "Really?"

Son nodded, "Yep."

He never asked what the house rules were, nor did he say anything about moving in with us.

Guests in our home are treated differently than permanent residents, especially those in that in-between stage of life: the high school graduate who is not married.

By that time I figure they are old enough to handle a job, wash clothes, make meals, and pay their way.

The first time we had an in-betweener came when my stepson arrived declaring, "I'm twenty going on sixteen."

I declared, "You either enroll in summer school or find a job."

He found a job and signed up for summer school.

The rule hit my oldest son full force a couple of weeks after he graduated. He thought he would sleep all day and sit up all night in front of the computer, calling bulletin board systems across the country. We got our phone bill before the younger ones finished school that year. I yanked him out of bed that morning and sent him to find a job so fast he made sure he was in school or working every summer afterward.

We all made an exception to the rule the summer our now college sophomore was sick in bed. As soon as he was capable of helping a little around the house, though, I handed him a broom.

Until this summer that was the only exception to the rule when both college sons had summer jobs lined up. Then one was offered and eagerly accepted a fellowship for summer session at Notre Dame. The youngest simply wanted to experience life somewhere else. He went to New Orleans and spent days filling out applications before he found a job driving an ice cream truck twelve hours a day, earning below minimum wages. He traded that job for sitting weekends with a terminally ill patient. During the week he packed a duffel bag and headed to church camp.

Our youngest son's work with that patient and our other son's summer school at Notre Dame both ended the same weekend. With eight weeks of summer left, we had two unemployed lunks hogging the couch and lounge chair as they waited to go to Rochester, N.Y. to help my aging father who needed companions and help getting around the city after an encounter with the medical world.

By the time they returned, college was a couple of weeks away. No more short term jobs or summer school: they slept, read, watched videos, visited family and friends, worked around the house, and teased me. Last week they finally left for college saying that next summer will be different.

I sincerely hope so.

September 2, 1996

To Drop Out or Not

OUR TEENAGER DISAGREED WITH EVERYTHING we said, declared we were too strict, and wanted more independence than we were ready to give. Inevitably we clashed. Late into that night we talked, reasoned, and argued. Nothing made any difference.

Finally, we simply declared enough. My husband had to be at work very early and the teenager had school. Back in the privacy of our bedroom, my husband said, "He is going to get up tomorrow and want to drop out of school. What are we going to do?"

Shocked at the unthinkable having been spoken, all I could envision was having a teenager with an attitude at home, every day, all day long. A teenager who already resisted afterschool chores and errands, even those related to a small afterschool job.

The resentment rose in me at the thought of dealing with that attitude every day all day long except when he was at work. We finally decided if he was determined to drop out, he would have to pay for his share of the household expenses. We mentally reviewed the monthly household expenses that everyone used: electricity, water, basic phone, food, and house payments. We totaled them up, averaged out the cost per day per person and fell into an uneasy sleep.

Next morning, the youngest got up, ate breakfast, and dressed. The elementary children crawled out of bed, dressed for school, and packed book bags. The teenager huddled in his bed. I went to his room and reminded him, "The bus leaves in fifteen minutes."

"I don't feel good," he whined from the security of his blankets.

"Probably not, after having stayed up that late, but, your dad had less sleep than you and he was at work an hour ago." I walked out.

He meandered into the living room and looked at me carefully, "What if I don't go to school?"

My husband's late-night premonition had prepared me for the question of the day. I was not shocked. I was fuming. However, I calmly said, "Your dad and I talked about that last night. We decided that if you did not go to school, you would have to pay room and board." I assured him that his small job could not cover the cost as I mentally doubled our late night estimate and told him the inflated price.

He looked at the floor thoughtfully, "What if I don't have that much money?"

"I guess you will just have to go out and get a job to earn the money."

We stared at each other for a while. He stood up and went to his bedroom silently. I took a deep breath to calm my shaking hands and waited to see what would happen. Five or ten minutes later he was back, completely dressed, books in hand. We never heard another word about dropping out. He concentrated on the classes he liked, chose to tolerate the ones he did not like, and eventually graduated.

When I told a friend about our crisis, she said, "I would not have given him the option. My son wanted out, found a job and dropped out."

Life with teens is like that; very unpredictable.

November 11, 1996

Life Without a TV

"Mom, why didn't we have TV when we were growing up?" I asked her once. My husband and I were debating getting a set.

"We thought you five had other things to do: homework; practicing the piano, trumpet, clarinet, or trombone; helping with the housework; farm chores; and basketball practice. Besides you had to go to bed early enough to do chores before catching the school bus in the morning."

With our children my husband and I embraced the same philosophy. Last year when my father visited, however, he asked if we would hook up to cable TV for his entertainment. We didn't have time to do it then; but this year it was hooked up before he arrived.

He enjoyed cable from our lounge chair a whole two weeks. Then he fell, broke his hip, and watched it from a hospital bed. Although my father no longer occupied the guest room and cable TV, my daughter did.

As I gathered up papers for an evening writing class, I reminded her, "You are not to watch that movie. I don't like what the previews showed." She didn't. I returned to a room cluttered with snack food with her in the middle watching the sitcoms I had missed as a teenager.

I sat down to see what I had missed. Not much. When I paid the first bill for cable TV, I discontinued the premium channel.

As I hauled in the groceries one afternoon, her books and papers were strewn across the floor. She was totally absorbed in a talk show.

"Hey, turn that off," I demanded.

"But Mom, they're talking about why fraternity hazing is bad."

I let it stay on as I fixed supper. It was interesting, but they made their point in fifteen of the sixty minutes we watched. The next time I received a bill for cable service, I cut back to the basic channels.

I didn't have a chance to watch cable TV or even say "turn it off" on Saturdays. I was out of town. Six Fridays in a row, I stuffed clothes and toothbrush in a duffel bag, closed my eyes to weekend housework, visited my new granddaughter, accompanied my daughter to academic competitions, and attended a church retreat.

My father, still in the hospital, declared he was going to my sister's as soon as he could. I had the cable TV disconnected. We had other things to do.

Friday as I left for the church retreat, I admonished my teenager, "I picked up and cleaned last night. I do not want to return to a cluttered, dirty house."

Saturday I dragged in at 9 p.m. The floors were vacuumed, beds made, dishes washed, even the minivan was washed and vacuumed.

I thanked and praised my daughter effusively.

She sighed. "Mom, why can't we have cable? It's so boring without a TV. I cleaned everything, washed the car, practiced the piano, laid out in the sun, and did my homework. There was nothing to do. Why can't we have the cable connected?"

In the midst of her whine my husband had entered the room. We looked at each other, covered our grins, and did not reply. The answer was too obvious.

April 28, 1997

Dennis the Menace II

MY SONS USED TO REMIND me of Dennis the Menace. Years ago my husband and I left them with a babysitter while we went to a company dinner. Our young, elementary aged son terrorized the babysitter until she ran out of the house. More than blankets warmed the backside of one Dennis that night.

I don't know how long it took the babysitter to recover from the trauma. I was so embarrassed I didn't talk about it for years. I am quite comfortable talking about it now, as long as no one asks what he did to scare a teenager twice his age and size.

A couple of years ago my college sons talked about one of their childhood exploits. It happened while I was gone, of course. A now mature Dennis began the revelation asking, "Hey, Mom, do you know why the cushions have those gashes in them?"

I shrugged, "Too many children using them for gymnastics, I guess."

He smiled at my innocence, "We were expressing our anger creatively. The cushions were shields to catch the knives we were throwing at each other."

"Throwing knives at each other?"

"Yeah, they stuck in the cushions every time."

My daughter piped up, "They did, Mom. I told them they shouldn't do that," she added like a prim little Margaret. "They just yelled at me to get under the other couch out of the way. I was scared. I hid under the couch and watched them."

"And you were how old when this happened?"

"Six or seven." She was driving a car before they confessed that secret.

I heard about it immediately when Dennis bothered our neighborhood Mr. Wilson. Wilson did not like kids in his yard. My son was running all over the neighborhood playing with a dog and forgot. In the excitement of the chase, dog and boy traipsed across Wilson's yard.

Wilson raged at Dennis and Ruff for romping through his flower beds. As always Dennis the Menace was sorry, but Wilson's wrath was not easily dissipated, especially not after he saw Dennis dancing on the street in front of his house. Wilson marched over to our house, found my husband, and told him that our son was mocking him.

By the time I came home, son had endured a serious encounter with father. After my husband finished telling me about the visit from Mr. Wilson, I turned to my recalcitrant son, "What were you doing out in the street in front of his house?"

He looked at me so innocently, "An Indian peace dance."

I kept a straight face as I admonished him, "Don't ever do that again. Be polite and stay out of his yard."

We no longer live in the same neighborhood as the Wilsons. And in spite of their impudence, each of our Dennis the Menaces lived to adulthood and horrified us with tales of what really happened when I left the house for a few minutes.

School is out for the summer. My children are away at camp, college, and work. Do you know where your children are and what they are doing? Are you sure?

June 9, 1997

Conversations in the Car

MY SON AND HIS DIRTY clothes piled in the family car with me to go home for spring break. We left the campus talking about people, classes, and philosophies. As we entered Union County he paused, looked at me and said, "You know, Mom, half the fun of coming home is talking with you."

With no television and telephone to interrupt and the car radio off, my children and I talk when we travel.

The hardest conversations are when one has disappointed me. After one such disappointment, I was in the car with the kid who should have known better. The offender turned to me, "You don't trust me, do you?"

I thought about that for a while. "I trust you with my money. I trust you will complete the chores you are assigned. I trust you to do your best at school. I trust you in everything but that area. My trust was demolished. I am not ready to trust you yet in that area." The transgressor used other expeditions to challenge the seriousness of the offense. I had a captive audience as I underscored the impact of what had been done.

My children are not the only ones who get feedback. Years ago as I struggled for the second time in as many days to parallel park, my three-year-old chirped, "You did it better that time, Mom."

When I took the thirty-three-year-old son to the store last year, he watched me negotiate city traffic for several blocks. "You are a lot more relaxed driver than you were when I was home."

Besides getting feedback, we dialogue about everything under the sun.

After a meeting in Little Rock, my teenager and I talked nonstop all the way to El Dorado. As we neared home my adolescent sighed, "I love being alive. I love being on earth. I don't want to die and go to Heaven."

Death was not imminent, but I knew the feeling. "That's how I felt when we first considered moving away from Indiana. For years I lived through one remodeling mess after another as your dad replaced wiring, plumbing, heating, walls, and flooring. When the house was finished, he began looking for a new job.

"I did not want to move, but now I know how good it is to move on. I wanted to enjoy that house without the remodeling. When your dad accepted a new position, we moved out of a house perpetually in need of repair, into a brand new house with new furniture, appliances, rugs, and decorations. No more remodeling messes. It was a breeze to keep clean. But before we moved, before I knew the reality of the next place, I did not want to leave what I knew for unknown territories."

Car conversations are not usually so grave, especially not when I'm driving a high school student to the state science fair in Conway. The first time, we both were so excited and involved in our conversation that I missed my exit. It was an hour before I realized we were going north instead of south. The extra hour drive back went by quickly; we were so busy talking.

Time does fly when you're having a real conversation.

March 9, 1998

Positive Peer Pressure

LIKE MY GRANDMOTHER AND MOTHER before me, I taught my preschoolers the alphabet, counting to one hundred, and how to print their names. I even held gym class for one because he needed special exercises to recover from an accident. I made him walk the plank, pedal his tricycle around the house, and go through the motions of jumping rope. In the eighteen months before kindergarten, he plodded through the daily exercises for muscle control.

The first day of kindergarten he found a chameleon on a bush during our walk to school and excitedly tucked it in his pocket to show his teacher, "Guess what I have in my pocket?"

"You tell me," she said. He pulled out his tiny reptile to show her.

She took a deep breath, "He would be happier outside, wouldn't he?" He let the critter go and eagerly went to meet his new friends who were building a house out of wooden blocks.

The teacher met with the parents to describe a new reading readiness class. "Many children do not have the physical skills related to the tracking necessary for reading. We will work with square foam blocks and slowly convert to round balls, then soft rubber, and finally basketballs. The children learn balance by walking a line on the floor before trying the beams." She described other exercises similar to what we had been doing at home for months.

I sat in the back of the room scoffing at the idea of reading readiness exercises. "He has been reading for two years. He doesn't need this."

He loved doing the exercises with his classmates. Within weeks I was eating my words. His coordination stabilized as it never had through all the months of work we had done at home alone. The use of his muscles increased almost immediately. The teacher pulled me aside one day, "His walking has improved in just one month."

Late in November parents were invited to watch their children demonstrate the new skills they had learned. I perched on the edge of the bleacher concentrating on my son as the teacher started the record player.

All the children stood in formation with two sheets of newspaper at their feet. At the signal, they picked up a sheet of paper in each hand and wadded the page into a little ball using only the hand holding the sheet. By the end of the song, each child held a wadded newspaper page in each hand, except the final third of the page held in my son's hand with the nerve damage.

Then the children ran across the room, picked up jump ropes, and jumped to the beat of the music. Okay, so my son wasn't the best, he was vastly improved over what we had done at home. He flew across the balance beam, bounced the ball to his partner, and caught it in return. A few weeks of group exercises at school had helped him more than the previous two years at home. Positive peer pressure had worked wonders.

When my other children entered kindergarten, the exercise program was defunct. They learned to read just fine without it.

November 16, 1998

Work Ethic Spills Over

MY PARENTS NEVER SAID WE had to work before we played. They never posted a list of rules by which our family lived, but it was the law nonetheless.

To make sure we did the tasks we were given, our parents checked up on us. When we lived on the dairy farm, mom had to be in the barn helping my dad. She kept track of our practice time at the piano by our reflection in the mirror on the wall behind us. She knew how long we practiced. We never figured out how she knew, but we knew we could not skip a day.

As teenagers, we felt safe from her watchful eyes; she worked an hour from home and dad was busy at the neighbor's ranch down the road. Both assumed as mature, responsible teenagers we would live by the rules and we did, sort of.

We set up the ironing board, pulled out the vacuum sweeper, and switched on the television set. It was the first time we had one in the house. We had to catch up on sitcom reruns.

The moment our dad's car turned into the driveway, the reruns shrank into a dot on the black and white screen. I yanked a blouse over the end of the ironing board, and my sister made sure the vacuum sweeper roared before he opened his car door.

He could see we were working, even if all he said was that he had come home for a sandwich.

Another mother and I touched on that subject recently. We both heartily agree that keeping kids busy is better than having them slouch around the house doing whatever they want, whenever they want, however they want. Just one little whine of "I'm bored," and we have the answer. "We have windows that need to be washed, a lawn to mow, a floor to clean, and a stack of clothes to sort and fold." Bored ingratitude dissipates under the duress of household chores.

I thought everyone understood my work ethic. When I was asked to sit with my husband's wheelchair-bound grandmother for a month, I handed her a pan of string beans to snap. She slowly worked her way through the small pile and handed them back to me. I thanked her for her help. She snapped, "Well, you told me to do it."

I did? I was shocked. I would never tell my elders what to do. But then, I did expect her to want to help out. She had two hands and nothing to do except read or watch TV. I had plenty of work to do and not enough time.

I thought she would want to have something to keep her hands and mind occupied, and that attitude is my own grandmother's fault. She always told us to leave the dishes. "It will give me something to do," she said and asked my mom to remember to drop off our clothes and socks that needed mending.

The year my husband's company closed down, forcing him to retire, he caught a whiff of my impatient attitude, "Don't just sit there, do something!" I had lots of ideas. He told me he could keep himself busy, thank you. I backed off.

Last week he volunteered at Habitat for Humanity and detailed their daily accomplishments. I stopped by to see what he had done. He told another worker, "My wife is checking up on me."

Not, me! I was just stopping by for a sandwich.

June 14, 2004

With One Hand

IN THE YEARS SINCE A car accident took his left arm, my son-in-love has developed quite a repertoire of responses to the inevitable question, "How did you lose your arm?"

"I lost it in an accident when I was two," he truthfully began in response to one inquiry. Then he paused, looked down, shook his head and added, "I shouldn't have been driving..."

More than one little kid has had him bend down, look them earnestly in the eye and say, "You know how they tell you not to feed the animals at the zoo? Well, I did, and the alligator ate it."

At a family reunion an older relative walked over, shook the empty sleeve, smiled, and said, "What happened to your arm?"

"Oh, I left it in the suitcase back at the hotel," he shrugged.

My daughter's favorite is the time he looked at the questioner in shock and gasped, "I don't have an arm?" He made a dramatic inspection of his body, and began wailing until he couldn't hold back his laughter any longer.

His attitude springs from his parents' determination to not treat their one-armed child disabled. His parents had him fitted with a prosthetic arm, but he found it awkward and inflexible. He learned to do things one-handed.

Before his first day of kindergarten, his mother took the teacher aside to emphasize to her, "Now you make sure that he does everything by himself. He can do it." She visited during lunchtime a few days later "and there he was with his classmates running up and begging to be the one who carried his tray, picked up his milk, or opened the carton. He managed quite well," she recalled with a laugh.

The only time his parents told him "No" was in response to his request to play football. The accident had also involved a head injury which they didn't want aggravated. To compensate, his parents worked to get a soccer league established in the community. He played competitively in the junior and senior high school soccer leagues, still plays in a local adult league, and avidly follows the Major League Soccer.

For several years his mother made one accommodation: Velcro closing sneakers. But at eight the kid who would be like everyone else told his mother that he wanted sneakers with shoestrings.

"Okay, but you will have to learn how to tie them yourself," she said.

He agreed. She showed him the trick the rehab doctor had taught her for tying a shoe one-handed. Then she set him on the stairs and told him to practice until he could do it himself. Several hours later, he came off the stairs, the proud owner of his first pair of tie sneakers.

Traffic violations have added another layer of one-armed misadventure stories.

One young officer mandated that he put both hands on the wheel.

"I only have one hand."

She stopped, looked carefully, turned red, began talking about the weather, admonished him to drive more carefully, and let him off without a ticket.

He was pulled over for reckless driving as a teenager. The officer demanded, "Get out of the car and put both hands behind your back."

He complied.

"Put your other hand behind you!" the cop started shouting.

"I don't have another hand."

"Yes, you do." The officer reached in and poked around inside his empty, long sleeve until he admitted defeat.

His parents did not beg 'disability' when he brought home the ticket; they made him pay his dues.

Their attitude guaranteed the independence which allowed him to play soccer, ride horses, and bikes, play baritone in the band, and earn a college degree as well as develop a sense of humor for dealing with the inquisitiveness of total strangers.

August 14, 2006

Drug Abuse: It Hurts Too Much to Laugh

WE DON'T JOKE ABOUT DRUG abuse at our house. We know its pain, disappointment, and cost too much to laugh about it. We see all too clearly how much our loved one has paid, not just financially, but physically, emotionally, socially, and spiritually. It's sad to look at him and remember his joyful grin as he helped me wash windows as a four-year-old, his eagerness to get on with his paper route after school, and his glow of adventure when he and his brother built an igloo after the blizzard in Indiana.

Sometime in high school his *joie de vivre* fell by the way as he experimented with street drugs. In time, drugs dominated him so much that even drug dealers told him, "Slow down you'll blow up."

He barely noticed the warning or the loss of family, friends and finances until eighteen months ago, when, with no other option, he came to live with us. He said he wanted to change but he took drugs the night before he moved in with us.

He arrived with black garbage bags stuffed full of his clothes, a handful of unpaid utility bills, bank overdraft notices, unpaid traffic citations, and a suspended driver's license.

His blood pressure registered twice that of his father's. His father took him to the doctor for medication. We took him to Narcotics Anonymous until he found rides with other attendees.

We encouraged him to pay off his traffic fines until he finally regained his license. We insisted he work at home, as a volunteer, or at a job. He did all three. He said he loved to mow our lawn but begged off from doing it time and again. He said the factory line moved too quickly for him to keep up. Fellow volunteers raised eyebrows at his inability to do the simplest job without close supervision. He received his six months' tag from NA for being drug free. We cheered for him and thought he had begun to tentatively turn things around.

He hadn't. With a large check in hand he shoved everything and everybody else aside for a twenty-four hour drug spree.

We gave him another chance. For seven months, he went to work, said he was paying bills and saving money.

Then one morning he left the house to get his daughter to celebrate her birthday and never arrived. Her wrapped birthday present sat unopened on his dresser.

Party food wilted on the platter.

A specially prepared dessert shriveled as the clock ticked off the hours without his appearance or phone call.

It didn't happen once. It happened twice; two weekends in a row he shrugged and left the birthday girl and her sisters tearfully waiting in vain.

The first weekend we listened warily to a story about deciding to go fishing instead of going to celebrate a child's birthday.

The next weekend he loaned his car for a couple of hits of crack to guys who took it for a joy ride, wrecked it beyond repair, and then ran away. He called the next day and asked us to bring him his clothes.

On our way to an activity we dropped off his clothes and told him he was welcome back after at least a year in a spiritually-oriented drug abuse program. He stared at us, silently defiant.

Drugs have cost him two marriages, his children's confidence in him, thousands upon thousands of dollars, dozens of jobs, his car, driver's license, health, home, and self-respect.

He found a place to sleep for a while, but friends who had once invited him to share quarters quickly changed their minds.

When he ran out of options, he signed-up for a short-term drug rehab program. Before he left, he had a few more hits of crack. Two weeks later, unable to cope with life in rehab, he landed in the hospital.

After six weeks, the doctors concluded he needed long term care.

Before he transferred from the hospital to the unit, a social worker told me, "This is how he will probably be until they come up with newer medications. We do not recommend that he drive. You should consider this a permanent placement. It is the closest unit to your home that we could find."

I hung up the phone in shock at hearing my hopes for his future crushed under the heel of twenty dollar hits of crack cocaine.

We pray the bleak prognosis will be wrong. For now, because he has less than a dollar a day to spend, he is 'drug free.' During our first visit to the unit his case manager recognized his financial limitations but cheerfully pointed out, "If he participates with the program, he can earn points and get things like Pop Tarts or cigarettes." Hearing him reduced to that level left me hurting too much to laugh at drug abuse.

August 28, 2006

Shared Sorrow Comforts

"I REALLY NEEDED THAT CONVERSATION," the young woman said as we pushed our chairs back at the end of the meal. None of us had said anything particularly insightful. We had simply shared our experiences and concerns in dealing with family members with a serious brain disorder.

The gathering had not been planned. We just happened to sit down at the same table at a women's conference, two sets of mothers and daughters with sons, brothers, grandchildren living with the nuances of severe mental illness and a mother of a young daughter living in the world of autism. I am afraid that we rudely ignored, talked over and around the other women at the table with us.

The conversation began when someone mentioned that the young mother had stepped back from community activities to deal with her daughter's perception of and presentation to the world. Having seen her older daughter's learning curve, the mother suspected her youngest had a problem. She related the heart-breaking experience of watching the staff at Arkansas Children's Hospital verify everything she suspected. She spoke of the triumphs of learning to calm her daughter by wrapping her in a specially designed heavy blanket.

I told her about driving home late at night with a grandchild with a brain disorder. Alert, awake, and quite energetically the child chatted for an hour.

"No more talking. You have to wait at least thirty minutes before you say anything else," we said.

She obediently quit talking. But she did not fall asleep as expected. She sat in her seat wide awake, watching the clock. At the end of thirty minutes, she started in exactly where she had left off, and did not slow down until, finally back at the house, she received the long-delayed nighttime medication which allowed her to sleep.

"Exactly," the mother of the autistic child sighed. Her daughter cannot simply switch to whatever is considered normal behavior. She gets 'stuck.'

Understanding those triggers bewilders us all. The mother of the middle-aged son shook her head helplessly. Her son had taken his medication faithfully for years, yet had recently needed hospitalization.

His sister recalled the number of times he told her, "Do you know what happens if I don't take this medication? I go crazy."

He took his medication, but, something changed, the medications quit working. Sadness hung over the family when the illness again overwhelmed their family.

The sisters empathized with their ill sibling and at the same time feared they or their children would succumb to the illness. We talked openly and at length because we saw 'the look.'

I saw 'the look' the evening I intended to just say a quick hello to another woman before heading home. We quickly became caught up in a discussion of our concerns about our loved ones with brain disorders. A woman sitting beside the mother looked up at me after a while, "I thought you were going."

The other mother understood, "It is difficult to leave when you see that little spark that says another person knows what you are talking about," she said.

It is the brightening of the eyes that comes after they have been washed with many tears. The look comes from having acquired one of the most difficult concepts of Christianity: Those difficult times teach us to "give praise to the God and Father of our Lord Jesus Christ! He is the Father who gives tender love. All comfort comes from him. He comforts us in all our troubles. Now we can comfort others when they are in trouble. We ourselves have received comfort from God." II Corinthians 1:3-4 (NIV)

No one wants these painfully gained insights. Having been drafted into a club we never wanted to join, the support of others in the same situation serves as a balm to our troubled spirits. Time spent with others in the same boat makes the most awful of events a bit more manageable through shared experiences and much needed conversations.

October 27, 2006

First You Work, Then You Play

YEAH, YEAH, THE KIDS HATED it, but I loved my rule when we had perfectly healthy, minor children around the house: "First you work, then you play, makes my life easier any day."

I'd like to say I initiated the rule, but in all reality I lived under the same mandate as a child.

First I had to do my work then I could go play. I never thought too much about it until my sixth-grade teacher gave us an assignment to write a friendly letter. I wrote one to my cousin. The letter included the sentence, "After we finish doing the dishes, we can go out and play in the woods" or something like that.

The teacher read it out loud to the class as a good example of putting work first, like I had any other option.

Our parents expected the work to be done. Play time (this was long before play dates existed) could be fitted in after we washed the dishes, swept the floor, cleaned rooms, made beds, fixed meals, and helped dad with farm chores, including working in the hay fields in the heat of summer, or whatever other job my parents dictated needed to be done that day.

Having learned this rule from early childhood on, I assumed every child automatically jumped up and did what needed to be done without being told. Then I married a man with a couple of able-bodied children and discovered the reality of all children.

Children and teenagers like to dawdle and play. They like to avoid doing work or to do it at their own speed, and in their own time. Children assume vacations are a great time to sleep in, play outside, and hang out with friends.

Sounds good on paper, but since I am a morning person, my sleep-in time ends around 7 a.m. Therefore the kids' sleep-in time lasted until 7:15 a.m. As my dad said, "You can stay up as late as you want, but you will be here helping with the work early in the morning."

So I yanked my children out of bed early, even during vacation. I wanted to get my chores done so I could do what I wanted to do. Plus, long, long ago, I looked at our family of many children and declared myself free from slavery. I say this because mothers, inevitably, have to be near slaves to newborns, babies, and toddlers.

My old rule came roiling out of me a couple of years ago after we opened our home to several immature people for an extended stay.

I had to work during their stay, but I also had to go home from work, and the last thing I wanted to see when I walked in the door was a chaotic house.

I talked it over with my husband. Pointing out that children behave much better when they have definite activities and responsibilities to complete before they can get the privilege of doing what they want, I suggested he come up with ideas of tasks to keep them busy.

I told him, and the expected guests, I would not be acting as the genie of the magic hamper, going around and gathering up dirty clothes, and washing them late into the night after everyone else has gone to bed. I would not be performing feats of magic with food and presenting wonderful meals twenty minutes after I walk in the door after a day of work. I would not be coughing up a bankroll of cash to pay for their entertainment.

Yes, I would find ways to entertain, ways that began with a list called "helping around the house."

We decided that they could help power wash the house, clean up yard debris, take care of the dishes, do their own laundry, prepare meals, and work on memorizing verses before they earned permission to do what they wanted to do.

And yes, once the work was done, we did play games, watch videos, read books, explore the neighborhood, go shopping, or just hang out and visit, just like I did when I was a kid in a large family.

It turned out to be a rather pleasant visit. I actually looked forward to a return visit.

December 28, 2011

Childhood Revisited

MY HUSBAND POINTED AT THE blue glasses in the cupboard. "You choose every glass except that one," he scolded.

I just looked at him and his fuss over glasses.

"That's the one with the egg under it," he explained.

I should have known. A couple of weeks ago he insisted on buying two bags of spring colored M&M's, repackaging them into our stash of plastic eggs, and hiding the eggs all around the house.

I have been finding chocolate filled eggs ever since: under my pillow, beside my toothbrush, in the tiny teapot my father gave me long ago, in the dresser drawers, tucked into stacks of fabric, and inside the bookends on the head of our bed.

Most folks think he is just another old timer with lots of energy and ideas. I think he verges on entering his second childhood with the advantages of all the experience and knowledge of the grandfather.

That's all very fine and well, but I had a grandson in mind when I bought that wooden kit to assemble that included a tiny machine to make it move. He looked at it longingly. "Who is this for?"

"I don't know. I thought maybe it could be done with a grandchild," I said as I dashed about preparing to go to work.

He studied the box. He opened it and dumped out the parts.

The kit had never been opened, but it had been by the time I returned from work that day. He had opened, assembled, tested, and found it wanting. "The machine is too small for the weight of the wood," he announced.

A month ago it was the child's electric car waiting for the trash man. I suggested we bring it home to see if it still worked or if he could get it working. I also insisted that he not put a lot of money into the repairs. Like every other kid on the block, he did not listen. He calls it his Cadillac. It is a two-seater with a working radio. He began making plans, BIG plans for that car. He quickly analyzed that an incorrectly sized fuse had melted the wires on the accelerator. He ordered another and went shopping for paint.

"Wait until you get the part," I reiterated.

"It will work. I know it will. I tested the circuits. They all work."

I could not park my car in the garage that night. He had turned it into a paint shop for the Cadillac Escalade. He gave the large plastic car a fresh coat of paint and waited for the part to arrive. It did not arrive before the grandchildren visited, but that did not keep him or his twenty-month-old grandson from having a lot of fun with that car.

Grandpa and Daddy pushed tiny tot up and down the driveway in the car. The kid grinned with sheer joy. He was driving a car. When they parked it, he didn't care. He stayed in the car and kept on pretending to drive. He loved it as much as Grandpa.

Long after the little driver left, the part came. Maybe the Cadillac would work, but hubby found other problems to resolve. He bought another battery and charger. It still did not go. He drew schematics of the electrical circuit. He studied the wiring harness, the fuses, the accelerator, and other linkage points. He talked with the neighbor, his building buddies, the guy at the repair shop, anyone who might or might not know something, including me.

With the accelerator in place and a careful sizing of fuses, he declared it running and went looking for a test driver. "You really can't tell for sure if you don't have a child driving it," he explained.

The neighbor's son showed that it went faster backward than forward. My husband switched some gears around and declared it ready for decals. He ordered them Monday. While he waited on them, I showed him the Lego soccer set I had purchased at a yard sale.

"I wonder if it has all the parts," I asked. I left the box on the table and went to work on an adult project.

Happy as a child at Christmas time, he picked up the Lego soccer game, dumped out the plastic bags, opened the instructions and began building.

"It only has ten men, and I think it's missing a flag," he said.

I walked over and looked at the box. "That's all the men it shows on the front of the box."

He sorted out the pieces and began assembling a green playing field. Long before I finished my project, he proudly called me over to demonstrate how it had all the parts and that it moved for playing the game. Then he took it all apart and put it back in the box until the next time.

He may be a kid at heart, but at least he picks up his toys and puts them away without being told.

April 18, 2012

Sew Much Fun

Gizmos

I BARELY STAY INSIDE THE lines of paint-by-the-number pictures, but I still can't resist buying craft projects at garage sales. My fifty-cent splurge on a child's how-to-knit-and crochet-kit I rationalized as something handy to have if my daughter got the urge to learn.

She never got the urge, but with my son's announcement that his wife was expecting their first child, visions of delicate baby blankets stirred a grandmotherly urge in me. I pulled the boxes from the back of my dresser drawer and opened them.

I had two plastic knitting needles, one plastic crochet hook, and four small skeins of yarn that wound into the tiniest balls of pastel pink, yellow, blue, and white yarn I've ever seen. And I have seen plenty of yarn: my grandmother made baby afghans as well as sweaters, mittens, scarves, and shawls for her children, grandchildren, and in-laws. One summer Grandma handed me skeins of black and blue yarn and taught me to knit. I knit and purled the cover for a pin-wheel pillow. As I remember it, the project was fun and fairly easy to do.

Thinking back on that, I decided I would knit a baby blanket.

No matter how I held the needles and yarn, something was always in the way. The first few rows of yellow yarn spiraled around the needle with my tight stitches. I worked to make big loops. The stuff sagged off the needles. I unraveled the whole mess and tried again. The longer I knitted, the more obvious that each day's stresses revealed themselves in sections of loose or tight stitches.

Discouraged, I discarded the uneven mess of yellow and picked up the tiny ball of pink yarn and a plastic crochet hook. Crocheting only uses one instrument. I had enough hands to hold the yarn and make requisite loops, twists, and turns.

The instructions may have been written for children, but I never figured out the knack for going from one row to the next. I added too many stitches. My intended square of crocheted yarn evolved into a wedge.

I tossed aside that flop and any idea of crocheting a baby blanket.

Finally I picked up the white and blue skeins of yarn and a gizmo to make yarn florets for an afghan. The instruction booklet showed pictures of models holding afghans that were gardens of colorful yarn flowers.

I'll bet those models never touched one of those gizmos. A knob at its base turned to expose metal pegs for holding the yarn I looped back and forth across the plastic head. Everything was just fine until I accidentally twisted the knob the wrong way. The pegs receded, releasing the unfinished yarn flower. It fell apart, but I persisted and managed to sew together several blue and white yarn flowers. The loops were uneven and the spacing irregular. The stitches were all out of kilter. My paint by number pictures turned out better than that!

I shoved all the unfinished projects out of sight and headed for the nearest garage sale in search of delicate, fluffy baby blankets. That was a whole lot more fun than fighting with knitting needles, crochet hooks, gizmos, and yarn.

April 7, 1997

T-shirt Quilt

MY DAUGHTER CUT UP ALL her husband's favorite T-shirts.

She also cut up her own. Maybe the fact that they each owned enough T-shirts to fill a drawer explains why it took her five hours to accomplish the deed. That and she cut out the T-shirt logos in squares to make a T-shirt quilt. She ended up with thirty-six big squares and fifteen smaller squares to line across the top.

The whole idea stretched my imagination. I'd never heard of a T-shirt quilt, but that didn't keep me from offering suggestions for putting it together and overwhelming her.

Determined to finish the project this summer, she started to pin the top line together. The edges were uneven. The task was difficult. The pile of squares began to look impossibly huge.

I offered to bring my portable machine and sew with her one weekend. Like the king in Rumpelstiltskin, she opened the door to her sewing room and showed me the impossible task: Convert fifty-one squares into a never-before-seen T-shirt quilt.

While she finished her last afternoon of a summer graduate class in education, I began basting together the squares. I thought I needed to stiffen the material. I tried tape. I pulled tape off the first foot long seam for ten minutes.

I decided not to use tape to stiffen the seams.

I used skills I learned one summer in a sewing factory and lined up the edges without pins or tape and basted them in place with the machine. Row by row I finished and arranged the quilt strips across her living room floor.

Two hours later she came home, saw the basted strips, and smiled. "This is so great. I had this on my list of projects to do this summer, but after I got started on pinning it together, I was not sure I would ever finish it."

"It's just basted in place. It all needs to be permanently stitched."

"Okay. Do you want to go shopping for the backing material?"

We went shopping and came home with seven yards of sale priced flannel, filler batting, quilting needles, and thread.

The flannel hit the hot water in her washing machine. We hit the sewing machines with a vengeance. A couple hours later, I held up the last seam. "You really need to be the one that sews this so you can tell people you finished it yourself."

She really didn't care; she just wanted to get done. I took a break. She sewed the seam. The quilt top was finished. The flannel was out of the dryer. She sewed together the back. We sandwiched the quilt batting between the top and the flannel and held it together with safety pins.

Together we figured out how to use quilting needles to tie off the quilt. Mother and daughter sat side by side on the couch tying off row after row, rolling up the finished part on our laps as we watched a video.

Around 10:30 p.m. she told me I needed to go to bed to be alert for my early morning departure the next day. "I know. I just want to see what this looks like finished," I said and kept on stitching until I didn't care anymore.

I stood up and stretched, "All you have to do after this is fold the edges of flannel up and over to make a finished edge and machine or hand stitch it into place." I bent over to demonstrate and ended up pinning the whole thing before I sagged off to bed.

The next day as I was recuperating with a nap, she called to announce, "It's done. It took another hour, but it is done! I am going to put it in my car and take it everywhere I go to show my friends. Thanks, Mom."

Sure thing, Hon! Anytime you want to chop up a few more T-shirts, just give me a call.

July 26, 2004

Decorating Baby's Room

MY DAUGHTER INVITED ME TO go to the fabric shop with her to "check out material for decorating the baby's room."

I agreed to tag along. That is about all I did. She already knew exactly what she wanted to use for making a valance, a crib sheet, a bed skirt, and a bumper pad.

She knew, but we looked at other options anyway. And then we walked back over to her original choices, and she began pulling out bolts of material: Dark blue with a vintage print of cowboys on horses, chuck wagons, and desert plants; tan with Roy Rogers' signature written in rope and cowboy-handkerchief red.

I provided moral support as she perused the pattern book to find out how much material she needed to purchase in order to make everything.

She showed up at my house the next week with material and two patterns in hand, expecting me to coach her through the sewing process. I did not have time to coach her; I had to go to work. Before I left, I told her to cut out the material and we would sew that evening.

That evening she told me it was a day of "carpenter Dad meets daughter's sewing project."

He pulled out his three feet long T-square, a large piece of left-over plywood for a cutting board, and his X-Acto knife. He plopped that plywood down on the kitchen counter, laid material over it, measured out yardage, lined up his long T-square as a cutting line, and whacked out chunks of material for a sheet, curtains, skirting, bumper pads, and tags in short order.

Cutting material, however, did not rate the same exactness as cutting

159

wood, "Hey! This stuff folds up into the right size," he said, "Why not just cut it along these folds."

The bumper pad pieces came out in various sizes. I raised my eyebrows and suggested adjustments.

"This is how you ruffle material." I began sewing a basting seam along the edge of the long strip of red bandana material. Afterwards I showed her how to pull the loose threads to make it ruffle. She did the rest.

We pinned and, for the most part, she sewed blue cowboy material into a blue valance and bumper strip and a Roy Rogers' signature into a sheet and bed skirt.

Back home she and her husband fitted it all into place and she declared it "great," until she decided that the bumper pad needed more filler.

A thrift store provided a barely used bumper pad. I provided two evenings listening to TV shows taking out the seams and reassembling it all into a thicker bumper pad.

I gathered up the abundance of scraps she had left.

"If you take these leftover red strips and cut out pictures of the cowboys, you could make a really cute quilt," I showed her what I meant.

"You do what you want," she said with a shrug and went home, leaving behind the assortment of scraps and a piece large enough to back a quilt.

I spent a couple of hours looking through my collection of cross stitch patterns for simple Wild West patterns. Two hours later with a stack of booklets in hand, I began sorting out embroidery threads to make a red cowboy hat, blue boots, brown saddle, cactus, a miniature Trigger, and a little boy riding a rocking horse. We centered the cross stitch pieces in plain blue. My husband cut quilt blocks with cowboys in the middle and strips of red to frame all the quilt blocks.

A long week of cross stitching after work plus a couple weekends of sewing yielded a red and blue baby quilt and a couple of baby-sized matching accent pillows.

Roy Rogers never had it so good.

August 4, 2006

I Just Need One More

Hi, my name is Joan and I'm a fabriholic. I am addicted to buying fabric for which I do not necessarily have any use.

My addiction isn't as bad as other fabriholics who have filled their attics, basements, and spare bedrooms with their stash of fabric.

All I have is a medium-sized cardboard box (filled with various shades of white material), two drawers stuffed with colored and patterned coordinated stacks of fabric, and that's it...except for the two stacks of felt and flannel material tucked in beside the craft, crochet, and quilting books and magazines. However, that huge plastic trunk of material which doubled my stash, which I picked up at a yard sale a month or so ago, I don't count. I am still trying to figure out how much of it I actually want to keep. The trunk takes up the space of a love seat in the guest bedroom.

I have not reached the level of the woman who wrote in a 1980's quilting magazine. She had packaged up all her spare fabric into boxes, stacked them, and covered them with tablecloths to look like end tables. She did not run out of fabric: she ran out of furniture to accent with end tables. She also ran out of attic space, space under beds, and space in the clothes hamper.

I may be a fabriholic, but I'm not that bad.

For one thing, I don't smuggle new purchases of fabric into the house so my husband won't see it. I leave the new stuff in the car until I am ready to show him.

Besides, my husband enables my addiction. Last month he brought home several pieces of fabric to add to my options for making a jar or bottle quilt. Even as I write this, he sits at the table designing a baby bottle or baby jar quilt for an upcoming addition to the Hershberger family. As a craftsman, he understands the need to have a wide spectrum of colors and textures for any artistic development, including quilts, cross stitch projects, and his wood-working projects. Our garage overflows with his tools, piles of wood kept for an unknown future need, and the remnant of the broken ceramic tile that I bought—which he used three years later.

I am a neophyte fabriholic. I only fit four out of ten characteristics of a fabriholic.

I do like to "pet" fabric. Fabric feels and looks good to me. It triggers all sorts of dreams of combining the material with completed cross stitch projects, my collection of lace and bias tape, and those unique buttons I found when the fabric store closed last year.

I buy fabric without having any idea how I will use it, nor do I care if I use it. I relish new fabric purchases and quietly put them away.

However, I do not stop total strangers on the street to admire the cloth used to make their shirts, nor do I ask others to leave me their stashes in the will, or refuse to find a use for the more unique pieces in my collection.

I should quit buying more material, and I will, as soon as I have some fabric printed with M&Ms, Hershey, and Coke insignias. I "need" those for my palette when making a jar quilt or an "I spy" quilt.

Unfortunately, those types of fabric cost a bit more than most. Fortunately, they do sell jar quilt bundles on eBay. Unfortunately, a tiny piece costs more than half a yard of most fabrics. Fortunately, I do have a thrifty bent. I can wait for a bargain, I think.

January 14, 2008

Making a Quilt, Making Work for Myself

IF I WOULD JUST KEEP my mouth shut, I could save myself a lot of work. But no, I had to tell my parents about the quilt family members assembled for my neighbor's fiftieth wedding anniversary. It had twelve-inch square blocks with a different embroidered picture for each family member. With my grandparents' golden wedding anniversary looming on the horizon of time, I mentioned it as a gift idea to my parents.

A couple weeks later, my father asked, "How's the quilt coming along?"

Before my next call to my folks, I went shopping for material.

Initially, my artistically inclined husband considered the quilt completely my project. In my haphazard way, I designed and embroidered blocks for our family. Those blocks were ready to sew into the quilt until my sister sent her precisely drawn and stitched blocks for her family. One look at her excellent work and my competitive man began cutting new blocks for our family. He used his talent and created fantastic pictures for me to embroider another set of quilt blocks for our family. I don't remember what happened to my unacceptable creations. My grandmother hung the quilt proudly on the wall in her sitting room.

Ten years later I made a similar quilt for my husband's parents and a few years later, a greatly modified version for my parents. Then I said I had finished quilting, I preferred cross stitch. I meant it, too, until I realized I could combine cross stitched pictures with quilting. Overnight I began collecting old quilting magazines at garage sales and talking about ideas.

If I could just make up my mind what I want to do before I start assembling a quilt, it would take a lot less time. I can't make up my mind, so my quilts are not so much created as evolved.

I literally have had quilts completely assembled when I realized another cross stitch picture suited the quilt better than the one stitched deep in the middle of the quilt.

Each time, my husband assured me that the one in place would do. Each time, after he left the room, I began ripping out stitches to replace the block. Replacing a block or two is one thing. The most recent quilt, which uses a technique I have never tried before, has evolved so much that I have stitched some seams half a dozen times.

Before the most recent grandchild's arrival, I told my husband, "I think I'll make an I Spy quilt," thinking of the ease and fun of assembling a multitude of uniquely patterned four-inch blocks for the child to discover.

"I thought you were going to make a bottle quilt," he protested, no doubt thinking of the bundle of fabrics with realistic patterns of hobbies and objects he had recently chosen with the older grandchildren's help. Both quilts use small patches of unique fabrics. However, an "I Spy" quilt consists of square blocks while a bottle quilt requires assembling the same fabrics into bottles with lids.

I know I said I wanted to make a bottle quilt. I asked him to pick up fabric. But after I read enough about jar quilts to understand the challenge it would be to my beginner skills, I realized I should never have mentioned it.

Since I had mentioned it, our kitchen table conference concluded with the bottle quilt evolving into a "baby bottle and baby food jar" quilt, which is an even more complicated version of the bottle quilt.

I chose a dark blue background fabric to use between bottles and spent one long evening assembling and remaking one bottle three times before the white material against the blue background and the pale pink fabric of the complicated nipple came out straight and even.

Last week I assembled the bottles into a quilt top. The background of my nearly finished baby bottle quilt is not blue. It is a soft orange and has a much simpler pattern for the bottle's nipple.

Initially I set aside deep orange and purple fabrics to create shelves to 'hold' the bottles and jars and to back the quilt. Last week I pulled out a warm brown fabric and used that instead.

The original plan included half a dozen extra things tucked between the bottles: items such as children's blocks, a teddy bear, and a camera. The quilt has none of those.

Over the months of puzzling my way through this quilt, I laid out the completed fabric pictures seven or eight times before I stitched them into place, declared it finished, stood back, studied it proudly, and noticed two minor flaws in the arrangement.

The baby won't care. Her parents won't know the difference, but my hand keeps gravitating towards that seam ripper. I expect to have it finished sometime before her golden wedding anniversary.

July 7, 2008

Simple Quilt

Leafing through a secondhand quilting magazine with colorful pictures of intricately pieced fabric, my daughter looked up and protested, "How do they decide whether a quilt is beginner's level or not? This doesn't look like a beginner's quilt to me." She thrust the photo of a beautifully stitched quilt in front of me.

So says this child of mine who pulls out a sewing machine once or twice a year!

She laid the magazine down, refusing to look at any more triangles and tiny blocks assembled into a queen sized quilt and labeled easy enough for a beginner.

She looked across the room at the baby quilt she had come to my house to make for a friend. "Now that is a beginner's quilt!"

Well, yes twelve nine-inch blocks with a two-inch sash around each is a beginner's quilt. It might even qualify as a simple quilt. I made a similar, full-sized quilt when I was about her age. With big blocks, colorful, simple to assemble, it really impressed my grandparents who hung it on the wall behind their sofa.

The simple quilt quickly and easily satisfies her need to create. She developed her own style last year as she helped me sort my stash of fabric. Stacking reds, pinks, blues, greens, and violets, she stumbled across a couple of yards of intriguing fabrics: one printed with colorful pages intended to be made into a toddler's fabric book about insects, and a piece printed with a child's map of a city traversed with a road just the right size for Matchbox cars.

"It would make a great, reversible play quilt," she said and began pawing through my stash of green fabric until she found a grassy print of shamrocks to sew between blocks as a border.

Within the hour her newly claimed fabric covered our dining room table, and I tried to show my lefty how to use a rotary cutter.

She tried but opted for shears for the cloth pages as well as the accompanying silhouettes of a dragon fly, butterfly, lady bug, and bright yellow sunflower.

Raiding my sewing cabinet, she hauled out buttons shaped like bugs and cars to decorate the finished quilt and bonding fabric to stiffen the cloth bugs to make them appear to have just landed on the little quilt.

Spools of thread and stray pins cluttered the floor of the sewing room. She insisted she wanted to machine quilt it.

I talked, coached, sewed, sighed, and insisted that we needed to take out and fix haphazardly cut seams and machine quilting.

The house was a mess, but we completed the play quilt for her son before she left that weekend.

I messed up her house in December as we talked our way through another simple, reversible baby quilt with blocks from a cloth book. She cut and sewed straighter lines, but I had calculated and cut insufficient framing strips so we had to refigure and make do.

She returned last week to make her friend's baby boy a play quilt similar to her son's.

She sorted through my thrift shop and garage sale finds and chose a Bob the Builder book to use on the reverse side of another kid's map I had found somewhere.

She ripped apart the completed book, trimmed the pages into blocks, figured out the spacing between the blocks, and the number of strips needed to sew it together.

Because of my work schedule, visiting with folks and taking care of her two-year-old, the simple quilt took us a couple of evenings.

Tuesday night she cut straight lines that sewed up quickly and easily into strips.

The blocks lined up evenly. The top and bottom sandwiched the flannel filler and pinned together smoothly.

Wednesday evening she machine quilted straight lines through the sandwiched material and finished it with a zigzag stitch on the edge of the red quilt binding from a reader.

A simple quilt finished with very few glitches.

One more simple quilt like that and the two of us just might be ready to make one of those beginner quilts.

April 13, 2009

Quilting with Lindsay

I opened the door to my sewing room for my visiting granddaughter. "Well, this is either the craft room or a junk room," I said. A pile of fabric slumped onto the floor waiting for a shelf. Piles of fabric for quilting projects waited my time. Idea books crowded the closet. Audio books waited to entertain me with background info while I worked. Photo albums still lacked all their pictures.

"It's a junk room," she whispered in a teasing voice.

"Yeah, with lots of fun things to do," I agreed. "Do you want to make a quilt?"

She began pulling out fabrics: a bold black and white racing flag, a jigsaw print of purple, orange, and cute pink girly patterns, and Irish green shamrocks.

I opened my variegated stash of fat quarters collected for bottle quilts. Her pile of choices grew.

"I might make a black and white quilt," she mused.

I looked at all the colors she had piled up. "I have enough for a black and white quilt."

She added a few colorful cartoony fabrics to her basket.

I pulled out quilting magazines to stimulate ideas of how to arrange all the wonderful fabrics she had found.

The blue and white quilts intrigued her as an option for a black and white quilt until she considered the amount of work and skill level involved.

A colorful quilt pattern idea on top of the Halloween fabrics caught her eye.

"That's sort of a strip quilt," I said. "Strip quilts are just long strips of fabric sewn together. You could take a long strip of each of the fabrics you like and do that."

The idea intrigued her, if we used multiple fabrics in each strip of color. She rummaged through the fabric and pulled out seven each of pink, orange, blue, black and white, green, red, orange and purple colored fabrics and an eighth collection of multiple colors.

Before we began cutting oblong blocks the width of a brick, she arranged the colors in strips to see if she still liked the idea and the color tones. Seeing all fifty-six fabrics lined up in rows, she pulled out three to replace with others in different shades or tones.

We washed and dried the fabric. I ironed and cut about half the blocks and left the fifteen-year-old to iron and cut the rest while I went to work.

I came home to a stack of wrinkled fabrics with a corner whacked out of each, and the blocks cut from the center of the neatly ironed smaller piece. I folded, sorted, and stored the fabric remembering my mother's saying, "Live and learn."

Saturday afternoon the teenager lined the blocks on my bed, not vertically as originally planned, but horizontally in color families. I liked it. "But what about the multi-colored blocks? Do you want to pick out a few others to swap out?"

She shook her head and assigned each to guard the end of a row.

The rows of red, blue, orange, green, pink, and violet turned my bed into a big box of crayons.

We took turns pinning, ironing, and sewing the rectangles into rows.

Near bedtime I had pinned and sewn a couple of rows together when the designer stepped in, looked at colorful banners, and began rearranging their order.

"We can take apart these two rows if you want," I offered.

"Mom, no! I like this," she smoothed out the purple row. I finished pinning together the rows. She sewed half.

A couple of days later we worked on the black border. I cut. She sewed. I ripped out half the seam and showed her how to work with the bulky pile of fabric. She finished sewing the border and ironed it flat. Another night's work on the black and white checked back where she wants to put cross stitched pictures of cats and we will make a quilt sandwich.

It's too bad she only plans to be here for a month. I have a lot of colorful fabric waiting to be used.

July 20, 2009

Sorting Through My Stash

I just had to open my mouth and mention my abundant stash of crafts and cloth to my sister. She heard 'abundant' and thought 'excess.'

"Our church gathers up unused crafts and sends them to a warehouse in Canada where they sort and ship them to outreach ministries. If you have extra fabric, quilt blocks, or yarn, we make and prepare baby layettes and quilts to send to new mothers in third world countries. I'll take whatever you don't want. You write down the details of the donation, and we will send you a receipt."

So, during her visit a few years ago, we sorted through my cupboards filled with crafts and fabrics I had purchased at garage sales or shops or received from someone else's stash. I gave to her charity until she could barely pull the zippers closed on a large duffle bag.

Weeks later I received a letter detailing how the group had used every single thing I had released to them.

My sister came again last week. I knew she was coming. I know she preaches "clean up, clear out, and quit hoarding more than you can use." So I looked at my excess and called to tell her I had some extra crafts for her to take home. I even pulled out an extra suitcase. "I think it's too big for what I have to donate," I said, "but I have a smaller suitcase if that works better."

Then I plunged into preparing for company and forgot to sort through my stash of fabric and pile of projects including the promised quilt for my youngest granddaughter. But neither my sister, nor my daughter, who both came to visit last week, forgot.

Before I knew it, my daughter talked her aunt into a day of quilting. We pulled out rotary cutters, cutting mats, graph paper for designing the already reserved fabric, plus more. With my daughter dictating the design and working as a quilting apprentice, the three of us cut, ironed seams, laid out quilt blocks, and sewed up the quilt.

I had planned to make a baby quilt. My daughter asked that I make it a twin sized quilt to use on the child's future big girl bed. My sister suggested a border of strip quilting. With the three of us working Friday night to Sunday afternoon, it took fifteen hours to finish either a full sized quilt or an oversized twin quilt that draped to the floor.

"I never knew how much work was involved. I appreciate a lot more what it takes to make a quilt," my daughter said as she sat admiring the finished quilt top. "I think it would be fun to have a quilting party with some friends," she mused and began planning one.

After she left with the quilt top and her two children, quiet settled over the house. I gathered up the needles, shears, leftover fabric, and toys. My donate-the-clutter sister turned her radar on just one spot: my overflowing stack of Christmas fabric.

"When I changed bedrooms this year, I made myself donate half of my fabric to the quilting guild. I think you should get rid of half of your Christmas fabric."

Like an obedient child I sat down on the floor and began pulling out bright red and green fabrics. She urged me to keep looking and thinking about whether I really liked the fabric, would use it, or could let it go. She snagged preprinted pillow fabrics for her guild and folded up the rest to donate to the sewing group at West Side Baptist Church. Any excess the church seamstresses have will travel to a mission outreach program in Texas, according to Pud McDade, who assured me nothing goes to waste. McDade said that the women in Texas use even the tiniest scraps for stuffing toys.

Once I finished sorting through the heap of Christmas fabric, I realized I needed to tidy and sort through my stacks of fabrics in red, blue, green, orange, purple, and brown tones. As I admired stacks printed with hearts, shamrocks, and fall designs, Sis mumbled her cleaning mantra. "Do you really need this? Do you like it? Will you use it? Should you keep it?"

She even maintained a very neutral face as I pulled out my cards of rickrack and seam binding. After I eliminated half of them, she slid them into her pile and gloated, "We use these on the layettes. We had run out of them. This will keep us busy for a while."

My sister hauled fifty pounds of fun and work home in that extra suitcase (she bought at least a third of the contents at a garage sale).

We took three boxes of fabric and notions to West Side Baptist. Others gained fabric and crafts which will eventually become finished items. I gained space and the joy of letting go and sharing my abundance with folks who can put it to good use right now.

June 14, 2010

Family Sewing Circle

I PACKED THREE SEWING MACHINES and all the extras for the family gathering along with my ideas of what to sew. But the young women and granddaughters had their own ideas that came out as soon as I lifted my Featherweight Singer out of its small black box.

First I had to deal with the crowd of curious little folks.

"What's that? How does it work? Can I try?"

"Sure," I removed the spool of thread and the bobbin, set the foot pedal on the table near the machine, and reached for a piece of paper.

"Come here and sit on my lap. We'll sew."

We dropped the presser foot on the paper, I controlled the pedal with my fingers, and the needle precisely punched a row of holes across the page. For the two-, four- and five-year-old preschoolers, a few minutes in front of the machine sufficed before they hopped down to play. The older girls and adults stayed. They had plenty of plans for the seven sets of sample fabrics from the fabric shop.

"Can we make doll quilts out of these Strawberry Shortcake pieces?" my daughter asked. Within an hour, we had two small quilts decorated with strips of lace covering the dolls, and three other block quilts taking shape. The fourteen-year-old granddaughter chose the sophisticated floral fabric for a small quilt. My daughter pieced a top for a promised Halloween quilt to accompany her son's yard of fabric printed with Halloween candy. His quilt lacked filler but it pleased him immensely.

"Thank you. This is awesome. It looks super cozy," he told me.

The seven-year-old granddaughter took the bag with seven strips of farm animals, fields, and hay and disappeared. The strips became quilt blocks which she arranged in rows. She even wrote down the sequence of pictures for each row. Her mom began chain stitching the blocks together. Before she went to bed that night, a large hunk from a brown fleece blanket backed her quilt.

As we folded up for the day the seventeen-year-old granddaughter sidled up to me. "Is that hard to do?"

"No. Sewing is easy. I can show you next time."

The next time we pulled out the machines, the fourteen-year-old agreed to make the Beatles fabric into a table topper for her St. Louis aunt. She mostly worked alone while I coached her eleven-year-old sister on the techniques for strip quilting to make a colorful Marie Engelbreit wall hanging. She amazed me with her ability to sew quarter inch seams and the precision of her lines of blocks. She finished it with a bright yellow seam binding.

The thirteen-year-old wanted to make a pillow. She chose fabric from the small stash I brought, cut out a square pillow, and sewed the pieces together. A rarely used car neck pillow provided stuffing, and she sorted through the decorative buttons to finish it.

Opening the tin of buttons caught the attention of every girl from seven months to seventeen years. With pacifier in her mouth, the baby grabbed fistfuls of buttons to inspect and drop. Her older cousins shouted out their finds, "Look, an elephant!" "This flower would look neat!" "Wow! Look at this one!" "I want that one!"

The four-year-old granddaughter pawed through the lace and seam bindings. The stiffness of the bias strips proved to be perfect for practicing her skills with the scissors. She reduced the bias tape to scraps. The two-year-old climbed up on the bed and practiced poking pins through fabric. When she had two pieces attached with the pins hanging down, she slid off the bed holding the pinned fabric over her dolls.

"Be careful, don't poke your babies," someone said.

"I'm going to poke my dollies," she assured us and laid the fabric over them.

The seventeen-year-old negated quilt making and made a colorful shoulder bag with a strap of quilt binding finished with an embroidery stitch. As we began gathering up the scraps, threads and machines, the fifteen-year-old appeared, "I want to make a pillow, but not one like hers. I want to make a round pillow."

Thinking of the trick of constantly turning a circular piece of fabric and the late hour, I said, "I think a square pillow is a better starting point." She picked out fabric and buttons and quickly finished her project with the help of her now experienced cousin.

As she proudly showed off her pillow, we gathered up dropped pins, buttons, snippets of binding, fabric, and threads, and put away my machines until the next sewing circle. It can't be too soon for me.

February 1, 2012

Time Well Spent

Outfitting for the Season

As the damp, overcast weather descended this fall, I felt mighty chilly. I scrounged around the back of my closet searching for warm clothes. Everything was short sleeved, lightweight, and summer. I didn't find any long, warm, fuzzy winter clothing to wear. Nothing.

I settled on a short sleeved, white shirt and jumper and wrapped up in my winter jacket.

After a chilly morning of work, I dashed to a clothing store at lunch time and bought a long sleeved, navy blue turtleneck to replace my short sleeved white shirt.

The next few days I searched our closets in vain for warm clothes. Finally conceding I had none, I wrote a list for a basic winter wardrobe: Slacks, shirts, and sweaters.

Thanksgiving Day my children and I studied the ads for the traditional opening day for Christmas shopping. Local shops lured me to visit their store first with special prices for early shoppers. Some of the early bird sales advertised items that filled my list of clothes to buy.

The day after Thanksgiving I felt energetic when I rose early to shop the town before going to work. I dashed from store to store. I bought a couple of Christmas gifts, but I stocked up on clothes for myself: Slacks and turtleneck shirts in white, burgundy, turquoise, and black.

I felt mighty proud of my purchases. I had found some terrific buys on warm shirts and slacks. I would be warm. I smiled contentedly as I parked and walked into the office. In a couple of predawn, pre-work hours I had done well real well.

The next week on casual Friday I thought I would wear something Christmassy. A vague memory haunted me of a hot summer day when I had purchased a Christmas sweatshirt at a garage sale. I rummaged through the drawers, the hall closet, and the bedroom rack of clothes. I even checked my daughter's closet. I could not find it. No Christmas sweatshirt, plus I realized I still had not purchased any sweaters. I compromised, wore the new burgundy turtleneck shirt with slacks, and promised myself another shopping trip when life was not so hectic with errands and holiday events.

Sunday morning as I again contemplated my wardrobe, wishing I had more options in winter clothes, I suddenly realized I had those options.

Last spring with gentle breezes warming the air, winter clothes suffocated me. Fed up with a closet overflowing with clothes for all seasons, I yanked every single one of my long sleeved shirts and sweaters off their hangers, folded them neatly, and laid them to rest in the cedar chest for the summer. When I looked for them in the fall, they were out of sight and literally out of mind until Sunday morning.

I felt ridiculous as I opened that cedar chest and pulled out maroon, white, black, and navy turtleneck shirts. Underneath the shirts I found my garage sale Christmas sweatshirt and three sweaters.

My momma once said, "Joan has it all together; she just doesn't know where it's at." Maybe my momma was right.

December 15, 1997

Family Trip to the Store

WE ONLY NEEDED PEANUT BUTTER, a gallon of milk, and cooking oil when we stopped at the grocery store. Well, those things, plus the cocoa butter my daughter added at the last minute! I figured all together it would cost me less than twenty dollars.

If I had been by myself, I would have been close. However, I wasn't by myself, my husband and daughter came with me. It was too hot to sit and wait in the car. Thinking of the electronic blood pressure cuff in the pharmacy, my husband made a beeline to the back. I yanked a cart away from its ranks of tightly packed companions. My daughter looked at the produce and announced, "We need more fruit."

We had a long mother-daughter talk over crisp heads of lettuce, glowing summer peaches, and a mountain of summer squash. We left the produce with lettuce and a honeydew melon.

The shortest distance to the milk passed the blood pressure machine where hubby was studying his robotic results.

"Oh! A new machine! I have to try it." I sat down and let the cuff get a grip on my arm. A minute later I stood up and announced my blood pressure was normal.

"How do you know?" my daughter asked.

"The chart says so," I pointed.

She shyly sat down to try the machine.

I walked away to give her some privacy and picked up that gallon of milk.

My family caught up with me as I weighed my options in cooking oils and joined me for a friendly stroll down baker's lane. At the racks of chocolate chips, nuts, and coconut, our entourage came to a halt.

"Do we have chocolate chips for cookies?"

"We have butterscotch chips."

They wanted chocolate chips to make cookies that day.

"Okay, get some. They have mega chips, mini-chips, chunks or regular." I went ahead with the grocery cart, taking the long way to the peanut butter department. A few minutes later I looked down the baker's aisle. They were in the same place debating the chips and nuts of choice for making cookies.

I strolled over to the meat department, added a package, checked out the canned fruits, and added a couple of cans to the cart, debated chunky or creamy peanut butter, settling for chunky.

My duet caught up with me in front of the salad dressings. They had decided to make white chocolate chip cookies with macadamia nuts. A block of white chocolate, a small package of macadamia nuts, and another of hazelnuts were added to the cart. All items I considered too pricey. My daughter glanced at the shelves of dressing: "We need more ranch dressing, Mom." I grabbed one and dashed for the checkout before they helped me shop anymore. My husband slipped over to the ice cream aisles. The clerk was scanning our groceries when he added two cartons to the cart.

Our six sacks of groceries totaled $52.84. Walking to the mini-van I heard myself echoing my mother, "I am never taking you to town again, never."

All that, and we still forgot to buy cocoa butter!

July 26, 1999

The Perfect Gift

I DISCOVERED THE WAY TO give grandchildren exactly what they want: take them shopping as I did just before Christmas. They held and studied several toys, lost interest and allowed me to re-shelve them.

I said we couldn't buy everything; they had to choose. My daughter had her almost three year-old nephew with her. I had my four and a half-year-old granddaughter. We looked at dolls, crafts and toys, but nothing interested her.

We were doing pretty well not finding anything until we reached the craft aisle with several intriguing projects that we selected. She was pointing out a couple that interested her when she saw the package of rainbow-colored clay with tiny animal shaped cookie cutters and four colored molds. Her interest soared. It was a great hands-on project for a little cash.

"We can't buy everything," I reminded her. "We will have to put some of the other things back." She didn't care. She held tightly onto her package of clay.

We found her little brother and my daughter exploring in the aisles of action toys. My grandson had found a display of small emergency vehicles that rolled forward, whistled or rang when a string was pulled or a lever pressed.

He picked out three and pushed them into his aunt's hand. "These are for you." He was so earnest. "When I come to your house, I can play with them."

"Why, thank you. You think I really would like these?"

"Yes, I am going to give them to you."

"Which one do you think I would like the best?"

He studied the three packages and picked out the ambulance and the fire truck that he would get for her.

"Of these two which ONE do you think is the best?"

He studied them again and selected the fire truck with the button that activated the wheels, a siren and moved the ladder up and down.

"You want to give me this?"

"Yeah," He looked longingly at the little fire truck.

"That would be very nice, wouldn't it?"

He nodded his head.

My daughter and I smiled at each other. She put all of the little vehicles back on the shelf and pushed their cart away. I picked up a fire truck and hid it beneath a couple other packages and whispered to his big sister. "Don't tell. It's a surprise."

Her eyes gleamed with the secret.

At the checkout she leaned over towards her brother and whispered, "We have a secret for you."

"Shhh, don't tell," I reminded her.

Fortunately he didn't hear us.

Right after Christmas we celebrated his third birthday. After he blew out his candles, we handed him the fire truck.

He danced around impatiently as grandpa cut the wires and plastic that bound the fire truck to its box. He ignored the rest of his gifts, placed it on the floor and pressed the lever. The little siren whined, the wheels turned and the ladder moved up and down.

"Thanks! This is the neatest present ever!" he yelled.

But of course it was! We had after all gotten him exactly what he wanted even when he said he wanted to give it to his aunt.

January 7, 2002

Shoe Shopping

IT WAS THE NEW PAIR of loafers on another's feet that dictated my shopping quest at the beginning of our second day of shopping.

The previous day I had vaguely remembered that I needed to purchase something for my wardrobe, but once I saw the book store I never thought about clothes again. Instead I bought books, lots of books—books for me, books for others, books to give, books to keep, books to share, but no clothes, and for sure, no shoes.

One snazzy pair of loafers reminded me. So I resolved, for one day, to join the other women and be clothes minded, especially since we had gathered in a place with three outlet malls with lots and lots of shoe shops.

I assumed that with all the shoe stores available, I would find the style I preferred, in the color I wanted and, of course, in the size I wear.

I should be so lucky. Most stores do not carry my narrow shoe size. Long ago I quit checking out cute shoes in a variety of colors. I learned to cut to the chase, find a clerk, and ask, "Do you carry my size?"

Most don't, but serendipitous moments do occur when I find a perfect fit at an affordable price. With all those shoe shops, surely a fortuitous moment awaited me somewhere. So I set out that morning, confident that I would return with shoes and not books that day.

I wore out a lot of shoe leather walking the sidewalks, going in, and out of the shops, asking sales clerks my question of the day, "Do you carry my size?"

I anticipated the "No, I'm sorry we don't," but I remained hopeful that I would hear at least one "Yes!" In the fifth or sixth store, in search of a clerk, I saw a style I really liked, only to be told they did not carry my size.

Like a leaky balloon, my hopeful, shoe shopping energy dissipated. Empty hands hanging heavily at my side, I watched other shoppers leave shops laden with shoes, slacks, and shirts. I plastered on a smile and admired their purchases. I shambled along feeling sorry for myself, tired of hearing, "No, we don't carry your size."

Disappointed and discouraged, I said, "Phooey to shoes," and headed for the nearest book store. As I perused novels, considered books on tape, and glanced through books filled with excellent photojournalism, the day's quest faded into oblivion.

Instead of luxuriating in the midst of the smell of new shoe leather, I breathed deeply the fragrance of fresh ink. If I could not look down and smile at new shoes, I could peek inside promising biographies.

Since I would not be taking home a box of shoe leather, I chose a box filled with audio book cassette tapes. I gathered up my favorite styles of books and left to drown my day's defeat in carefully polished tomes. Shoe shopping would just have to wait for another day.

February 20, 2006

Well Spent Weekend

MY HUSBAND DIDN'T SAY A word, not a word, but he certainly did clear his throat and raise his eyebrows a few times last weekend.

I don't know what his problem was. He knew that, besides celebrating our child's anniversary, the purpose of the visit to Indiana was to go shopping.

And early in our marriage my husband once observed, "Joan, when you do something, you really do it." When I answered that I had spent the entire day reading books, he said it proved his point. So, true to form, I spent the entire weekend shopping and spending money.

On the way north, we took my St. Louis son shopping for tools for an early birthday gift. The next day my chauffeur tracked down two out-of-the way shops which yielded a couple of items I have been trying to find for some time.

Then we arrived at our goal, the oldest son's house, just outside an organized subdivision's neighborhood garage sale. Coordinated garage sales are very popular events in that neck of the woods. About a third of the homes in the subdivision (with the goods of their friends and family from other neighborhoods) fill up their garages and driveways with tables loaded with unwanted miscellaneous items, furniture, racks of clothes, toys, and tools. They roll up their garage doors and await the invasion.

School clubs anticipate the yearly event and set up fundraising barbecue dinners and refreshment stands to sustain the garage sale shoppers. Signs and police officers direct the flow of traffic and parking in an orderly fashion. Many shoppers park at the nearby mall, unload a cart or wagon and walk.

Early in the morning I arrived with pocket money, a good pair of shoes, and a list of items I wanted to purchase if I saw them. My daughter-in-love brought her sense of humor, her own pocket of cash, and a daughter to help her spend it.

We walked up and down the streets for five hours. We bought bigger items and left them with the original owners, noted their addresses, and promised to pick them up when the crowd thinned out.

As always, I gravitated to children's toys, crafts, and clothes. There is nothing like visiting grandchildren to give me an excuse to go to a garage sale and justify buying two chunky Tonka trucks. Give him a year, and I expect one toddling grandson to be sitting in the bed of the dump truck.

In the afternoon my husband drove our van to five or six houses to pick-up purchases. Okay, he had to make three stops for me, but I wasn't the one who bought the couch.

While the women walked around the neighborhood, the men drove around the county to buy a gallon of freshly made maple syrup from the farmer and uniquely flavored cheeses and breads at the cheese factory and bakery. They returned to home base with their own stories and purchases.

Eating out that evening took about as much as I handed over at the yard sales.

Still, we spent about what we had planned until we headed home and stopped at the outlet mall for a break. That's when we broke the budget. I found a shoe store that carried my hard-to-find shoe size and came out with four pairs of discount priced shoes. My husband did mention that his shoes cost a half or a third of what one pair of mine had cost. But still, the shoes have been on my list for months.

Then I saw it, a gift shop and book store in the last throes of closing! Looking ahead to various gift giving times, I piled up a tab that matched the price of the shoes. We moseyed home, tallied up that gas and hotels had cost us more than everything, tightened our belts, decided to stay home for a few weeks and save up for our next expedition.

May 8, 2006

Mail Order Fun

EATING MY MORNING CEREAL, STUDYING the back of the cereal box, propped up in bed leafing through a catalog satisfyingly fat with pages, or curled up in the lounge chair browsing my way through Internet websites, I relish shopping at home. After days of drooling over my options, comparing cost with cash capabilities, I take a deep breath and make the plunge. I order and sit back to wait for the promised package.

In the early 1960's my imagination zoomed in on the black and white line drawing for one hundred dolls advertised in the back of the magazine for a dollar plus twenty-five cents shipping and handling. I loved dolls. The text assured me the expensively molded dolls measured up to four inches. Small dolls, yes, but one hundred of them, such riches! I wanted all one hundred dolls dressed as nurses, babies, brides, grooms, dancers, ballerinas, clowns, cowboys, and Indians. I saved up my allowances and ordered a set.

The dolls arrived in a small square, cardboard box. The inch and a half high, unpainted, very detailed figurines were made of pink, pressed plastic depicting dancers, nurses, cowgirls, and Santa with a sled which measured four inches in length and about three copies of each design. I was so disappointed. I felt robbed of my $1.25.

Sure, it came with a money back guarantee, but I was a little kid. I swallowed my disappointment, shoved the cheap, plastic figures aside, and forgot about them until recently. A search of the Internet for "One Hundred dolls" pointed me to a website with a picture of the ad and the dolls. In the late 1950s and 1960s the company captured the imagination of many little girls perusing the ads in the back of magazines.

No warm fuzzies accompany that bit of memorabilia but the experience did not dampen my enthusiasm for sending off for stuff.

As a twelve-year-old, our club of cousins saved up box tops and cash to order a doll advertised on a box of cereal. We may have aged out of playing with dolls, but that did not matter. We wanted that doll because it came with several outfits.

Together we only had enough money and box tops to order one doll. That satisfied our need for a secret club project. We puzzled over the phrase on the order blank, "No stamps, please." We could not understand how the mailman would deliver our order without a stamp, so we ignored the sentence and stuffed an envelope with cash and box tops anyway. I know, I know. Today every offer dictates, "No cash, please; checks, credit cards, or PayPal only." But this was back when we confidently taped a quarter or two to a piece of cardboard to pay for our purchase and knew we would get it.

Once we received our doll we did not know what to do with her. Planning, purchasing, and receiving the package in the mail proved the better part of the fun. We changed her clothes and admired her during our sporadic club meetings. The rest of the time she remained in her pristine box. It was not until my family moved across the country and broke up the club that she found a permanent, loving home with a younger cousin.

I still am a little kid savoring the ads and pleasure of pulling a package out of the mailbox with my name on it. These days, however, I study electronic catalogs with popup windows for a closer look at the product, rotating pictures of all sides and magnifiers to study even the stitching.

Better yet, last year I discovered digital product premiums: unique codes added to each individual package of the product. I can log in to the company's website, add my codes, and contemplate the choices for redeeming my premiums. Besides receiving coupons for free beverages, I have signed up for free magazine subscriptions, restaurant gift certificates, a printed photo book that I filled with pictures of my family, and a most satisfactory, name brand backpack with custom designed zipper tabs. In other words, enough premiums to compensate any day for one disappointing box of one hundred dolls!

December 8, 2008

With God in
the Center

Spontaneous Thanks

THE BEST THANK YOU I ever received was from one of my sons when he was about five years old. I was at a garage sale. Under a table of slightly worn clothes I saw a perfectly good pair of child sized cowboy boots. No price tag.

It was late in the day. I turned to the seller, "How much for these?

"Oh, a quarter," she yawned.

I decided my five-year-old might want to pretend he was a cowboy sometimes.

I tossed them in the car with the other items I had purchased at garage sales that morning and headed home.

I had lots of help hauling my "finds" into the house. My elementary-aged children acted like it was Christmas without all the trimmings.

I handed the boots to the five-year-old. "Here, try these on for size. I thought maybe you would…" I never finished.

"Thank you, Mom. Thank you!" he yelled as he grabbed the boots, shoved his feet in them, and pronounced, "They fit! Thanks, Mom! It's just what I wanted."

He did not just wear his cowboy boots pretending to be a cowboy. He decided "these boots are made for walking and walking's what they'll do." He wore the soles of those boots all the way through.

The boots wore out, but the memory of his uninhibited, spontaneous "thank you" will always be with me.

I wish I could have been as uninhibited on my fifteenth wedding anniversary.

Our simple wedding fifteen years before did not include a reception with a decorated cake. My husband decided to amend that.

He took me out for dinner. When the waitress served dessert, it was a multi-tiered decorated cake he had secretly brought to the restaurant in the back of the van. The waitresses had brought knife, forks, and plates. I was very pleased, but I felt very conspicuous as the other diners stared at me.

I declined to cut the cake and share it. I wanted out of there. I wanted that cake, but as everybody knows, "You can't have your cake and eat it, too."

I had my cake. I rode in the backseat staring at it all the way home. I left it in the middle of the dining room table to admire for a couple days, refusing to let anyone touch it.

If I could have, I would have worn that cake out by staring at it. Once I cut it and served the first piece, it vanished as my children helped me eat it. If my husband thought I took his gift for granted, let me say, "Thanks! It was just what I wanted."

As we take time to be thankful for the things we have taken for granted, or for blessings we have that we have "always wanted," also look around for items you never considered before.

One Thanksgiving we each took a turn praying around the table. The kindergartner mumbled his thanks, ending with, "Thank you for the walls, Amen."

I looked at him questioningly, "The walls?"

He reached for the rolls. "Yep, they hold the ceiling up."

Of course, I just never thought about the walls that way before.

This Thanksgiving as I look for things I take for granted, I am looking for something that is holding up a very important part of my life.

November 22, 1993

Peanut Butter Prayers

I WAS CONSUMED WITH SADNESS, anger, grief, loss. I wanted to have everything returned the way it was. As I made lunch for my preschooler and the baby, I emphatically told God what He needed to do for me.

Before lunch I said the perfunctory grace of gratitude even though I felt none, and we ate. My son chattered about his morning and ran back out to play. I cleared the table and sat down with the baby.

As I rocked her back and forth, my thoughts returned to my problem and the perfect solution that God should give me.

The little guy, back in from play, interrupted me. "I want a peanut butter sandwich." The baby stirred, looking at him sleepily.

"Not right now. The baby is almost asleep."

"I'm hungry."

"We just had lunch you can wait a few minutes until the baby is asleep."

His face hardened as he looked at the intruder, "I want a sandwich, now."

"Sorry, you have to wait."

He contorted his face as if in major pain, "I can't wait. I need one now."

I tried to divert the oncoming temper tantrum, "Look. I'm not going to go make a peanut butter sandwich right now, but if you want, we can read a book while I rock the baby. OK?"

He scowled at me, stomped over to his bookshelf, and returned with several books. By the time we had read all of them, the baby was asleep and the preschooler was yawning.

"Want to go upstairs and take a nap?" He nodded.

I took the baby to the crib and walked with him up the stairs to his bed.

He melted onto his bed. I tiptoed away to enjoy the quiet house while internally I raged with pain and made demands to God that He give me what I wanted when I wanted it and the way I wanted it.

An hour and a half later as I folded clothes, my preschooler woke and came to me.

"You said you would make me a peanut butter sandwich."

"Right, I did say I would fix you one." I made one and went to load more clothes into the washing machine.

When I returned, he was out in the back yard playing. The sandwich was on the counter. He had taken only a couple of small bites.

I looked at the counter, still hearing his absolute insistence two hours before that he needed that sandwich. As I gathered up the leftovers, my persistent prayer returned to my thoughts.

I started to remind God one more time of what I wanted right now and stopped.

Was I praying "peanut butter sandwich prayers"? Demanding more when I was already full?

My grief, rage, pain, sadness continued. I still wanted what I wanted when I wanted it. But I sat down, read a book, tried to take it easy while I waited.

I never did get what I wanted at that time.

A few years ago I began finding reasons to be very thankful that I had not gotten what I prayed to receive. Sometimes when I am ready to make my demands and needs known, I think about that peanut butter sandwich. I ask myself, "Am I asking for a real need or making a lot of noise and fuss about something I am not ready for?" Sometimes that long gone sandwich causes me to rethink my prayer requests.

March 13, 1995

Prayerfully Resolving Family Problems

"WOULD YOU PRAY FOR US? We are having problems with our son stealing." I was at the end of my parental rope.

"If a child is raised right…" my listener began. I took the issue up with God myself. He understood. The two perfect people He created and taught had not kept their fingers out of His fruit tree. My kid could not keep little fingers off other people's property.

Everything that had worked with our other children did not work with this one. About once or twice a year I would have to deal with yet another incident of my elementary child having stolen some small item from a store, a friend or a sibling.

My listener had not even bothered to ask how we had dealt with our child.

First, we insisted every item had to be taken back, personally with an apology. The other children had only needed one time before they learned.

Responses had been mixed at best: "Oh keep it. No one missed it." "We don't sell that item. It must have been left on a shelf." After a clerk said, "My children never took anything," I felt about two feet high that mine had chosen to steal.

Spankings made no impression.

When stolen food or money disappeared, my child had to earn the money to pay for it. We had applied the Biblical mandate that "those who have been stealing must never steal again. Instead, they must work. They must do something useful with their own hands. Then they will have something to give to people in need." Ephesians 4:28 (NIV). For our child that meant wash the floor, clean the garage, or pick up pine cones from the yard.

And still things were stolen.

Finally, frustrated, I asked for prayer, only to be told that we as parents had failed. I slouched down, said no more, but determined to find a way to teach my hard-headed child self-control, even when I was not supervising.

That's when I remembered that the Old Testament punishment for stealing was not jail, nor physical punishment, but repayment at four or five times the object's worth. "If a man steals an ox or a sheep and slaughters it, or sells it, he must pay back five head of cattle for the ox and four sheep for the sheep."

We established a new rule: The next time he stole, the child would have to pay back twice as much as was taken. The multiplier would increase with each subsequent incident. The message did not register with twice, thrice or four times the value. It took having to pay back five times the value of the item before my child decided, "I don't like this."

That final time my hard-headed learner came to me with cash in hand and confessed to me before I found out.

I wasn't angry. I was relieved. My child had finally accepted responsibility for personal actions. It made a big dent in a child's savings account, but it was worth every penny.

A couple of days later we were riding together. "How come, Mom, although I did the right thing this time, I still feel awful?"

"That's your conscience teaching you never to do that again."

He hasn't, either. I have not been as judgmental of parents with a problem child.

May 20, 1996

The Impact of One Teacher

MR. NOSKY, MY JUNIOR HIGH public school English teacher, expected a lot from his classes of thirty-five to forty students. He expected us to write, and write a lot. We wrote out speeches, book reports, essays, and friendly letters.

Oh, yes. I had almost forgotten writing a friendly letter with Mr. Nosky.

We had to lay aside our ball point pens and use an old fashioned fountain pen and unlined paper on top of a page with darkened lines meant to keep our writing in neat lines. Mr. Nosky forbade us to end our letters, "Well, I have to go." Students who failed to bring envelopes and stamps to mail the letters on completion had to buy them from Mr. Nosky. Letters were folded neatly in thirds and inserted into the envelope so that it opened with the top of the page up.

Everything that we wrote, including friendly letters, began with a penciled rough draft. He thought we were capable of writing complex sentences and graded accordingly. He was adamant, "If you make a mistake, cross the word out once. Do not scribble over the word. Write a correction beside it."

Final drafts were written with our fountain pens.

We lived with notebooks, library books, and literature texts as well as the mandatory spelling books. He lived with stacks of papers to read and grade. So when he had to supervise study hall, he laid out his rules the first day: "Bring your homework, text books, enough pens, pencils, and paper to last, and a book to read." No one slept in his study halls. No one talked. He had too much work of his own to do to tolerate any goofing off from students in his study halls. Mr. Nosky didn't like unnecessary noise. He liked written words. He expected a high level of achievement from everyone.

My older brother and I endured three years and two years respectively under the man before my parents moved to another state. We secretly mocked subsequent English and literature teachers' surprise at the level of our abilities to communicate on paper. We told our younger sisters and brother that they were sadly lacking in their education.

Of course, that was back in the era when teachers were still next to God and parents, but it was after the Supreme Court ruled that prayer could not be mandated in schools. Mr. Nosky, a Catholic, never mandated prayers, but one day he told our primarily Protestant class, "I pray for each of you every day." Writing wasn't his only concern. He cared about us, too.

I was reminded of him when I went to a Moms In Touch prayer group last week. The open, interdenominational prayer group of mothers with children in school was led by a teaching mom. She wanted to pray with others for her school. When I substituted at the high school, I met other, similarly concerned, teaching parents and nonparents. With praying moms and teachers, like Mr. Nosky, who are concerned and expect the best from their students, any school has a prayer of a chance at succeeding.

October 14, 1996

Answered Prayer

I TOSSED CEREAL AND MILK on the table for my grade school sons to eat while I gathered up a change of clothes and snacks for my preschooler and found my pocketbook. My two-year-old daughter and I were heading out for a morning of garage sale shopping.

One of the boys came out wearing one of his two remaining pairs of jeans that still fit him and did not have holes in the knees. "Mom, I need some more jeans."

He did. It was not the era when it was fashionable to go to school with ragged, torn jeans, especially not in grade school. It was, however, our financially tight spell of the year.

"I am going to pray that I find some jeans for you at the garage sale today," I told him.

He looked at me skeptically. I was not in the habit of telling him what I talked over with God.

"I am. God provides in a lot of different ways." The child looked at me skeptically. "Never hurts to ask," I said. I left wondering if I had been too bold in telling him that.

Within a mile I stumbled across a small unadvertised garage sale. Usually I drive by yard sales set up hastily on chairs and boards, but this time I stopped. The first thing I saw was a pile of little boy's jeans. I picked up the top pair to examine them. The size was right in fact all six pairs were the right size. They were rugged little boy jeans with reinforcement material behind each knee, marked at less than a dollar a pair.

As I studied the seams for wear, the seller commented, "My mother bought them for my son a year ago. A month later he had a growth spurt

192

and could not wear anything he had. I tried selling them last spring, but no one was interested."

I stacked all of the jeans on my arm. I knew one little boy who would fit all six pairs for the price of less than one pair at the store.

It took my skeptical, active son several months to wear them out.

The memory of his skepticism bemuses me these days when I receive his email. He knows God listens to the simplest of prayers. This fall he was asked to serve part time as an associate pastor while he continues his graduate studies. After a few months of trying to pedal his ten-speed bike everywhere, he grudgingly admitted he needed a vehicle. He didn't say anything to us, he prayed about it.

At Christmas time he announced that he had the use of another student's car for six months while he studied abroad. All he does is make the monthly insurance payment and maintains the car.

His prayers go beyond his own needs. Every week he emails me a praise and prayer list from around the world. I pray as I read it through. He joyfully records answered prayers, awed at seeing God work around the world. Many of the answers are as easy to measure as jeans at a garage sale. When the results are more elusive, he prays on because he has learned even when nothing seems to be happening, God is still listening and will honor those prayers in His time.

February 8, 1999

Praying for Help

As AVID DO-IT-YOURSELFERS MY HUSBAND and I planned a blueberry Saturday. We would pick and put them in the freezer. However, the washing machine shaft broke; I knew who would fix it. Saturday morning before we went to pick berries, my husband tore apart the machine reluctantly stopping only to go berry picking.

We returned with twenty-five pounds of berries and four bushels of corn. My three grade school sons and I stayed outside for a corn husking party. My repairman returned to the washing machine.

As I hauled the corn into the house, the heap of fresh blueberries reminded me of work to do. I told our two oldest sons they were blueberry factory workers. They began sacking berries for the freezer. I helped them as I waited for the water to heat for blanching corn. By 9:30 p.m. all the blueberries were in the freezer and the factory workers were in bed.

I still had heaps of corn to do, a kitchen floor covered with washing machine parts, and a husband who needed an extra hand.

Several times I begrudgingly quit cutting corn off the cob to play mechanic's apprentice. Finally my man said, "I think I have this fixed. Help me put the tub back in place." I put down the knife I was using and helped lift the tub through the front of the frame. He reattached the belts.

All I had to do was hold the seal, counterweight, and clamp all in place. The cast iron counterweight turned in my hands, the metal clamp had shrunk and the rubber seal had grown. For an hour we fought to position and balance everything as we screwed the clamp in place.

At almost midnight we stopped. "While you try to figure out another way," I said, "I'll take this corn down to the freezer."

Wearily I stumbled through a trail of cobs, corn silk, squashed berries, tools, and machine parts to the basement. I slumped on the steps beside the freezer and dropped my head into my hand, "Oh God, I just can't go on. You know how those parts go together. Would you please put our hands in the right places and show us how to put the parts back in place? We need You, the God of the Impossible, to help us."

My prayer was interrupted with the persistent man's call. "Let's try again." I went back upstairs. The pieces flowed together without slipping. We screwed the clamp in place. My husband lifted the front panel over the machinery. It didn't fit. We had a part in upside down. We quickly undid the clamp, repositioned everything, and fitted the panel in place. We were done.

I didn't say anything about my prayer. I pushed my hair back and returned to the counter and the last of the corn. At 1 a.m. Sunday we crawled into bed.

Two weeks later as we weeded our garden my husband asked, "When did you pray?"

"About what?"

"That we fix that washing machine."

"Why do you ask?"

"After an hour of getting nowhere, we put those two pieces together twice in less than twenty minutes."

He knew that we may try to do it all by ourselves, but we don't really do it all by ourselves.

April 5, 1999

Post the Ten Commandments

THE SUPREME COURT DECLINED TO hear an appeal from the city of Elkhart, Ind., to keep their six feet tall statue of the Ten Commandments located in front of city hall. I didn't drive by to see it during a recent visit to the city, but I had just reread The Ten Commandments in a 1942 printing of a Common Book of Prayer. Accompanying service notes suggested that the commands be read once a month in conjunction with communion.

Once a month? It has been ages since I have heard them read in church or used in a sermon, let alone read them myself.

A few minutes after reading The Ten, I entered a beautiful church filled with worshippers who would support displaying The Ten Commandments in front of city hall or in a courtroom. The church atrium is warm and welcoming with beautiful pictures of gardens, a supply of books and floral arrangements but no display of the Ten Commandments.

I am not picking on that church, but I haven't seen the Ten displayed at any of the churches I have attended at home or while traveling. Other than the billboard on the northern end of the city's business district, the Ten are not generally publicly posted.

They are not in the businesses owned by those who protest every time another governing body is reprimanded for posting The Ten.

Not in private schools.

Not in my home or the homes of folks I know.

Not in any of the places where anyone would dare prohibit the posting of the Ten.

While we wait on the legal system to decide if, at this time, it views

The Ten as part of our legal heritage or a religious statement, no law prohibits posting them in other more accessible spots.

Reading the command, "Do not commit adultery," while picking up a divorce decree at the court house merely rubs salt in the wounds.

Posting the Ten Commandments in shops and restaurants with "Do not steal" highlighted, might keep potential culprits from having their first encounter with the command on a court room wall while awaiting judgment.

Having The Ten in plain view when making financial decisions would underscore, "Do not covet." Reading the tenth command, while waiting for a bankruptcy hearing is too late to stop the quest to satisfy an overwhelming desire to have more than the paycheck can cover.

Before a child reaches juvenile court with a willfully defiant attitude, post The Ten in the home. There the command "Honor your mother and father" can be demonstrated with respectful attitudes and actions.

Deacons, pastors, choir directors, and Sunday School teachers, especially need to be reminded, "Remember the Sabbath Day to keep it holy."

Write it and the other nine in big, bold letters in the church foyer to remind worshippers to take one day out of the rush of life to rest and worship before exhaustion flattens them with lots of time to read and contemplate The Ten.

If the Ten Commandments are important enough to make a legal fuss regarding their display on civil property, surely they are important enough to post in our places of business, our homes, churches, schools and, most especially, in our hearts by living them out in our daily lives.

July 23, 2001

Lifting Hands in Praise

IT SOUNDED LIKE A GOOD idea when we talked about initiating the ministry.

I was one of the first to volunteer.

Some weeks I enjoyed talking with the man in his nineties who played championship level checkers and enjoyed computer chess. He also studied math every day just to keep his mind sharp.

At times I needed the pat on the hand and hug from the grandmotherly woman as much as she did.

One Sunday a wheelchair-bound middle-aged patient and I exchanged grins when he took off his glasses and hooked them onto the top of his shirt as I had hooked mine on my blouse.

But other times I slouched in my chair and wondered why I had agreed to go to the nursing home twice a month for Sunday School. I shrank back from the wraparound reminder of the fragility of the human body, the inevitability of aging, the effects of a stroke, or the onset of Alzheimer's.

As we sang about God's love for all of his creation, I looked away from the harsh reminders of the vicissitudes of age. I didn't want to know that I would not always be a healthy young woman. I didn't want to think about the fact that someday I might be like that lady in the high-backed wheel chair unable to even wheel her chair into the service. Lost in the confusion of dementia, she did not look at anyone but stared over our heads.

I shuddered inwardly, looked away, and focused on the worship leader preparing to do a special number. She popped in a cassette tape with a simple song. She did not sing. She let the vocalist on the tape sing while she signed the message of the song in a ballet of the hands. I watched fascinated as always, studying the repeated signs, wishing I would remember them later. Lifting hands to worship God in sign language always adds richness to the worship service.

The room of elderly folks watched quietly, politely—except- what was that movement?

I turned.

The wheelchair bound woman, the one who could no longer communicate because Alzheimer's had robbed her of her speech, was sitting up as straight as she could in her high backed chair. Her eyes lit up with recognition. A small smile creased her face.

She knew this song.

She knew these signs. She lifted her hands in praise and signed in unison with the worship leader.

From one side of the room to the other, the two women looked knowingly in each other's eyes and performed a hand ballet of worship to God.

My grumps, my complaints, my questions faded.

We brought these folks little that they did not already have. They knew all the songs, they knew all the words, and from a life time of living they had tested the reality of their faith. We had simply come to worship the God of our faith with them.

This woman bound by a wheelchair and a fading mind had forgotten many things: once familiar names and places, the years of life with her husband, and how to perform simple tasks. Speech failed her, but she had not forgotten God's love or how to worship Him in sign language.

She worshipped God that day. And in her worship she ministered to me. She reminded me again that God so loved everyone, even those incapacitated with age and dementia, that he gave His only Son that none should perish if they only would believe and receive God's gift of love. (John 3:16.)

It was the first and last week I saw her there.

A month or two later I read her obituary in the newspaper and blinked back tears as I remembered the smiling, frail elderly woman, trapped in a wheelchair, bound by a fading mind, but still smiling and lifting her hands in praise of her God.

April 12, 2004

When God is Not Fair

No fair, God. No fair! That is exactly how I felt that long ago winter as a young mother.

It began with a really bad mistake in my check writing.

We had agreed to send something each month to help some missionary friends of ours. As Christmas time neared, I felt like we should give them a bit more as a Christmas gift until I looked at our typical young family's tight budget and decided we really could not afford it.

Well, God decided differently.

I wrote down in the checkbook ledger the amount I was going to write for their monthly check. I subtracted it and proceeded to write their check not for the amount I had planned, but for the second number I had written everything we supposedly still had left in the checkbook. I did not catch my error until the bank statement came and I was flicking through the checks.

Ouch!

I mean, really, OUCH! We did not have enough money to have a lot of errors and flexibility in our budget. We kept a garden and canned everything. We shopped sales and had decided that taking ourselves and our children to the dentist would just have to wait for a while. We simply could not afford it.

I called my mom and told her my shocking discovery. She mentioned it to my brother who shrugged, "Hey, if God wanted her to give that money, He will cover the check."

With sinking heart I began to tick off checks as I balanced the check book. I had made a lot of mistakes that month. At least one was a one hundred dollar subtraction error.

All totaled, they offset the amount for which I had written the Christmas bonus check.

The check was covered. We had given them a Christmas gift.

When we spoke with the missionaries later that year, we mentioned the odd circumstances for their Christmas "bonus." They said, "It came in very handy to pay off some unexpected dental bills."

What? My check provided funds for their dental bills?

I could not believe that God had provided money for their dental bills and He did not provide any for ours.

I was silently furious with God. It was so unfair. He provided a huge checking mistake to take care of their dental bills and didn't bother to get around to sending me anything for even check-ups.

That lack of provision gnawed at my soul for months. It gnawed at me when I prayed, when I looked at the budget and wanted more money for taking care of what I considered simple needs such as dental check-ups. It gnawed at me when I looked at toothpaste.

Eventually, our situation changed, and I scheduled dental check-ups for everyone. One by one, the children went in. One by one each came out smiling, "No cavities."

Nor did my husband and I have any cavities.

We had not needed to go to the dentist.

And God knew that all along! In spite of my lack of trust in His provision for us, He had taken care of our dental health.

God did not provide the same for each family. He gave our missionary friends funds. He gave us excellent dental health. But in both cases, He took care of our family's needs.

For months I had prayed, "Give us this day our daily bread," said "Amen," then walked away to worry, fret, and stew over where the bread was going to come from for that day.

Jesus said, "Why do you worry about the rest? Consider how the lilies grow. They do not labor or spin. Yet I tell you, not even Solomon in all his splendor was dressed like one of these. If that is how God clothes the grass of the field, which is here today, and tomorrow is thrown into the fire, how much more will He clothe you, O you of little faith!" Luke 12:26-28 (NIV)

If I had walked in faith, I would have said, "Thank you, God, for using me to meet our friend's needs. I trust You to use whatever means You choose to meet our needs."

The great thing about God is that even though I did not remember to "thank God no matter what happens" I Thessalonians 5:18 (NIV), He continued to provide for our need in His way, and in His time I found out about His provision.

August 21, 2006

Waiting on God

THE RAIN FROM TROPICAL STORM Ike left two feet of sewer water in my son's basement. His black Sunday email read, "Our basement flooded yesterday. Since our insurance excluded flood and sewer backup in the coverage, we will be on our own for the cleanup and replacement of anything that was damaged: washer, dryer, furnace, hot water heater and treadmill. Also the '91 Honda Accord died yesterday."

Helplessly I considered my family in the midst of that mess as I watched my husband in the midst of building his long-dreamed-of workshop, trying to get it in the dry before the winter rains drenched building materials stacked in our backyard. He could not see his way to go to St. Louis to help.

In the middle of the night I frantically dictated to God a pile of solutions I had figured out and determined to go up over the weekend by myself. I kept telling God a lot of ways He could work out everything.

None of it seemed right.

As my emotions whirled, I stopped praying and waited to discern God's message through all this turmoil.

The only message I got was the lesson I taught that week to the children at church, "Don't be like Saul who could not wait on God." Samuel told Saul he would come in seven days to offer the sacrifice and offer a prayer before they went into battle. While Saul waited to confront an enemy with thousands of well-equipped men, he watched his own army slip away into hiding. By the morning of the seventh day, Saul had six hundred men left. Samuel still had not come. Saul took matters into his own hand. He prepared and offered the sacrifice himself. His army needed the ceremony as encouragement in the face of such an enemy.

As he finished the sacrifice, Samuel walked in and rebuked Saul's lack of faith. "You have acted foolishly," Samuel said. (I Samuel 13:13 NIV.)

I knew Saul's feeling. I did not want to act foolishly, but I could not let go. While I waited for dawn, my meditations focused on "Wait, I say on the Lord." Finally, I relaxed, yawned, and headed back to bed. I was tired of trying to tell God how to work out everything. I would wait.

Nothing happened the next day or the next.

The work did not go any faster for us. It did not go any smoother for my son who had to work four twelve-hour days after the sewer lines flooded his basement. The tow company hauled their car to the repair man they had used the last time it acted up.

They asked nearby friends and family for help, and they waited.

201

At our house, over the next two weeks, building buddies came and helped my husband hoist trusses into place and covering them with plywood and tar paper.

In St. Louis the mechanic said the problem was related to work they had done previously. They fixed it at no cost.

The sewer company accepted responsibility for water backing up into basements. In recent months the community had voted to deal with the inadequate lines, but the storm hit before the work could be done.

A neighbor told them to take plenty of pictures documenting the extent of the damage before they began emptying out and power washing their basement.

They weighed the price of renting a power washer versus purchasing a machine. The sale on power washers at the Big Box Store for a few dollars above the price of one day of renting finalized that decision.

Saturday friends helped drag their soggy possessions out of the basement and watched their baby while his wife enjoyed kicking out a water-logged wall. The town established nearby collection sites for the trash and saved them the cost of hauling it all to the dump. In three other days by themselves and with other friends they finished the hauling, power washing, bleaching, and rinsing.

Now comes the process of sorting out expenses incurred with purchasing and installing a new hot water heater, furnace, and the various irreplaceable losses. Now I must process and recognize that no matter what plans I develop, God has a better solution waiting for them if I will just trust Him and wait.

September 29, 2008

Thoughts on Redefining Marriage

IF YOUR PRIMARY OCCUPATION ON Sunday morning avoids anything to do with church, don't bother to read this column. If you weary of one more discussion on the importance of defining marriage as a heterosexual experience, stop reading. If you just want a warm fuzzy tale of family events, take a break and come back next week. This week I will be sorting my way through a few thoughts I have on marriage as a believer in the eternal, sovereign God. This week I explore what I think about the covenant which joins two souls in marriage, a decision which modern society has made into a very complex, controversial issue.

Reading through the Old and New Testaments has left me with a deep impression of the repetitive description of God's relationship to His believers. Throughout the Bible God plays the role of the husband.

Time and again Isaiah refers to Israel as God's bride or wife. "I made you. I am now your husband. My name is The LORD WHO RULES OVER ALL. I am the Holy One of Israel. I have set you free. I am the God of the whole earth." Isaiah 54:5 (NIV).

In Hosea God tells the prophet to marry a prostitute to represent the way the Jewish nation turned from worshiping God to worshiping idols. When his wife returns to prostitution, Hosea seeks her out in the marketplace, buys her back, and takes her home as his wife just as God sought to redeem and restore His loving relationship with Israel, even after they had prostituted their beliefs to idols.

In the Old Testament the nation of Israel is the bride, the promised and cherished one. In the New Testament the followers of Christ are similarly portrayed as a virgin coming to her bridegroom. For instance, in II Corinthians 11:2 (NIV) it says, "I promised you to one husband, to Christ, so that I might present you as a pure virgin to Him." And again in Ephesians 5:25 (NIV), Paul admonishes, "Husbands, love your wives. Love them just as Christ loved the church. He gave himself up for her."

All the references to the relationship of God with those who believe and follow Him reflect a husband and a wife, a male/female relationship.

There is no portrayal of God as a female or wife, nor is the analogy ever of two entities with essentially interchangeable roles or capabilities. God provides, protects, and leads. Believers, whether they are Israelites or Christ's followers, are those under His protection. We are the loved ones receiving His provision and watchful care.

Believers look to God for leadership, submit to His commands and enjoy the protection of a sovereign, strong God. And, in spite of all that, believers break His commands, follow false gods, and walk away from His protection.

For that reason God has already done what no human can ever do. He came to earth as the ultimate provision, the perfect sacrifice for our lifelong predisposition to trespass over His boundaries. We can never do what God does for us. The roles are not interchangeable.

Today some push for a different understanding. Today some want marriage to be redefined as any two persons choosing to share their lives regardless of their birth gender. Voices ring out loud and clear on both sides from church halls to city halls, from annoying talk radio to trash talk television shows. But putting all the popular yammering aside, the issue comes down to this: as followers of the eternal God we do not exist merely for our personal happiness. Our mandate as believers is to live in every way possible that brings honor and glory to the God of the universe including within our marriages.

We do not glorify God when we twist His analogies of His love for us by equating the union of a man and woman to the union of two women or two men.

We do not glorify God when we seek personal happiness and embrace a union diametrically opposed to the picture He regularly uses to describe His love for His followers.

We do not glorify God when we shrug our shoulders and say, "Times are changing. We need to reconsider what is socially acceptable."

People change. Their viewpoints, their rules, and their focal points change, but God does not change. Because I follow an eternal, unchanging God, I cannot consider a redefinition of marriage structured to suit a temporal, social environment. I choose instead to glorify God by adhering to His analogy of marriage demonstrating His unchanging, sacrificial, eternal love for mankind.

February 8, 2010

A Respectful Blend

"You're not my mother!"

Right, I knew that before the child ever said it. I never said I was, but as a parent for nearly four decades in a blended family, I've definitely been reminded a time or two of that fact. I know it isn't easy for the children, but then family living never has been and the blended family is nothing new.

My mom's father had two step-mothers after his own mother died. His first step-mother treated him as if he were her child. When she died, his father remarried, and Grandpa moved in with his first step-mother's parents who loved him as their own. During Grandpa and Grandma's early childless years they parented a relative's son for several years. Both my dad's mother and my aunt housed foster children as did I for one year.

Although I have not lived on the child's side of a blended family, I do know the struggle as an adult to treat each child the same. Sure, I might not be their birth parent or grandparent, but that is not the kid's fault, and it is my responsibility to provide godly, loving parenting.

My mom-in-love also housed unrelated boys for a while. One day she and I were having a discussion about blended families when she stopped and pointed at a seasonal picture. "Look at this picture of the Nativity. Mary's husband Joseph was not the father of Jesus." She stood staring at a picture of "the holy family" realizing that even Christ came from a blended family.

At twelve Jesus acknowledged His birth father when He said he had to be about His Father's (God's) business; but then Luke 2:51(NIV) records that having said that, He returned to Nazareth with Mary and Joseph "and obeyed them." Christ submitted to the man who was not His father and "Jesus became wiser and stronger. He also became more and more pleasing to God and to people."

Similarly Samuel, the last prophet leader for Israel, left his parents' home as a very young child and went to live with the high priest. "The boy Samuel served the LORD under the direction of Eli." 1 Samuel 3:1 (NIV). Except for the earliest years of his life, Samuel did not live with his parents, but he honored God by subjecting himself to Eli's authority even if it meant he had to wake up and go help aging Eli when he called in the middle of the night.

My family's experiences and the Biblical examples came together recently when I reviewed the rules for expected behavior with some in the family. I count six children, fifteen grandchildren, and a couple great-grandchildren. Some are not related biologically, yet the goal still is to treat each one the same way, and I expect the same from them.

We are not a unique family. Whether in a blended family or not, many adults and children need an occasional reminder to treat others with respect and to follow the examples and mandates in the Scriptures.

In Exodus 20:12 (NIV), every person is commanded to "Honor your father and your mother, so that you may live long in the land the LORD your God is giving you." It doesn't say "if they are good enough, have not offended you deeply or have not made some horrible mistake." It says to honor them. As an adult that meant that even when my father was difficult to be around, I was to choose to speak respectfully to him. I could not obey his every whim, but I could respectfully decline.

At the same time, we each have many people who are in authority over us besides our parents: teachers, pastors, work supervisors, police officers, and government officials.

Our job as followers of God is simply laid out in Romans 13:1-2a (NIV): "All of you must be willing to obey completely those who rule over you. There are no authorities except the ones God has chosen. Those who now rule have been chosen by God. So when you oppose the authorities, you are opposing those whom God has appointed."

I know it is not easy for children or adults to honor everyone in their lives. I also personally know it is not easy to deal with intact families, let alone blended families, but I know by faith that God honors and blesses those who follow His way.

September 6, 2010

Prayer Meeting in the Park

THE ECONOMIC CRUNCH OF RECENT years hit real estate related businesses hard. The number of homes sold dropped along with the price of houses. Even the task of appraising houses for their market value declined. This job that had once supported my friend left her looking elsewhere for employment.

Month after month, calls asking for an appraisal grew farther and farther apart. Some months she received only a couple of calls compared to previous years of being asked to appraise at least three or four houses a week.

Week after week the cost of living and the income from working failed to agree.

Discouraged, the once busy appraiser began looking for other means of covering her household expenses. She opened her home to a woman needing to rent a room. She looked into working at a department store or cleaning houses—anything to get her through the rough time in the fallen economy.

Fortunately she no longer had children at home. The two oldest were married with children. Her youngest, finishing college, worked to cover his out-of-pocket expenses. As the holiday season approached, she suggested that each person make personal gifts rather than purchase them.

One Saturday morning as she left her quiet home office and headed to the park to walk her dog, she resolved to make it through Thanksgiving and Christmas and then consider another field of employment.

She pulled into a parking spot, opened her door, and reached for the dog leash.

"Excuse me, Ma'am."

She turned and smiled, "Yes?"

A young woman stood shivering hesitantly before her.

"I'm supposed to go to the park this morning and pray for someone. You are the one. Is there something you would like me to pray about for you?"

That question had an easy, obvious answer, "My business. Pray for my business. It has been rough the last couple years."

The teen did not give her name. She did not ask the business woman for hers. She simply prayed earnestly over the business. She prayed for more phone calls to come. She prayed for wisdom for the woman. She thanked God for the answer and closed with a quiet, "In Christ's name, Amen."

The young woman lifted her head and smiled at the older woman, "May God be with you," and she left.

Pulling her dog's leash, the business woman started to walk her dog unsure what it all meant yet still pleased that God had sent someone to pray for her. The time of prayer calmed her through the rest of the weekend.

Monday, she received two phone calls for appraisals.

By the end of the week she had had enough calls to keep her busy for another week.

In the year since the prayer meeting in the park, the phone has continued to ring. Each business call leaves her keenly aware that: "If the LORD DOESN'T BUILD A HOUSE, THE WORK OF ITS BUILDERS IS USELESS. If the LORD DOESN'T WATCH OVER A CITY, IT'S USELESS FOR THOSE ON GUARD DUTY TO STAND WATCH OVER IT." Psalm 127:1 (NIV).

She could not build a business without God. Only He could make this happen, and He did in His time.

I called her recently to ask her if I could share her story. She apologized for not lingering to talk; she had too much to do to sit and chat. She said she might need to hire an assistant.

Our brief conversation testified of God's provision as He answered the young woman's prayer and demonstrates the walk of faith when we pray asking God to provide our daily bread—not a whole year's worth of bread at once but enough for the day. That is a thought to consider as we enter another year in economically uncertain times. He is the One providing the work and the energy we need each day for our daily bread.

January 3, 2011

God Still Answers Prayers

LIFE HAD NOT WORKED OUT the way that the middle-aged woman had thought it would. She was no longer married, no longer in her suburban home. Her minor children had moved hundreds of miles away to a western state with their father, and the hotel job she found to support herself paid the meager salary of $12,000. She did not understand how or why, but for seven months she remained stuck in that job at the hotel, struggling to make ends meet with no other job opportunities opening for her.

She found a room to rent in the home of another struggling single woman whose children had grown and left an empty bedroom available. Economic hard times had hit her landlady's business with a vengeance, nearly closing it for lack of activity, but she had been able to keep her home, used one room as an office, and rented the extra bedroom. Not that the office served much use as the weeks and months piled up and the phone remained silent.

The two had much in common until the landlady's office phone began ringing. Her business increased overnight and continued to increase to the point that she considered hiring an assistant to help with the paperwork.

The renter continued to put out applications in search of finding some way to use her experience and education, but month after month passed and nothing happened in the job market.

Nothing.

Then she heard the rest of the story about her landlady's changes in business.

During a family visit, the landlady pulled out an earlier column I had written telling about the day the landlady took her dog for a walk in the park and met a teenager who asked if she could pray for her, and if so, for what?

"Certainly my business is not doing well," the landlady answered.

The young woman prayed for this total stranger, and the two parted their ways. The next business day she received two phone calls providing her with half a week of work. The rest of the week and subsequent weeks were profitably occupied.

The renter's children came to visit just before Christmas. After they returned to their father, a deep remorse settled over the renter. The landlady noticed the sadness.

"Would you like me to pray for you?" the landlady asked.

"Yes. I was a commercial loan originator with twenty-one loans in the works and not one went through. I lost a six figure income. I have sent out a hundred job applications, and most don't even acknowledge the effort."

So the landlady, took her renter's hand, bowed her head, and prayed for the other woman.

A few days later, the renter came home one evening and said, "Guess what! I have a job interview. I think this is going to be the one that I get. I don't know how, or why; I just know."

And it was! The interview went well with a promotional agency that needed someone familiar with the hotel business to come to their headquarters and help set up conventions and conferences. They had been looking for someone for six months. All those months spent working in the low paying job at the hotel had provided her with the experience she needed for the opening they had.

"The headquarters is twenty minutes from my children!" the renter happily reported. "When you told me about the prayer and your business increasing, I thought 'Yeah, I wish something like that would happen to me; and now it has!'"

"Now you have a story to tell," the landlady said.

"No," said the renter. "Now I have a testimony." Within the month she resigned her position at the hotel, packed her bags, found an apartment, and moved to the better paying job within minutes of her children.

Before she left, her landlady said, "The day will come when God will send someone your way for prayer. Don't forget to take their hand and do so right then." She said she would.

And when she does, she will glorify God through the answered prayer in her own life as she experiences Christ's promise in John 14:13-14 (NIV): "And I will do anything you ask in my name. Then the Son will bring glory to the Father. You may ask me for anything in my name. I will do it."

May 16, 2011

God's Timely Christmas Gift

TIME AND AGAIN, I HAVE met folks who believe and practice, "If we are faithful to God, He will be faithful to us."

But no one said it was always easy! As my coworker said, "I have always tithed. Even when I did not know how I could do it, I tithed, and it always worked out. I don't know how, but I always had enough money."

As with any family, she experienced times when the money was tight, as she did the year her husband had been off work for six weeks with medical problems.

"We were not starving, but it was tight," she said. "I did not know how I would be able to buy any Christmas for the kids that year. I was a stay-at-home mom with a two-year-old at home. The older children were seven and nineteen at the time.

"I was talking on the phone with my really good friend. I was standing at the kitchen window when I saw a white truck pull up that said something about the Bell Phone company on the side.

"I told my friend, 'A white truck just drove up.'" She paused and watched as the driver opened the door and got out.

"There is someone here with a red shirt, white beard, and gray hair. He looks just like Santa Claus," she half laughed as she told her friend.

"Keep me on the phone," her friend urged.

"I'm sure it will be fine," she said, but stayed on the line anyway as the man walked up to the house and knocked at the door.

The stay-at-home mom went over to the door, opened it, and asked, "May I help you?" The man in the red shirt with the white beard said, "I heard you were having a hard time this year at Christmas." He reached in his pocket, pulled out a white envelope, and said, "This is for you."

She took it, and before she could open it or even say "Thank you," he turned, walked quickly back to his truck, climbed in, and drove away.

Her friend's voice came over the phone, "Who was it? What happened?"

"He looked like Santa Claus, that's all that I can tell you because it happened really fast and quick."

"What did he do?"

"He came up to the door, said 'I understand things have been a bit tight this year,' and gave me a white envelope."

"What's in it?"

"I don't know. I haven't opened it. I am kind of afraid to open it,"

"Open it! Open the envelope, and see what it is," her friend insisted.

"Okay!" She slipped her finger behind the flap, opened the envelope, pulled out five one hundred dollar bills, and began screaming.

"Oh my, it's five one hundred dollar bills," she half cried and half screamed. Her friend screamed happily with her.

"And I never had a chance to thank him," she said.

"Did you give him my address?" her friend teased.

The family never did find out who had brought the cash although one person did try. They called the phone company and asked, but no one there fit that description.

"Some people say that Santa Claus visited me," my coworker said. "But I do not think it was Santa Claus; I believe it was an angel.

"It is like I heard at the Bible Study the other night, 'Jesus is Sweet.' I have heard that 'He is good.' I have heard that He is 'real,' but that year, Jesus was 'sweet.' He was so sweet to us. We had a nice Christmas dinner. It was just amazing," she said. In the years since that event, her children have all entered full time ministry.

Yes, Jesus is good. Jesus is real. When times are tough, He is sweet as my co-worker discovered the day when a man who looked like Santa Claus gave her an envelope with much needed cash.

December 21, 2011

You Did What!?

Hazardous Halloween Candy

I'M GLAD HALLOWEEN IS OVER for another year—not because of the trick-or-treaters. I love the puzzled looks on the toddlers' faces, the older ones' expectant grins, and the escorts who feign disinterest even as they take a treat.

I like passing out gifts to so many for so little. I enjoy watching that half-blind walk as they leave with their head bent to peer deep into their bag and see what we gave them. Sometimes I am rewarded with a pleased shout as a little one holds up his treat to show his mommy.

I even like the ones who are trying so hard to cover the entire neighborhood that they barely have time to say 'thank you' before they dash away.

My problem is my family.

They won't believe that they have outgrown trick-or-treat. Every year it is the same discussion.

"Now this year you really are too old to go."

"But, Mom."

"No. Aabsolutely not. You're too old."

In our neighborhood it's hard to quit. Halloween is a huge block party with candy, kids, and cars lining the streets.

I really thought they were too old when I said, "Anyone old enough to fill out a college application is too old to fill up a trick-or-treat sack."

That year I thought I had found a happy compromise. I asked my high school aged sons to hand out the treats while I took the younger ones begging candy. They arranged a trick so that each 'beggar' heard a ghostly moan instructing them to take a piece of candy from the bucket. One son waited on the roof to drop a bucket on a rope while the other manned the phone. They were so intensely involved I breathed easy as we left to join the street party. I threaded my way between cars and children, cautioning my own to be careful.

We finished and returned down our deserted street to our similarly deserted house. They had not left a message, but I immediately knew where they were and fumed, "When are they ever going to grow-up?"

I barely had my lecture outlined when the doorbell rang. A box and a white lab coat with four familiar feet stood there holding out a white plastic bucket with a lid.

"Evening, ma'am. We are the hazardous candy crew come to pick up all your leftover Halloween candy to keep you from getting sick. If you will carefully place your leftovers in this container, we will take care of it for you."

"You didn't!" I gasped.

"Yes, ma'am, we have been visiting the homes in this area. We would like to take care of your hazardous Halloween leftovers."

I lifted the lid and looked in the container. They had! I blustered and faded out as they began doing some fast talking. As the crowded streets emptied, they had dressed up and gone door to door with their unique trick-or-treat message. The pile of candy they dumped out reflected the many people who had exactly followed their instructions.

They spent the rest of the evening perfecting plans for the oldest called "Next Year When I Am in College."

The next year when I called him at college, he didn't mention his grand plans. I didn't bother to remind him, either.

November 1, 1993

Hooked on Games

IT STARTED SO SIMPLY: A birthday gift of an electronic game. I was curious. What was so great about a happy face munching its way around a maze? I found the personal sized game on the after-Christmas markdown shelves at K-Mart a few weeks before my son's birthday. We had discouraged plunking down quarters to play the arcade version. I rationalized the economy of an at-home version, bought it, took it home, and took it out of the box to try my hand at the popular game.

That was my big mistake.

Directing the cheerful yellow ball around the maze, I avoided the ghosts and bounced to the next level. An hour later, having figured out how to get into the third or fourth level of the game, I stopped, looked up, and realized that I had better things to do than play with my child's video game before he ever received it as a gift. I pulled out the wrapping paper, taped it shut, put it on my closet shelf, and started supper.

I was busy cleaning the morning dishes when I felt the irresistible pull of the Pac Man game. I just knew I could get to the fifth level...if only birthday gifts didn't have to wait to be opened by the recipient.

I slit the tape at one end of the wrapping paper, slid the game out of the package, and promised myself just a few minutes of play.

Much later I looked up, shoved the game back into the box, and re-taped the gift. That night, my husband caught me sneaking another game. "That is the first time I have ever seen a birthday present played with so much before the birthday," he gently scolded.

"I'll put it back soon as I finish this game," I promised. "I just want to make sure it works. It was a demonstration game." The game worked fine, just fine. I mumbled a halfhearted, "I'll wrap it as soon as I finish using these three extra turns." A couple of hours before my son opened his game I wrapped it up and stuck a bow on top. After he opened it, I had to make sure he knew how to play it. The game wore out very quickly.

In the summer I found a master board to be connected to the TV with half-a-dozen game cartridges at a garage sale. A neighbor kid had tagged along with us. He whispered a shocked, "That is a good price. Buy it!" I found out later that the whole thing cost less than the cost of one game. It was a great buy, except we didn't own a TV. We never had in our fourteen years of marriage. Another garage sale remedied that and I was on my way to electronic paradise where supper could wait, phone calls might be returned later, and sick children were told to take a couple of aspirins and go to bed. Momma was heading for the top banana on the maze game.

"Mom! MOM! I want to play. It's my turn."

"In a minute; I want to finish this."

Three games later he was still waiting, and I was telling him he had to wait, "Because I am the mother, that's why."

We slowly accumulated a large library of game cartridges. My children used my favorites as legal tender in the neighborhood swap meets. I found more games that I liked. I was up early and sat up late, wearing out the controls and my wrist.

One day I stopped, looked up, and realized the house was in dire need of a mother. "I am not going to play this game again for a least a month," I said. I stayed away for a while. Then we bought another maze game, and I simply had to try it out. I reached for the game's controls and lost my own.

Time and again I found myself in the cycle of the pull towards and push away from the electronic games. Only with time did my interest wane. We sold the game. I was free from the pull and demand of an electronic master.

When we bought our first computer game, I was determined to remain uninvolved; but our in-house hacker stayed up late one night and found a three-D building block game that was irresistible.

Within days my name was in every slot on the high scorers' board. The easy levels lost their challenge, so I chose levels that I could rarely score in and played into the night trying to score anyway. Only the sharp pain in my wrist stopped me. Repeatedly I've kicked the habit. Occasionally I sneak in a couple of quick ones on the game I promised my son I would never play, but this time I really have this habit under control. I'll tell you how I did it, as soon as I finish this game.

Excerpts from May 8, 1995 and June 27, 2005

Welcoming Fall

ON THE FIRST DAY OF spring eighteen years ago, my husband came rushing in from work. "I just heard on the radio that during the hours surrounding the fall and spring equinox, an egg will balance on its larger end."

He headed for the refrigerator and took out an egg. I watched as he carefully held the egg upright, steadied it, and cautiously moved his fingers away. It stayed! In fact that egg stood at attention until sometime in the night when the equinox was over.

I picked up an egg and tried. I held it gently as I steadied it. I moved my fingers away. The egg rolled over on its side. For years since then, I have tried time and again to stand an egg on end during the spring and fall equinoxes.

I even told a general science class about it the year I taught junior high science. A couple of the students went to the school kitchen for eggs. They proudly returned to announce that their eggs were pointing to heaven. Mine laid down for a nap.

Until this past spring I have never been able to stand an egg on end during the fall and spring equinoxes. But this spring when the magic hour arrived, I grabbed a dozen eggs at 6 a.m. and paraded a few of them across the countertop. My husband noticed what I was doing and added a few more. By the time my children were up, we had seven or eight eggs standing at attention.

With a dozen eggs we discovered that not all eggs are shaped geometrically equal. Some come into the world permanently off balance.

My son grabbed a camera and snapped a picture of my astonishment and joy that I had finally stood an egg on end.

A couple of months later I happened across a column by Marilyn Vos Savant. She supposedly has one of the highest IQs in the world. The question of the weeks was, "Did Christopher Columbus really stand an egg on end during the spring equinox?" She flat out denied it was possible, suggesting that he had gently broken the end of the egg to make it happen.

After disparaging the whole concept as a myth, a trick that Columbus had played on the people of his time, she said, "Consider how hard it is to stand a boiled egg on end."

I don't know about the boiled eggs, but raw ones work if the hen laid one that was smooth and evenly rounded.

The fall equinox is this Saturday, the 23rd. The gravitational field that causes the phenomenon lasts more than one day. We had some eggs standing as long as thirty-six hours. If you remember in time, begin trying Friday morning to see when is the earliest that you can balance an egg and then note when the eggs start falling over. It may be as late as Sunday afternoon.

I would be interested to know about your experiences in balancing eggs. Write and tell me: how many eggs you tested, how many would not stand, how long they stood, how many people tried. Some folks will have my luck and not be able to balance an egg, no matter which egg they use. I'm still working on an explanation for that fluke. I'll let you know what I hear.

September 18, 1995

Egg Fun

ROBBYE HOGGARD CALLED ME EARLY Friday, "When are you going to start standing your egg on end?"

"I began trying a dozen at 6:30 a.m.," I said. "By 7:30, two of them stood, the rest refused."

By Friday afternoon, folks were shouting, "I did it! I made an egg stand on end!" The accomplishment has no use, but what a feeling when it happens, as the students at Rogers discovered on "Egg" Friday.

Notice, I said, "When."

Janna Tolbert called. "I was so angry with that first egg that I broke it and mixed it in the muffin batter and called my friend Irene Ross."

Irene suggested she try balancing the egg on a single layer of towel. With the towel, Janna got that "I did it!" feeling and called me.

As did others—Kay Patterson said she was going nuts. She began trying Thursday evening but could not get an egg to stand until about 8 a.m. Friday. Kay did notice, "When I use only my fingernail on top to balance the egg, it makes a slow spin."

When my husband came home, he used a towel crutch to balance twelve; but by 7 p.m., half did not need a towel. We had a little army of eggs guarding our counter top.

Terry Clark said her son, Patrick Antoon, was working on his third egg as she called. He had done it that morning at West Side Christian. I told her about Kay's observation of the spin. As we chatted, Patrick set up the egg and reported the same slight turn.

At home, my in-resident scientist said, "Put a mark on the egg and see if it always moves in the same direction."

The eggs rotated the shortest distance it took to return the egg where it had been when I marked it. The spin has something to do with the egg balancing.

To me it feels like a bolt being screwed into position. Our bolted-down eggs did not move.

Wednesday morning Kathryn Box called to say that her egg had been standing since Saturday, despite the vibrations of the dishwasher. I'm still trying to figure out what's different this year.

The first person to report balancing the egg was John Day. I told his wife Penny about my column before it was published. John mixed up the weekends. He tried balancing an egg on the sixteenth. He lucked out, picked a well-balanced egg, the right time of day, and the egg stood for thirty minutes. The rest refused to stand. A couple days later he tried again and the cooperative egg stood until his sons tried to duplicate his accomplishment and shattered the egg.

A few years ago I told Jan Cooksey about egg day. She went home and tried unsuccessfully before going to bed. At midnight she woke up, walked through the kitchen, saw the egg, and tried one more time. She did it! It was the middle of the night when everyone else was fast asleep and would not see her accomplishment, but she didn't care. When the ovoid balances, what a feeling!

Thanks to all who tried and called. The fall equinox fed my appetite for learning. Speaking of which, does anyone want a scrambled egg? I have two dozen waiting to be cooked.

October 2, 1995

Duct Tape

"YOU WANT WHAT FOR YOUR birthday this year?" I held the list of suggestions my son had handed me.

"Duct tape."

"You want that two inch wide gray sticky stuff with strings in it?"

"Yep."

I really do try to accommodate, but duct tape! Why? Because my son who pinches every penny twice uses it everywhere. Before he ever hangs posters he reinforces the corners with patches of gray. His notebooks are securely edged with duct tape when he first gets them. The hole in his suitcase sports a tidy gray square. Packages are not ready for mailing until they are duct-taped shut.

When his vinyl Bible cover ripped in the middle, I mentioned buying another one. He shrugged off my suggestion and reached for the duct tape. I think the stuff was originally intended for fixing something in the house, but I'm not sure exactly what.

I do know that its handiness is not a family secret. While visiting the newlyweds this fall, I saw the most extensive use of duct tape ever. An elderly hippy had converted his many-windowed, vintage van into his home. The back door had been insulated, then taped shut literally and liberally with hundreds of strips of duct tape. Even if the hinges had fallen off, I doubt if the doors would have.

It seemed an appropriate reminder of the tape's versatility. My husband had taken a package of tools as wedding gifts to our oldest son. He included a huge roll of duct tape.

This from a man who has screw drivers, hammers, saws, squares, levels, wrenches, various kinds of glue, nails, and staples cluttering his tool room. He knows how to use all of them to put together, take apart, balance, repair, and build any number of pieces of furniture. He also fixes the plumbing and car engines.

Hundreds and thousands of dollars' worth of tools line the floor, walls, and tool shelves. And what does he give his son for a wedding gift of essential tools when setting up his household?

Duct tape.

Can't live without it, you know.

I did think my pinch penny progeny had gone too far when he returned from college with the ever-present duct tape wrapped around a pair of shoes. They also sported odd bits of wire carefully bent and hooked precisely to help hold them together. I would have assigned them to the trash heap ages before that.

"Looks like you could use a new pair of shoes," I commented.

"This pair is fine. They're finally broken in enough to be really comfortable."

Looking at the wires and tape surrounding his feet, I doubted that. "I'll buy you a new pair."

"No. No, thanks. I like these."

The duct tape kept out the rain for a while longer, but after the third or fourth time, the duct tape wore off, he formally declared them too threadbare to repair and placed them lovingly in the trash. (I don't know which loss he regretted more, the shoes or the duct tape.)

I promised that the next time I see duct tape patched shoes, he would get new shoes, or I won't give him duct tape for his birthday ever again.

October 23, 1995

Breakfast Dr. Seuss Style

I YAWNED AS I SCANNED the ads recently until one caught my eye. I reread it carefully and flew to wake up the sleeping teenagers.

"Hey, do you want to go have green eggs and ham for breakfast today?" I shook the sleeping bodies awake, loudly announcing my find.

The first one's eyes popped open fast, "Sure Mom, why not." He sat up, ready to tackle the task of dressing and getting out the door quickly.

The second one bounced out of bed. "All right! Yeah! I want to go. Do I have time for a shower before we leave?"

I thought about his forty-five minute showers. "Probably not, it's only supposed to be served for another hour."

We piled into the car and headed out for our great adventure in eating.

The eggs were green, scrambled eggs, but the ham was the usual pink. Actually, I wasn't surprised that the ham wasn't green. Several years ago I fixed a Dr. Seuss meal of green eggs and ham, in honor of his book, "Green Eggs and Ham." I discovered that the oils in the ham resisted food coloring. It looked horrible, but it all tasted the same as usual, just as it did at our recent buffet breakfast.

Besides the green eggs and pink ham, there were biscuits and gravy which tasted great, but the gravy was a candy apple red. No one had bothered to disguise the pale white grits or to add color to the orange oranges, bright red strawberries, and delicately colored melons.

It was a feast fit for a king, if the king could forget that eggs are usually a warm, cozy yellow, not brilliant green, and that the gravy tasted better than it looked.

It's not the first eating adventure I had discovered in a *News-Times* advertisement. The most surprising one was a small notice several years ago at the bottom of a grocery store ad. The store would be holding a cookie stacking contest in several age categories with savings bonds for the winners.

Sounded like a fun way to get free cookies and do my shopping. I took the family grocery shopping. We all stacked chocolate cookies filled with white frosting. Mine toppled after about twelve or thirteen cookies. But the toddler and grade school student stacked theirs high enough to be winners.

Several weeks after being given a savings bond for the unusual knack of being able to stack cookies, my son was asked to participate in the regional cookie stack-off. The stack-off was scheduled for the halftime of a professional soccer game in Houston.

The cookie company sent us tickets for the game and a list of prizes, including a computer. We already had a computer, but a chance to see a professional ball game was too much to pass up. He would stack the cookies.

The official family cookie stacker was given an official cookie stacking T-shirt and taken to the center of the stadium where turkey roasting pans were heaped high with oversized cookies. Official cookie stacking judges read the rules and watched the stackers. A whistle sounded the beginning of the timed stacking contest. Our cookie stacker did his best but didn't come close.

I still look over the ads for another cookie stacking contest. Haven't found one yet, but I did find a great breakfast of green eggs and ham. You just never know what treasures are hiding in *News-Times* ads.

August 27, 1994

If the Shoe Fits

WE WERE ALREADY PRESSED FOR time when I picked up my son to take him to the airport to catch a plane to El Paso where he was to attend a banquet. As we drove to the Little Rock airport, we talked about the books he had read, his classes, professors, and life at home.

At the airport he pulled out his driver's license to prove he was himself and answered all their questions to ensure he was a safe passenger. We strolled to his gate where we waited for his flight to be called.

I glanced down and noticed his boots: permanently, liberally sprinkled in red, blue, and yellow paint spots from a summer of work.

"You do have your dress shoes for the banquet Saturday night?" I asked nervously.

"This will be the first call for flight 154 to Dallas," the intercom interrupted me. "Please have your boarding passes ready."

He hoisted his backpack onto his shoulder with a grin. "Nope, I just brought my boots."

My instinctive scolding blustered into hopeless silence. The plane was waiting, "I guess those will have to do," I moaned.

He chuckled. He had once again pulled my maternal chain with his footwear.

I'll never understand why he bothered to take dress shoes, loafers, and sneakers to college. He has avoided wearing them since he was a senior in high school.

At that time he wanted to go barefoot, but it was prohibited. He did the next best thing. He cut off the cloth over the toe and heel of his sneakers, ripped out the lining, and declared that he had a pair of sandals.

The remodeled sneakers were definitely light weight, airy, and exposed his hairy toes as much as any sandals. He had no interest in replacing them with a pair of sandals.

He is a frugal soul and a bit obsessive about keeping his possessions long after anyone else would have replaced them. With another pair of sneakers he repaired the tears and outrages of daily wear with wire, duct tape, and glue. Anything to hold them together was used until, for the second afternoon in a row, he sat down to pull the shreds of cloth back together and nothing held. At last he reluctantly deposited them in the dumpster.

The next summer he served with Teen Missions International where sneakers were prohibited. Every teen had to wear sturdy work boots all ten weeks. After wearing boots all summer, he continued to wear them through the next two years of college until the once thick soles were thin. When they proved irreparable, he sadly released them to the trash bin.

Those boots were replaced this past summer when his job at Lion Oil required safety boots. He bought brown camouflage boots that, through a daily baptism of paint, became the multi-colored pair he wore at the airport.

Hey, he wears shoes and is studying at college. I should be happy, right?

I'll try to remember that the next time he attends church attired in suit, tie, and multi-colored camouflage boots.

February 26, 1996

The Saga of Bill Overdue

"I'M HOME," I CALLED AS I entered the house. "Come help with the groceries."

"Shhh," my son greeted me. He motioned across the room where his friend was spelling out our address over the phone.

"What's he doing?" I hissed, setting the bag of groceries on the table beside a pile of magazines and ads for computers, services, accessories, and information.

"We are calling up companies offering free diskettes about computers and telling them to send it here to Bill Overdue," my son said in a low voice. About then his friend hung up chortling, "This is so funny. No one has said anything about the name. They just ask how to spell it and take down whatever spelling I come up with."

They laughed and started to paw through their collection of advertisements looking for another place to call until I reminded them of the groceries.

Because all of the calls were to 1-800 numbers, I never did find out how many phone calls they made for Bill Overdue asking for free information. I do know that for the next couple of years, Bill Overdue got everything except dunning notices for not paying his bills.

Initially the mailbox was filled with a variety of brochures, fliers, and sample diskettes from the places the guys had called. They sampled computer programs and rearranged the diskettes for personal use. Through Bill's benevolent sharing of his mail, they found out about the most recent developments in technology and games.

When his friend could not visit and check out Bill's mail, my son would gather up Bill's current haul and take it to school to share. The young technophiles relished the bargains on computer equipment and magazines that flowed through our mailbox.

The flood of mail in response to their calls had begun to slacken as their requests were fulfilled, but the advertisers began selling old Bill's name to advertisers in similar fields. Bill Overdue was invited to join international computer information systems.

He was offered samples of a variety of magazines, bargains on computers, and computer programs on credit, all with no concern for his source of funds. His original inquiry, along with an address, first, and last name, were sufficient reason for competitors to send more mail.

Eventually he had enough mail to fill up a paper grocery bag.

Long before the avalanche of mail ended, the two friends graduated and went off to college, leaving me to collect Bill Overdue's mail.

Slowly his interests have expanded. In recognition of his growing need for more funds to support his technological hobby, Bill Overdue recently received an offer for his very own credit card with a credit line of up to $3,000 depending on how his application cleared his credit card referrals.

Because of his incriminating last name and lack of Social Security number, we have forbidden him to apply, but his mailbox still fills up with offers to spend that overdue money.

March 4, 1996

Fashion Statements

"YOU ARE NOT GOING TO wear a T-shirt to the formal!" I gasped. "Wear your suit!"

"I can't. It doesn't fit me anymore."

I marched him back to his closet, pulled out the jacket, and told him to put it on. His shoulders stretched the seams to their limits. His forearms dangled below the sleeves.

"At least a nice dress shirt?" I pleaded.

"This is a nice shirt," he said, and pulled on a black T-shirt with rich gold lettering and symbols for Arkansas Governor's School.

I gave up.

After years of trying to get him to dress up for anything, let alone the school formal, I quit.

In the class picture taken that evening, he stands straight and tall, smiling confidently in the back corner of the picture.

Actually I should have been glad he decided to go at all. His older brother sold candy bars, collected money at fund raisers, and helped decorate for two days before he finally decided (the afternoon of the big event) that he would go, a bit too late for a date, and definitely too late to arrange for a tuxedo. His church suit had to do.

A similarly reluctant friend decided to join him in broadening his social experiences. He also had to wear what he had in his closet.

They showed up at the Junior-Senior Formal in suits and ties and discovered that the party was for the students, not a roomful of formal clothes that happened to cover up teenagers.

Tuxedoes weren't even discussed the next year when my next son joined them. Standard dress-up apparel has never been a particular hang-up for my nonconforming second son. When his older brother left, he felt even freer to make his own statement about fashion and parties, especially at the formal party at the end of his senior year, which he did not intend to miss. He had sold his allotment of candy bars during the fundraiser as a junior. By gum, he was cashing in as a senior who sat back and enjoyed.

His enjoyment absolutely did not include wearing a tuxedo—not even one that another family had purchased for their son recently. Not even if it was his size.

Not my "I have to be me" son! I did not realize, until too late, that all the time he had been wearing slacks and dress shirt to church, he had been outgrowing his suit.

That's why the night of the Junior-Senior Formal he wore dress slacks, his Arkansas Governor's School T-shirt, and a big smile.

When my third son became a junior, he insisted he needed a suit for Future Business Leaders of America competitions. He did not insist on a tuxedo for the formal. The FBLA suit was fine with him when he was a junior.

The next year he shocked me, "If I had a date, Mom, would you give me the money to rent a tuxedo?"

"Sure," I agreed. I was shocked. Break with his brothers' tradition of going stag and wear a suit?

"I don't have a date, and I don't want a tux, but I do want the money it would cost to rent one. Can I have it?"

He didn't get the money. He didn't wear a tux.

He went in his "Sunday go to meeting clothes" just like his brothers.

May 6, 1996

Super Bowl

OVER THE HOLIDAYS WE SAT at my brother-in-law's kitchen table talking about church youth activities in Indiana and Arkansas. That cued my husband to relate a telephone conversation he'd had with their mother. She had casually mentioned to him that one of her grandsons was going to the Super Bowl with the youth group.

My husband was amazed. "Wow! How did they get tickets?"

"From the youth director."

"How did he get tickets?"

"I don't know. The youth director makes these arrangements. He does it every year," she brushed aside his question.

But his interest was at an all-time high, "Every year? Do you realize how much that would cost?"

"It's only a hundred to a hundred-fifty people who go to Super Bowl every year, counting the chaperones that the teenagers have to have."

"Sure," my husband scoffed, "what man wouldn't agree to take his sons to the Super Bowl? They probably have lots of volunteers for chaperones. How do they get there?"

"On the bus."

"Every year? They don't fly to California?"

"No, they always take the bus."

"Every year he makes arrangements for the whole thing and they take a bus? Even when it's in California and New Orleans?" He was amazed.

She shrugged off his question. "I don't keep track of these things. I just know that the youth director takes care of the whole thing. It's an evangelistic kind of thing."

"Evangelistic?"

"Well, yes. Everyone has to listen to a message on the bus."

"I'm sure any drunk would listen to a message on the bus if he got to go to the Super Bowl." He paused and shook his head in disbelief. "This is just amazing to me. It must cost a lot of money to take one hundred to a hundred-fifty people and get a block of tickets like that. It is incredible. I wonder how they do it."

"I don't know how. That's the youth director's job. It's a long trip for them. This year they are going to Indianapolis on the bus. They will leave early, stop for something to eat, and have devotions on the bus. Then they will bowl all night long at this huge bowling alley in Indianapolis."

"Bowl all night!" My husband choked on his surprise. "I thought you were talking about the Super Bowl, not an all-night bowling tournament."

At that point, my brother-in-law looked at his mother. "I bet Mom doesn't even know what the Super Bowl is, do you?"

She looked at him questioningly. She glanced at me and everyone sitting around the table for a clue.

Finally, she smiled hesitantly and cleared her throat. Evidently thinking back to her own sons' activities at this time of year, she tentatively ventured, "Does it have something to do with basketball?"

The men cracked up laughing.

"No," my husband said. "It is the playoff of the best teams of the two national, professional football leagues. It's the equivalent of the World Series in baseball."

But that's another story: She didn't know what the World Series is all about, either.

January 27, 1997

Stargazing Amateur

IT HAPPENS EVERY TIME SOMEONE shouts, "Look, A shooting star!" I look and see a quiet, still sky. I plan to stay up to watch lunar eclipses only to sleep through the whole thing. When that once-in-a-lifetime comet passed nearby, it was lost in the haze along the horizon. On the day of the partial solar eclipse, the skies were overcast with sun blocking clouds. I was an astronomical failure until my husband took Astronomy 101.

He came home with star charts and tables, excited about the oldest field of scientific study. The August after his final exam in astronomy he hauled mattresses, pillows, blankets, camera, binoculars, and family outside to watch the yearly meteor shower. It was a most satisfying experience. I saw shooting stars until they no longer interested me.

A few years later when yet another partial solar eclipse was announced, the kids and I waited in the yard with two pieces of cardboard. The top one was punctured once with a pin. The other we held underneath as recommended for a safe view of the solar eclipse.

During the eclipse we studied the speck of light on the bottom cardboard. Except for the odd dip on one side of the circle, it looked like someone had shone a flashlight through the tiny hole.

"We must have pricked the cardboard unevenly," I told the kids. Only as the partial eclipse waned and the speck of light returned to a full perfect circle did I realize that the dip was the moon eclipsing the sun. Better luck next time understanding what I'm seeing, I decided.

With star watching (except for the star of Bethlehem) there is always a next time. A couple of weeks ago I heard that the other eight planets would align with the moon in the southwest sky shortly after sunset for a week. Seven nights and all before my bedtime, I couldn't miss it. I mentioned the once-in-a-hundred-years show to my husband and waited in vain. The clouds descended, the rain poured, the skies did not clear up all week.

I gave up on the planetary show and prepared for a business meeting in Little Rock. My husband drove. On the way home, I was sleeping when he shook me awake, "Look! There they are. All lined up with the moon."

As predicted, the brightly shining moon pinpointed the head of a clear, celestial path to the southwest horizon. I spotted the faint light of the two planets, the brilliance of Venus, a planet of lesser light, the red of Mars and the blue of Mercury. We lacked the requisite telescope to see Neptune and Pluto, but it was enough for me. We paused briefly at the crest of the Calion Bridge for one last clear view before we descended back into the pine forests of home.

So—I've slept through an eclipse or two. Never did see the comet of the century, but, with a little help from my amateur astronomer, I have seen the yearly shower of shooting stars and the once-in-a century planetary path to the moon.

December 22, 1997

Cub Scout Magic

IT HAD NOT BEEN A good morning for checking out the neighborhood garage sales. I had found only a couple of books that interested me. I was ready to quit for the day when I spied one more sign. I pulled over and parked. The usual rack of clothes, tables of knick knacks, and boxes of toys were on display. Off to the side near the money box was an unusual table with a cardboard box draped with a blue handkerchief.

Noticing my puzzled look at the box, a uniformed Cub Scout called to me, "Do you want to see some magic tricks? It's free."

I looked at his mother. "The whole garage sale is to benefit the Cub Scouts," she said.

"Do you want to see a trick?" he persisted.

"All right," I leaned against a post of the carport.

"This is an ordinary pack of cards and four jacks. The first jack went to the first floor." He slid a card into the bottom of the deck. "The second jack went to the second floor." Another card squeezed between the cards a bit higher up on the deck. He repeated his chant with the other two cards.

"All of the jacks took the elevator to the top floor." He turned it over one, two, three, four jacks from the top of the deck.

"For my next magic trick I will take an ordinary playing card that has been torn up and place the pieces in an ordinary envelope."

He held the envelope almost covering a matching envelope behind it.

"Now I will say the magic words, and the card will become one piece."

He flicked his hand holding the envelope dramatically in the air, "Badada boom," and reached inside the envelope. He pulled out a whole playing card.

"Now I need one penny, just one penny, for my next trick. I won't hurt it, and you will get your money back. Do you have a penny?"

I found one penny tucked in a corner of my change purse and handed it to him.

He folded the penny into the blue handkerchief and stuffed both into a small leather purse, "Badada boom."

He emptied the handkerchief and purse over a glass of water. A penny sized, clear disk settled into the bottom of the glass.

"Now I will make the penny reappear."

He reached into the water, removed the invisible penny, stuffed it back in the handkerchief and bag, took out my penny, and returned it to me.

His repertoire of magic tricks was finished, but not his magic show. "Now which trick would you like to see how I did it?"

His offer surprised me, but I knew immediately. I wanted to know how the cards got back to the top of the deck.

"The card trick."

His shoulders slumped as if to say, "That old trick, it's easy," but he reached for the deck of cards. After explaining the sleight of hand involved, he couldn't resist; he proudly reached for the envelope with the torn card. "To do this trick I..." he proceeded to show me every trick he had done.

I knew the show was over when he zeroed in on another garage sale shopper. "Do you want to see some magic tricks? It's free."

I walked back to my car smiling to myself. It had turned out to be a great day to check out the local garage sales after all.

November 9, 1998

Is that the Right Foot or the Left?

THE KID COULD NOT FIGURE out which shoe went on his right foot. As often as not he got it wrong. I showed him repeatedly how the shoes looked when they were right.

We tried various methods to help him remember, but he still started his days with his shoes on the wrong feet.

The summer he was five, we camped out at Mammoth Cave National Park in Kentucky. Our then family of three boys included a three-month-old. My mornings in the tent were rather hectic as I packed diapers, extra outfits and snacks for everyone. The day we planned to explore the caverns I tossed commands left and right, "Hurry up and get dressed. Get the outfit for the baby. Load the jugs of juice in the car." The older boys dressed themselves. My husband loaded the car, and we headed for the caves.

Under the artificial lights inside the earth, I belatedly noticed that the five-year-old had his shoes on the wrong feet. Since there was no place to sit down and they weren't bothering him, I said nothing.

At the rest stop, Wrong Way Hershberger joined the line at the water fountain. As he bent over the fountain, the man behind him, chuckled and turned to the guy beside him, "Hey, look! That kid has his sneakers on the wrong feet."

That kid heard. He went off to the side, sat down, and changed his shoes. It was the last time his sneakers were ever on the wrong feet.

I empathized with him. My mom used to look at my feet and shake her head. "No, it's the other way around."

Eventually I figured out how to match my left shoes with my left foot. I should have learned to match the styles of shoes. A couple years ago I was sitting in an open circle of chairs with a dozen, well-heeled women when I noticed I was wearing the left shoe from one pair of black shoes and the right shoe from another pair. I tried to hide one foot behind the other. The ladies never said a thing.

I think I've learned to wear my shoes correctly, but my mind still reverses other things. As a college student of the 70s, I did not have access to a spell check. At the end of one assignment, the professor wrote, "Either you have a lot of typos, or you don't know how to spell the word receive."

Actually I just kept thinking 'receive' was an exception to the rule: "I before E except after C, or when it sounded like A as in neighbor and weigh." Since receiving his note, my "I's" and "E's" are always in the right order.

But something is still crossed in my brain.

Last week I was assigned to get a picture of a ribbon cutting at 2401 W. Hillsboro. I noted the assignment, figured out where it would be on Hillsboro, counted the minutes I needed to get there, and left on time. I was almost to the 2000 block when I realized I was on the east side of the city and the address was for West Hillsboro.

I sped around the city on the bypass. I arrived too late to take the picture. I left feeling like a little kid caught with my shoes on the wrong feet.

January 18, 1999

Our Second Car: a Red Wagon

MY HUSBAND DISMISSED STROLLERS AND bought red wagons for his children and himself.

He returned from his first foray into the Red Wagon Dealership with a metal wagon that he insisted I take out for a spin. He gave me a push and the neighbor's a grand laugh.

It was a sturdy wagon. It had to be to drag our mound of dirty clothes down the street to the Laundromat and back. While I washed clothes, the two oldest sons entertained themselves with the wagon or used it as a bench for sitting and waiting.

A couple of years, a broken axle, a warped handle, and worn-out tires warranted our declaring it old and ready to retire. For his second foray to the Red Wagon Dealership, my husband selected the deluxe model: the largest wooden wagon on the lot, the kind with red rail sides. When the children were babies, it served as Mom's Reliable Transportation Service around the small village where we lived. For the weekly children's hour at the library, I typically loaded an infant in a covered carrier and a child or two into the wagon bed, plus a diaper bag and snacks, then dragged the lot of them a mile over the uneven sidewalks to the library.

The wagon served my husband through several years of house remodeling and family camping trips east to Washington, D.C., north to the mountains in Maine, and west to the deserts of Arizona.

When my husband decided it was time to take a trip, he removed the rail sides and stacked them on the bed, tucked the handle underneath, and wedged it all into place. With little ones we always found room for the wagon. It served as an extra chair at the camp site, a stroller, a lunch wagon, and a bed for sleeping children. When we were in Washington, D.C., if I wearied of walking, we took off the sides, let the children out to chase the pigeons strutting down the mall, and I sat down.

At home the wagon entertained the children. Big brother hitched it to the back of his bike and hauled the preschooler up and down the overgrown alley beside our house. On yard work days the kids tested their strength and the wagon's by using it to haul loads of leaves, limbs, and once, a huge root their dad had dug out. During the summer and early fall harvest of our garden we balanced loads of tomatoes, green beans, and corn on its bed.

Mostly, though, I remember its usefulness as we converted the most unacceptable house in town into a premium priced, real estate quick sale. The wagon hauled loads of crumbling plaster and scraps of the fresh dry wall away from the house to the junk pile.

The two years we spent creating a basement out of a cellar were hard on the wagon. My husband and the big boys used it to carry concrete blocks from the stack left by the building company. They loaded it down with bucket after bucket of sand to make mortar to seal the blocks into place beneath the house. Finally, they used it to haul stones out of the yard before we seeded it and declared the house done.

We covered the work scars and cracks in the wagon with blankets when our last child arrived, but it was never the same after that. We sold the house to the first couple who looked at it, moved to the suburbs, and bought a second car. The wagon ended its days bereft of its rails, unused, a worn-out toy, left in the back yard to disintegrate.

It has never been replaced.

February 22, 2005

Grandkids are So Much Fun

"How come you don't have any kids?" the next to youngest granddaughter asked me as she leaned out the window of the family van just before she went home from the family campout.

"All my kids have grown up," I explained. Besides, I thought, why should I have kids when I can have much more fun being a grandmother to my sons' children?

Late Saturday afternoon of our family campout the kids kept getting underfoot. "Hey, kids. Come here. Let's do a nature scavenger hunt. You go find a rhododendron and moss on a stick. When you find them and show me, I will give you a treat," I said, and pulled the unopened bag of trail mix out of its hiding place in my car.

Racing to be first, six pairs of little feet and their grandfather, who had to help them, scrambled away from the campfire and the adults seated at the campfire.

For the next half hour to forty-five minutes, they kept me busy sending them out to find colored leaves, seed pods, and ferns. With each bit of plant they brought me, they selected their favorite parts of the trail mix. One preferred the nuts; another, the banana chips; others, the raisins.

As my made-up game wore out, the oldest child wandered off to find more seed pods to add to her collection, the only grandson explored the differences in trees with his grandfather. The similar-aged children organized a game.

Only one child remained. "Grandma, tell me to find something else. I don't care if I get a treat," she said.

"Okay, how about you gather up some twigs and make a little house right here. You could use ferns for the roof and moss for the floor." Her face brightened and she began gathering twigs. She built a charming little cabin for the wood elves.

The next day after a hearty swim in the chilled water, they restlessly converged and swirled around the picnic tables. "Would you like to paint?" I asked, grabbing and unzipping the bag of water colors and paint brushes while I looked around for something to paint. My notebook had already sacrificed most of its extra pages. I saw a stack of one hundred cheap, paper plates and began peeling them off.

The paper plates' crinkle edges flattened under the weight of paint and pressure of little artists' hands as plates became pizza pies, smiley faces, beautiful flowers, and collages of colors. For the next half hour, they painted plates, leaves, their clothes, the tables, and anything else they touched.

Quickly an art gallery of painted plates spread out around us— drying in the patches of sunlight in the deep woods. An hour later as we packed up, the children grabbed their plates and gave one, two, or three each to their childless aunt and uncle. The rest of the plates went home or disappeared during the camp clean-up.

Back home the oldest visitor discovered a rather thick book of crafts for children. "I want to do all of these," she declared. "Can we?"

"Well, maybe we could try to do one or two," I suggested. The next day the paints came out again. I stuck with the simplicity of explaining potato print cards. My husband picked ferns and leaves and worked at the fine art of leaf prints with the middle child.

By bedtime colorful greeting cards painted or printed with sturdy potatoes or delicate ferns covered the dining room table. Reluctantly we closed up the paints and arranged the cards on the shelf to dry and finish another day. The book's other activities may have to wait for another visit at grandma's house.

August 1, 2005

Tool Auction

My husband enjoys the feel of a new hammer in his hands, the grip of a well-made wrench, and the engineering of his new table saw. Over the years he has accumulated more than his share of tools, but, he still could not resist the great buy on tools that he found late last summer.

"Look at all these wire and metal cutters," he said, holding up a package of ten to fifteen nippers sized from very small to hefty. He may have needed one or two tools of the forty-five in the three sets.

"What are you going to do with all those tools?" I asked.

"I think they would make great Christmas gifts for the guys. Any family can use another wrench or two."

He really wanted to divvy them up with all of our sons present, but he couldn't. So he gave tools to one son at Thanksgiving, sent some in Christmas packages, and set others aside for our after Christmas family gathering.

Before we gathered, he heard about a family who had a lot of fun distributing heirlooms using play money at a family auction. He decided to have a tool auction. He bought play money and labeled tools for auctioning.

New Year's Eve he handed out a bundle of cash to each guy and told the granddaughters they would take turns drawing cards to choose which tool was auctioned.

"I've always thought being an auctioneer would be fun," my daughter's husband said. He got the job of selling the family tools.

A granddaughter drew a letter and picked up the matching tool. My husband lovingly described the right handed circle metal cutting tool.

"All right, what we have here is a right cutting tool. This one cuts to the right and not to the left; we want to stay to the right and not too far to the left," our auctioneer chattered. "So, do I hear five dollars for a tool that leans to the right?"

A hand went up.

"Do I hear ten dollars for a right handed metal cutter?"

The bid crept up a dollar or two at a time until the auctioneer saw no more bids and began the countdown, "Going once, going twice, sold to the blue and purple man," He indicated the oldest son.

For the next hour he sold tools not only to the blue and purple man, but to the Family Pack: the son whose three daughters sat around him and urged him to bid on everything and yelled out bids when he didn't.

Because he was auctioning, he told my daughter, "pretty, little lady," to pay attention; he would wink and nod when a tool came up that he particularly wanted. Sometimes he had to wink and nod very emphatically.

As the bidding wound down on some of the tools, his brother "Wild Hog" would suddenly raise his hand or up the ante another five dollars or twenty dollars just for the fun of watching everyone squirm.

Sometimes a bidder wanted the item, but did not want to go higher, so they upped the bid one cent.

The auctioneer gave them "the look."

He also gave folks "the look" when they giggled and bid $77.77.

He rolled his eyes, sighed, "I'm bid all those sevens. Does anyone want to say eighty?"

At first tools sold for low amounts of ten to twenty dollars in play money. Then the price edged up as bidders realized just how much cash they still had.

By the end of the hour, Booger Pickers (so named because no one could figure out what the tool actually did) sold for one hundred fifty dollars and Noggin Knockers (okay, a crescent wrench) sold for three hundred dollars.

It took about an hour to sell the assortment of twenty tools.

It was an hour of fun, laughter, and slipping of money to help out siblings.

It was an hour of family bonding over a few inexpensive tools as a one-night only auctioneer made up the rules, the names, and the rhyming phrases as he went along.

It was a night for collecting tools and family memories.

January 7, 2008

Eaten in Secret

THE RAIN FELL GENTLY JUST outside the open end of the aging shed where the rusty drag for smoothing over a plowed field awaited another season of planting. My mom's chenille house coat hugged me gently as I sat on the wide seat, swinging my legs, and licking my ice cream cone of raspberry swirl. With no one else around, I had slipped out to the back porch and scooped up my frozen sweet from the five gallon cardboard carton left over from the church ice cream social.

Tucked behind the rest of the property, the ancient weather-beaten porch, partially enclosed and missing two-thirds of its floor, served primarily as a shelter for the cats, a place to hold the deep freeze, and a pathway to my perch. In the solitude of the ancient shelter, I could eat a sweet all by myself with no one to silently stare, reminding me I wore chubby girl clothes. Ahh, bliss!

Such secret bliss ended recently for a family member when another family member reached into the stash of candy and discovered that the expensive chocolates meant to be shared by several more members of the family had nearly disappeared at the rate of a couple of pieces a day.

Shocked, disappointed faces stared accusingly and asked, "Why did you eat all of it?"

"You need a spanking because you did not share those! You need to apologize for eating all that chocolate," one of the youngsters pronounced with a wagging finger.

I sympathized with both sides. However, no one ever discovered my own yielding to chocolate temptation.

Nobody discovered it because only I was home to greet my neighbor the morning she showed up with a freshly baked, dark, chocolate cake, one piece for each member of my family.

I thanked her, placed the paper plate of cake on the counter, and mentally declared the evening's dessert prepared.

It was a good plan until I could not resist taking just one little taste of the rich, dark frosting. It was delicious.

Maybe I would have just a little corner of my piece of cake and not wait eight hours for dessert. I carefully slid my fork through another bite of the delicacy. It was very delicious.

Ahh, the luxury of rich chocolate! I sighed, turned, and walked away to tend to the laundry only to return a few minutes later to nibble a bit more of my piece of cake. Here a nibble, there a bite, and I ate my entire piece of cake. Well, that was it. I had had my share and savored it in peace and quiet without children spilling milk across the table or arguing about which one had the biggest piece.

I began unloading the dishwasher where I could keep an eye on that plate of chocolate cake. That chocolate cake whispered my name. I grabbed the fork and relished the flavor and texture of my husband's piece of cake. I still had chocolate cake for the children to enjoy as an after school treat, until temptation won and I ate one of their pieces.

Washing that third piece of cake down with plenty of cold milk, I decided I would cut each of the remaining pieces in half for dessert that night.

Having grown up in a family where we cut birthday cakes into eight slabs, with one leftover for the birthday child to eat that same meal, I definitely know how to enjoy a good cake.

It felt like my birthday all over again as the next three pieces quickly and easily disappeared.

By the time the kids walked into the house, the paper plate, the smell of chocolate, and the dirty fork had disappeared.

I made something else for dessert that evening. I have no idea what it was, but I'm sure I enjoyed my share plus any extra I could get, and then I wondered 'why' the chubby clothes still fit best.

With sincere apologies to my family for eating their share of the cake, I am Joan Hershberger, a sugar addict.

June 28, 2010

Spare Change

Grocery Shopping

I MOSEYED MY WAY THROUGH the grocery store after work, picking up a few items and checking for items on sale.

As I entered the cereal aisle, a little girl sitting on the bottom of the cart protested as her mother paused by the Frosted Flakes. "Don't buy them! Why do you always buy that cereal?"

As I walked by, I glanced down at the price tag. "Because it's a really good sale," I said, and picked up a couple of boxes.

When I glanced back the mother had a box in her cart, and the child was asking her to buy other kinds of cereal.

"No," she said firmly, "I have certain things that I buy at certain stores. And I do not plan to buy any other cereal here."

That sounded familiar.

Recently my child said, "Mom, I don't mean to criticize you or anything, but you and the youth pastor's wife sound the same."

"And what is that?"

"Oh, you know. Buy it on sale and save money."

"I don't consider that exactly a criticism. Which would you rather have, one outfit or two for the same amount of money?"

"Same amount of money?"

"Uh-huh."

"Well, two if it was the same amount of money."

"So I shop around and wait for a sale. I get more for my money that way instead of buying 'right now' only because I want it right now."

But then there was the time I invited thirty-plus teenagers to come over after church for tacos.

For weeks beforehand, when I saw a sale on tacos, taco seasonings, and ground meat, I stocked up for the expected horde.

Tuesday as I shopped, I noticed that lettuce was a reasonable fifty-cents a head. Because I wanted to ensure freshness, I put off purchasing enough for the party until the weekend.

Saturday we cleaned, arranged places to sit, and I sautéed the ground meat to be reheated with taco seasoning the next day. We double-checked the menu, made a last minute shopping list, and headed for the stores.

At the produce bins I stopped in shock. In three days the price of lettuce had tripled.

I knew that severe weather had hit the growing area since Tuesday, but I found it hard to believe it would affect the price of lettuce that quickly.

"I am not paying that much for lettuce," I muttered. "Pick up some tomatoes. I'll get the rest of the stuff we were planning on buying here; then let's go."

At the next store the price of lettuce was ten cents higher than at the first. My child went hysterical with laughter. "Are we going to another store?"

Clenching my teeth, I grabbed a couple of heads of lettuce, jammed them into the grocery cart along with refried beans, and stonily proceeded to the checkout. My child, sounding like a hyena, followed me.

I bit my tongue to keep from complaining to the cashier. She had nothing to do with the price, but the cashier read my face. "One time I was going to have a Mexican party, and the price went up the day I went to buy tomatoes and lettuce."

"I know the feeling," I sighed. "My party is tomorrow. I didn't buy this earlier because I wanted it as fresh as possible."

We empathized with each other. I paid the higher price because I needed it then. But the next time that kid won't be laughing at me because I'll serve hot dogs.

March 7, 1994

Twenty Gallons of Milk

I WOULD NEVER EMBARRASS MY teenagers, but it takes so little to do it. Things I have done for years with no embarrassment are unacceptable when they are around.

Take the summer day I walked into the grocery store to pick up a few items and noticed that low fat milk was on sale. For years when I have seen low fat milk at a good price, I have purchased fifteen or twenty gallons. My children have helped put the milk in the freezer for later use.

They have struggled to yank a gallon loose from the rest after the jugs have been put too close together before freezing.

As long as I remember to have one gallon thawing while another is being used, I save money and a lot of last minute trips to the grocery store. However, my family is rarely with me when I buy that much milk. Recently though, one was with me—a teenager to whom low prices are not as important as appearance.

As I began loading twenty gallons into the cart, the teenager gave a sigh of exasperation and moved away from me in embarrassment.

"Ooh, Mom, how embarrassing," she said.

I squeezed gallon number ten beside number eight and nine and smiled, "Oh, no, it isn't. Actually it is kind of fun."

For my words of encouragement, I received this huge look of doubt as I piled a second layer on top of the first.

"No, really, just watch the people's faces as we go by them." I found a place for gallon number twenty of moo juice and began wrestling the cart down the aisle.

The teenager followed at a distance that said, "I am not related to that woman." In about a minute, however, the teen moved up close to me, hand covering the biggest grin ever.

"Mom, everyone you walk by stares at the milk without looking where they are going. One lady almost ran into someone; she was so busy looking at our cart." Maneuvering the 164 fluid pounds of milk ahead of me, I made my way down the aisle to pick up five pounds of sugar.

A couple stopped beside me as I reached for the sugar and looked at my cart, "Why are you buying so much milk?"

"It's a good price and low fat milk will keep in the freezer for a long time."

"Really?"

I smiled reassuringly, "I've been doing it for years."

I manipulated the overloaded cart through the produce department and picked up a quart of strawberries and headed for the checkout.

The lady at the next checkout stared at my cart for a while. I guess she added up milk, sugar, and strawberries before she asked, "You're making strawberry ice cream tonight?"

"No. I freeze the milk to drink later. The strawberries are for short cake."

My teen and I went to the car laughing. After the milk was in the freezer, I didn't think anything more about the incident. However, the next time we were in the grocery store, as we passed the dairy section, I heard an unembarrassed, mischievous whisper, "Let's put a lot of milk in the cart and watch the people's faces."

March 6, 1995

Hooked on Garage Sales

I LOVE TO WATCH PEOPLE's faces when I say, "I found it at a garage sale." If the listener goes to garage sales, the face lights up, and we swap stories of great finds. If I see a startled reflex and mental search for the right words, followed by, "My, isn't that nice," I know this one has never had the garage sale bug.

One friend used to beg her sister to go to garage sales. For years she heard a scornful, "What would I want with other people's junk?" until the sister went "just this once." The sister hasn't missed since.

I see her occasionally. She wears comfortable clothes for getting in and out of the car quickly, a fanny pouch, so her hands are free to look at the merchandise, and a no-nonsense attitude. She has little time to stay and chat for she has many garage sales to check out before the morning is over.

I go for the elation I get when a risk pays off.

Like the stainless steel mixer and matching bowls on my counter— initially I saw only layers of dirt and rust. I nudged a rust spot. It came off. I asked if it worked. The seller plugged it in and it roared to life with a surge of power. "We haven't used it much, we prefer the hand mixer."

Fifteen minutes of hot sudsy water and I had a shiny new stainless steel mixer and two bowls. It was time to test it on creaming butter and sugar for cookies. The mixer did the job with a fervor I had forgotten after years of using a rechargeable mixer.

It is finds like this that keep me looking after I have spent a whole morning tromping from garage sale to yard sale and found nothing. When my children were younger, I could always find something. Good condition clothes, toys, and books topped my list after I discovered garage sales. Before garage sales, toy purchases were limited to birthdays and holidays. After I discovered garage sales, we had Christmas all year.

My favorite was the day I found a huge box of interlocking building blocks priced at four dollars. My children spent the rest of that day and many others designing, building, and rebuilding.

By the end of my first year of garage sales, the toy box overflowed. We were ready for our own sale of toys to another set of children. Mothers with children cleared the tables. I took the money we made and spent it the next weekend buying more toys at garage sales.

One Saturday I came home after garage sale shopping, and my children were having their own garage sale. They had sold all my favorite toys. That was the day I began cutting back. It became harder to find them something they wanted at garage sales.

This summer, however, one rented his first apartment. He called recently with a few things that he could use and said second hand would be fine if I could find them. I did. Now I am begging him to let me go find more stuff for his sparsely furnished apartment. He is considering my proposal. I am crossing my fingers, hoping he will accept. I would have so much fun.

July 17, 1995

Newlywed Economics

"How are the newlyweds coming along?" asked a middle-aged friend who has four married children.

"Oh, they are experiencing the usual financial problems: not enough money, learning how to handle a budget, stuff like that, but doing fine otherwise," I said.

She looked over at a mutual friend who has two married children. They exchanged the knowing looks of parents who have watched their married children go through the same stage we all did twenty-five years ago, and we all began laughing.

Welcome, son and wife, to the early years of poverty! Fresh from college with education bills, marriage and moving expenses, they are still suffering sticker shock for their simple efficiency apartment and a budget that cannot buy everything they want right now.

But they are making progress. When my son first moved to Austin, he cleaned out my extra kitchen supplies and household furnishings. A twin mattress on the floor was enough for only him, but adding a wife complicated matters.

For their first Christmas her mother gave them the ideal set of pots and pans, and his father built them a bed. My kitchen equipment came back and their bed went to them. And what a bed! Under the queen-sized platform, my husband built in a dozen oversized drawers for storing. Hidden in the bookshelf headboard are secret drawers with trays of divided compartments and pop-out mini-shelves for eating in bed. Disassembled, it fit into the back of an extended minivan barely.

"If I had built it a couple inches larger, I would not have been able to shut the gate," hubby said. But he didn't, and it did fit.

He was proud of his work, and they felt rich. With their mattress and sheets, they suddenly moved up in the world. They moved off the floor, into the air. "You don't know what it's done for my self-esteem to be sleeping off the floor," the bride sighed after the first night.

Sunday night they had to tell everyone of their good fortune at their weekly discussion and Bible study group with other young couples. While they waited for the group leaders to come, Alexis described their wonderful bed. She told how it made their mini-apartment feel more like a real place and how important she felt moving up in the world.

The group leaders, who have only been married a year or so, arrived just as she was at the height of sharing the excitement of finally having a bed. Alexis went bouncing over to them. "Hi!" she smiled up at them. "Guess what? We got a bed!" She waited for their questions and approving comment.

The couple, in their late twenties, past the initial years of paying off college bills and setting up apartments, looked at each other. They looked at my sweet young things in their early twenties and smiled.

"That's nice. We got a house this week."

And then there are those who never experience the early years of poverty. But that's another story.

February 5, 1996

Quest for the Dress

ALL SHE WANTED WAS ONE beautiful prom gown suitable for a princess. All I wanted was to stay home, read a book, and not spend any money.

She says I make Silas Marner look extravagant. I say plan ahead and buy things when they are on sale. We began shopping very early for her prom dress.

I started out optimistically sure that we would find The Dress in the first place. It would be marked way, way down, and I could go home and read a book.

It didn't exactly work that way.

I waded my way through bouffant skirts, metal racks, and tiny hallways into crowded dressing rooms to evaluate the half dozen dresses she tried.

She found The Dress. It was not marked down, and we did not go home. She looked mournfully at the powder blue gown with keyhole back, squared her shoulders and marched to the next shop.

I lounged on a comfortable couch beside the three-way mirror while she carried a handful of gowns back into dressing rooms with wooden louvered doors and freshly swept carpeted floors.

She loved the deep purple formal with spaghetti straps and ground sweeping skirt. But Scrooge and Marley, Inc. frowned at the price tag and raised eyebrows at her bare shoulders.

Four shops later I slumped on a shiny metal stool held up by one curvy post while she dragged armfuls of gowns to the dusty dressing room. She giggled at the form fitting aqua gown, "I feel like a mermaid in this thing."

I had a very quick look at a stretchy sequined black gown that left her digging her nails in for a good itch. A gown with a fitted white top over a full black skirt captured her imagination. Its price tag fit my pocket book. She said, "Let's check out one more store."

Yeah, sure, one more place. After one too many malls and boutiques with dusty dressing rooms and nonexistent dress hooks, I was burnt out. We stopped for lunch. I collapsed saying, "Just order something. I'm so tired I can't think."

We ate, talked, revived, and headed back in search of The Shop with The Dress.

At The Shop, The Clerk actually asked, "What are you looking for today?"

"Do you carry formals?"

"Yes, and they are all on sale today."

I felt better immediately. A cushioned chair awaited me. The dressing room was clean, brightly lit, and had hooks enough to keep the full length formals from resting on the floor. The Clerk swept the rejected gowns from my hands, insisting, "No, no, let me hang them up."

My princess loved the imperial purple gown with the black sequins on top. She adored the royal blue princess formal that swept the floor as she twirled in front of the mirror. After figuring out the actual price after the discount, I approved of either one. She picked the more expensive one.

She smiled as the clerk bagged it up for her. I smiled as I paid for it. We both went home happy. At home, she put on her gown and pirouetted in front of her brother.

I just went to bed, too tired to even read.

June 1, 1998

Step Away From the Purse Strings

MY DAUGHTER ENROLLED FOR THE second semester of college, bought books, and called me in shock. "Mom, I don't have any money left. My books cost way more than I thought. What am I going to do?" I went on emergency alert, adding up our extra cash. My child couldn't go an entire semester without any money.

As she bemoaned the amount of money she now wishes she had not spent last semester, I did a reality check. "Are you counting the money in your savings account? How much will you get paid for the last bit of tutoring you did last semester? How much will you get paid for tutoring this semester?"

During the Christmas break, I mentioned that her brother had limited himself to one fixed amount of cash he could withdraw each week while avoiding ATM cards and checks. If he didn't have cash, he didn't buy. She said it was a good idea. So I also asked, "How much will you need if you stick with a weekly spending allowance?"

On each end of the phone line we both figured it out. If she didn't throw any wild parties or go on any major spending sprees, she would end the semester with money to spare. She would have cash for her immediate needs, a little weekend fun, and all those wonderful meals the college provides.

"But what am I going to do about my tithe?"

"Pay it first. God will make your 90 percent of the money go further than if you keep all 100 percent. If you wait to give to God after your bills are paid, you never will give to Him. You will always have something else that has to be bought or paid."

"Yeah, you're right."

She began listing her reserves: a huge stack of paper left over from other semesters that she could use this semester for taking notes and the simple gifts she received for Christmas—toothpaste, laundry detergent, and quarters for the washer and dryer. Faced with having to provide her own basics, she really appreciated the plain, ordinary gifts given her last month.

"I closed out one of my credit cards last month that I had actually overpaid on. They sent me a check for $3.22 this month. I was so ecstatic. I got $3.22!"

Having been there myself at times, I knew what she was saying. I waited for her to wind down before I said, "I am not going to send you any money. I know you won't have a lot of money, but you can make it."

"I know. I didn't expect you to, but it is scary."

"Yes, it is. Now you understand why sometimes I have not been in the happiest of moods when things have been tight financially."

We hung up, and I immediately felt like the meanest mom in the world for refusing to send more money to my little girl when she had none. Then I told myself to get a grip; if she is old enough to be engaged, she is old enough to experience the harsh reality of personal finances. I don't carry her all the way anymore. It is time to step back and let her carry herself.

Easy to say; no one said it would be easy to do.

January 22, 2001

Independent Kids

REARING CONFIDENT, INDEPENDENT CHILDREN BEGINS the first time we hold our breath as we let go of their hands and they take those first, tentative steps alone.

Recently, I watched as my two-year-old grandson played with a new, simple wooden tray puzzle with his sister and me. They dumped out the puzzle then grabbed pieces shoving each other aside as they fought to pick up and fit the most pieces in place.

Eventually both wanted to work with it alone. Daddy was watching and told them to take turns. Big sister had her turn first. When it was his turn, big sister reached across him and snatched up a puzzle piece. He squawked and elbowed her out of the way. It was his turn.

Their dad distracted her. Little brother dumped out the pieces and one by one wiggled them back into their proper places, conquering the puzzle. The last piece in place, he sat there smiling down at it, exulting that he had completed the puzzle.

If only it was all a simple wooden puzzle! Last month I held my breath and told my daughter I would not financially cushion her this semester.

At fourteen, she had a checkbook and spending allowance for her expenses. It was time for the next step.

She had a huge stack of text books to buy, a semester of clothes to wash, and the miscellaneous of life to handle. I knew she did not have a lot of money, but she had enough.

She called me back that weekend. "I talked with the financial aid officer today. He said there is a four hundred dollar alumni scholarship that I am eligible for. He said he sends them out to all of the students who are eligible, but most do not return them. He said most would get the money from the scholarship if they did, but they don't bother to fill them out and return them. I didn't know where mine was, so he gave me another one. I am filling it out today."

"All right, thank God! That should more than cover the cost of books," I calculated out loud. The other end of the line went silent. I had said too much. It was her decision now not mine on how she would allocate any funds she received from her efforts to take care of herself. It was time for me to sit back and simply watch.

Last week she called again to talk about funds. She had received a reimbursement for last semester's tuition. Since I had made up the tuition difference last semester, she was hesitantly asking if she should return the money to me or could she use it for a state test and other college fees that I had already agreed to cover.

She presented a wise, carefully thought out financial plan. I approved her distribution plan, hung up, and quit holding my breath. I could relax and watch my child enjoy the thrill and confidence of stepping out on her own.

Eventually, she will realize the same thing her oldest brother and his wife realized. They had piled into their first new car for their first cross country trip to visit us. He said they looked at each other and realized it was just the two of them with no parents to tell them which route to take, where to go, or anything.

"We looked at each other and grinned," he said, still amazed. Independence is fantastic.

February 5, 2001

Welfare to Work

I WAS IN FAVOR OF Welfare to Work long before the governmental programs were instituted. It is a no-brainer for me after mothering a houseful of children. Each child began life on the family dole and thought they were set for the rest of their lives. It was my job to slowly disillusion them. We practice, "No free lunch around here. You're either in school or at work!"

The first to come up full face against my Welfare to Work plan was in high school. He came to me early one school day, "What if I don't want to go to school?"

"Then you will have to pay rent."

"What if I don't have the money to pay rent?"

"Then you will have to get a job to pay rent." He quit asking questions, dressed quickly, went to school, and stayed for graduation. The necessity of getting a job was a great impetus.

That's what I like about the Welfare to Work program—the necessity. My plans as a mother did not include having unemployed adult aged children returning home to live. I assumed they would be out and working. However, when one son, after a hospitalization, asked to recuperate at home. I reluctantly agreed. When he arrived, I announced, "You will have to pay room and board." I named a price below apartment rental.

Once the shock wore off, he asked, "Do I have time to recuperate and look for a job?" I felt like a Grinch, so I added a touch of compassion, "Okay, a month or so." Two months later he was earning enough for rent, gas, car insurance, and had a few coins to jingle in his pocket. Plus, he fixes supper a time or two each week, does his own laundry and his share of house and yard work. I can live with that.

My Welfare to Work philosophy began as a child in religious education memorizing Bible verses, including II Thessalonians 3:10 (NIV) "The one who is unwilling to work shall not eat." That sentence has permeated much of my adult life and thoughts. Because my husband agrees, it is easier to insist our children work and pay their own way.

But it isn't always easy to get to that agreement. Friends of ours did everything they could physically, emotionally, socially, and financially to help their adult child make the transition to independent living.

They stretched all their resources for one who wanted the expensive trappings of an adult without doing everything it took to get them.

Finally they simply gave up and, along with the rest of the family, said, "No more help. It is time to sink or swim." Then they held their breath waited, and watched. The adult child began swimming. When she could breathe again, the mother told me, "Once I made up my mind to draw that line, it was so easy to do."

When Welfare to Work was passed, some nonprofits that work with the unemployed to assist with legitimate financial needs held their breaths, anticipating they would drown with requests for help. However, the line was drawn during a period of years of low unemployment. People found jobs and began swimming.

It is absolutely amazing how big a difference a little forced necessity can make.

April 2, 2001

Hush Money

I WOULD NEVER BRIBE MY children to behave, but I have at times figured out what each wanted that I had and the rate of exchange to get them to do what I wanted them to do in return. That is not bribery; that is just good business.

Take the three-week trip we made with our children when they ranged in age from early elementary to high school age. My husband came home in a generous mood, ready to give them each a wad of money to spend on souvenirs for the trip. He started to hand it over to them, but I snatched his generosity away from him and twisted it to my own purposes.

My plans and purposes were simple: peace and quiet on the road. I hate having "Are we there yet?" whined in my ear, or "He's bugging me" screamed from the one tortured by the one bored enough to do it. I also weary of children whimpering "It's not fair." A few hours in confined quarters with a passel of kids, and I don't care about fair. I want quiet.

So with my husband's money and the kids' allowance in hand, I quickly called a family conference, laid out the amount of money their father wanted to give them to spend on souvenirs on the trip, and set down the law.

"Now here's the deal. You each will get your share of the money. It is already yours, but I will be holding the money and only giving you each a part of your share each day. You can spend it, save it, throw it away, buy whatever you want, but you forfeit part of your share if you fight, whine, scream, or holler."

I proceeded to outline how I would divide their days of travel into time segments.

The high school-aged kids looked up from their books, glanced at the money, yawned about my proposition, and went back to their reading. We packed up and crawled into the car.

I looked at our screamer; the one who tortured us with long wails about the misery of being in the car. I took out a couple of cups, put them in the cup holders, put all the screamer's money in nickels and dimes into one cup, looked that child straight in the eye, and said, "It's all yours, but if you scream, holler or fuss in any fifteen minute period, I get the coins for that time."

We fastened our safety belts and headed down the road during the hottest part of summer.

The first day I had the screamer sit in the middle seat of our minivan. Anytime the screams or whines threatened the peace, without a word, I picked up a dime or two and moved it across to "mom's cup."

Protests, promises, and petulance followed but the money stayed put. After a couple more losses, cooperation and amicability became the rule. I moved the time checks to every hour and finally every day.

The kids read books, colored and cut, or played road games. My daughter and I did makeovers in the back of the car a couple of days and discussed many things. I made them memorize a Psalm or two on the long stretches of interstate.

One of our fun stops came after several days of travel when their pockets overflowed with cash. Tables of summer clearance items begged for their attention. They loaded up on discounted baseball figures, baseball cards and books. My daughter found paper dolls which she carefully punched out and clothed for a couple days before we lost them at a hotel room. The boys collected a basketful of computer magazines and comic books.

My husband bought souvenirs. I bought silence and sweet spirits and it was worth every penny of the money I did NOT pay them as a bribe to get them to do what I wanted.

November 10, 2003

AARP Advantages

IT IS OFFICIAL. I HAVE become an old lady.

It wasn't official when the grandchildren looked at me in total awe and said, "You are fifty years old? Wow! You are old!" Children think fifteen is awesome; thirty-five is barely possible, and they find it astounding that anyone would be alive at seventy-five.

So, I'm a grandmother. I'm a YOUNG grandmother, right? At least so I thought, until my daughter, the mother of the youngest of our twelve grandchildren, looked at my hands the other day. Now I look at my hands a lot. Some days when I look at them I see my mother's hands. But that day my daughter looked at my hands and saw age spots. At least that's what she called them.

Age spots! I thought. No way! Those aren't age spots. They are freckles. I ought to know: my mom had freckles just like them. My daughter just does not know the difference between freckles and age spots. But, even having my daughter declare me old enough for age spots did not make me officially old.

Nor was I officially old when the AARP sent greetings on my fiftieth birthday. I mean really, how many fifty-year-olds do you know who are officially retired? I declined their invitation to join their not-so-exclusive club and enjoy all those wonderful discounts. I didn't need them. I'm married to an old, old man who has enjoyed retirement discounts for years.

Nope. None of that made me officially old.

It was the sweet, young clerks behind the counter at the fast food joints who made me old. The sweet, young folks who gave me a senior citizen discount without my asking if I was old enough to qualify.

The first time I shrugged it off. After all, I had rather cavalierly concluded my order, "And, because my dad is a very old man, he gets the free soda."

The sweet young thing behind the counter looked up at me and said, "You can have it, too." That shut me up and taught me my manners. I took the two cups and filled them with ice and free soda.

But another time without my father around, I ordered an item from the ninety-nine cent menu and had the change ready to pay the tax. The clerk refused to take it all. She said my total came to a few pennies less than I anticipated.

"No, it would be more than that," I insisted.

"I gave you the discount," she mumbled.

Oh. Well, thank you. A penny saved is a penny earned.

Like many old folks, my husband and I count our pennies and consider the best buy for our appetite and our pocketbook. He likes buffets but as my mother sadly said when she was about my age, "I just can't eat as much as I used to eat."

That truth really hits home when we go out to eat which we do more frequently now that our children live many driving hours away.

Near the end of one trip, road weary and sagging with exhaustion, we stopped for a break, scooped up the spare change we had accumulated through our travels, and decided to use it to buy something to break the monotony of the cold, healthy foods we had brought with us.

My husband ordered fries, one small sandwich, and a couple free glasses of water. He looked at me, "That should be enough, right?"

I agreed.

The clerk took the order and patiently watched us count out nearly all of the coins in our fistful of pennies, nickels, dimes, and quarters to pay for the food.

She filled a couple cups with ice water, grabbed fries, sandwich and then a whole lot more food than we had ordered, and stuffed it all in a bag.

When we pointed out we had not ordered the extras, she shrugged, "Oh, it was just sitting here. You can have it."

We raised our eyebrows, grinned and said, "Thanks." Hey, if some sweet young woman decides to give a couple of road weary old folks more than a discount, I'm not complaining.

After all, I'm officially old enough to know that "A penny saved, is still a penny earned."

April 16, 2007

Lottery Tickets

ALL RIGHT, I CONFESS. SECRETLY, I have always been a bit intrigued with the idea of winning the lottery, the big one, the Powerball variety that sends a person into untold wealth and unbelievable financial opportunities.

Really, who doesn't at least dream a few minutes here and there of having enough cash for anything and everything, enough funds to finance one's retirement, and enough cash to help out a few friends and family members? The life of Reilly and role of Santa Claus has its appeal.

So for the past year of having a lottery in Arkansas I have toyed with the idea of purchasing one, just one, lottery ticket for a dollar in the hopes of winning the big one. I just never got around to doing that. To insure no one knew about my purchase, I would promise myself, "Next week when I go out of town, I will buy one of those things. Really, this time I will do it." And then find myself short on time, lacking the cash or promising myself, "I'll buy it on the way back through."

But I never did.

So, I had no clue how to go about buying a ticket other than knowing that this is one purchase a person cannot put on their charge card. It's a good thing, too, as I discovered during a road trip through the forests of Arkansas.

The ding of low gas had sounded just as the miles ahead promised to be devoid of a gas station on every corner. I found a gas station with the old fashion kind of pump, the kind without a credit card slot allowing me to buy, fill, and leave without ever seeing the inside of the store.

So I filled up and meandered into the little country store with my credit card. I stood right in front of the dispenser for lottery tickets.

While the clerk did the paperwork, I studied the lottery display in front of me. Bright, bold fonts declared the tickets cost three, four, and five dollars. I looked in vain for anything that said one or two dollars, something I might consider purchasing with my spare change.

"Wow! I did not realize that the lottery tickets cost so much," I commented to the clerk.

She looked up. "We have tickets for less."

"Yes, but those are not the ones that get the big award. I just don't have the money to pay that much," I said. "I prefer the sure thing of a simple fast food lunch to the quick loss of cash for a worthless piece of cardboard."

"I haven't purchased one yet, myself," the clerk admitted, shaking her head probably thinking of the many losers who had purchased tickets.

I left, slid behind the wheel, and drove away thinking about the variety of fast foods that could be purchased for three, four, or five dollars rather than line the pockets of those serving on the lottery commission.

After that stop I had a much better understanding why folks say the lottery robs the pockets of the poor. I thought I knew it all until our most recent trip on the interstate with stops for gas at the big truck stations. Stretching my legs, I meandered around the shop and found a vending machine selling lottery tickets for five, ten and . . . Hold the phone! Twenty dollars!

I could not believe anyone with limited means would spend that much grocery money on something with such improbable odds. Still suffering from sticker shock, I mentioned the horrific prices to a relative.

"Some places sell them for one hundred dollars," he nodded knowingly.

That much! I thought about all the groceries, clothes, or Christmas toys one hundred dollars could purchase. With the odds of being the one person in eight million who wins, the folks who need cash for those things buy the ticket with visions of sugar plums dancing in their heads, only to wake up to find coal in their stockings. The odds of winning equal a 100 percent chance of having less money for basic needs.

I still have not splurged on a lottery ticket. However, if you lend me the cash to buy one or two, I promise that when I win I will pay it back with one hundred percent interest.

Really, I will.

December 6, 2010

Inconveniencing Your Child

Report card

REPORT CARD TIME AGAIN. I married a man with a son in second grade so I have had twenty-two years of children in school. I've parented conscientious students, average students, and "needs help" students.

I've seen excellent, average, and could be better report cards. I've tried spanking, lecturing, and bribing.

Spankings, I tried that once. Hated the noise and saw little change.

Lectures on "You need to do better next time" yielded promises that were forgotten.

I decided encouragement and recognition of any small effort to improve was necessary.

It took commitment, but I preferred a system with a daily review of work assignments at home to earn points for a reward. The bribes—I mean rewards—were chosen by the child. I still remember our most impressive prize request: a table size castle with miniature knights in armor, horses, and weapons.

Other children chose rewards that took less time to earn such as a trip to the ice cream parlor or extra family fun times. With one child we had to insist he either earned a reward or lost a privilege. The rest did not need the threat of a loss of privileges to be motivated to earn the bribe.

When they became men, the childish ways were put away. Upon entering junior high, they were expected to have good study habits and to do their best. Most of them did.

However, there was one. He decided not to do the homework in seventh grade spelling. His grade was almost an 'F.' The teacher informed me the grade reflected the lack of daily homework.

I was enraged and disgusted with the child.

I had no intention of returning to checking his homework every day. That was his job. I don't demand A's, just a reasonable effort to do the homework and study for tests.

He had not even made a reasonable effort.

I did not want to move back to the close supervision level, but I wanted to make my point.

As a family we saved candy and snack foods as special treats. I decided to use that to make my point. I went to the store and purchased a candy bar for each child and took it home.

"These are for your report cards. Good work." I started handing out candy bars.

"Except you with the low grade in spelling," I looked at the guilty one and opened the candy bar enough to shake it out a bit.

"You did not do your homework in spelling. You do not deserve candy for THAT grade." I grabbed a long knife, laid the candy bar on the chopping block and chopped off the end of the candy bar.

He screamed—the student, not the candy bar. "That's my candy bar!"

"Uh-uh," I said as I popped the piece into my mouth and began chewing.

He was so angry; his hand started for my mouth.

I shook my head and chewed as I looked him in the eye, then said, "Next time, do all your homework and you'll get the whole thing."

The next time the spelling grade went up three letter grades.

Since then, I've eaten the ends of two other candy bars.

I wish everything about parenting came that easy.

October 25, 1993

I Don't Want to Go

FIVE-YEAR-OLD KENNY ROBERT WAS QUITE adamant about one thing: He did not like heights, and he had no intention of going up the wooden steps of the sturdy, if breezy, four-story observation tower at the park.

The fit he threw at the base of the tower was meant to convince Uncle Randy that he would not go. He did not care that Cousin Lindsay, also five, looked down at him curiously from her perch halfway up the first flight of stairs.

His uncle, our son, smiled. He had determined one thing: Kenny Robert could, and would, go up. As he told his wife, "My dad made me do things I didn't want to do, and it didn't hurt me."

Okay, I admit my husband did make the children do things they didn't want to do, but it was safe stuff like learning to pick up crayfish and shoveling dirt out from under the house until our cellar turned into a basement. Well, there also was that time he insisted that Uncle Randy, as a child of eight, could and would leave the inside wall of the observation room at the top of the second tallest building in Chicago and look out at the city through the break-resistant glass wall. It took a while for him to let go, but once he did, Randy loved the view.

Kenny Robert did not know about any of that. He only knew that, looking up from the base of the observation tower to the top, it looked high and scary.

"I don't want to go up there." The child wrapped his hand around the guardrail.

"Oh, so you don't want to go up the tower? Why?" Uncle Randy held tightly to Kenny Robert's other hand. He stepped onto the bottom step.

"Because I might fall."

"So you might fall." His uncle took another step. The child had to move up.

"Tell me another reason why you don't want to go up the tower."

"Because my mother would not let me go up."

Above them his cousin giggled.

"Oh, so your mother would not let you go up. And you might fall." Uncle Randy moved up another step.

"Do you have any other reason?"

"Going up that high will make my stomach hurt."

"So going up will make your stomach hurt, your mom would not let you go, and you might fall. Any other reason?" another step up.

"My head will hurt," another step, because his head might hurt, and then one because it was too windy.

All the way up three flights of stairs and across three levels of platform Kenny Robert told his Uncle Randy why he was NOT going up that tower.

He protested all the way up the ladder and through the hole to the observation platform.

They had run out of stair steps and ladder rungs.

They had reached the top.

"You tricked me! You made me go to the top!" Kenny Robert was angry.

But not for long; the view enchanted the child. He was on top of the world. He had climbed the tower. He had conquered his fear. Kenny Robert joined his cousin checking out the view and the small people in the park beneath him.

On the way down Kenny Robert did not have to cling to the rail or his uncle. He raced ahead freely.

At the bottom of the tower he looked up at his uncle, "Let's do it again! Let's go back up!"

They went back up, much more quickly than the first time, and stood victoriously at the top.

Afterward he told his mother, "I was really scared to go up, but Uncle Randy helped me all the way up, and it was really cool!"

His mother never said she would have forbidden him to go, or that she would have allowed him to be controlled by his fears and to stay at the base of the tower. She just listened with her mouth open that someone, anyone, could make her child do something like that.

January 24, 1995

The Perpetual Plodder

FROM THE DAWDLING DRESSING ROUTINE in the morning to pokey preparations for bed, the unhurried child tests my patience.

"It's your turn to do the dishes."

"Sure, Mom." He squirted soap into the sink and turned on the hot water.

I left, sorted clothes, started the washing machine, and cleaned a bathroom sink. When I returned, he had washed three forks, and wore a soap bubble beard.

"Come on, you still have homework to do." He nodded and poured water from a tumbler so he could explore the bottom of the sink through its glass bottom.

His daily ritual of putting on his socks was more than I could tolerate. The child would stare at the socks as if he had never seen them before. His whole demeanor said, "I have no idea of what to do with these things." Eventually he picked up one sock, turned it around three times before resting it on the tip of his toe, then paused, and stared out the window.

"Hurry up!" I hissed, watching the clock move swiftly toward departure time. He looked up at me vaguely before returning to study the sock on his toe. Ever so slowly he reached down and began moving the sock past the ball of his foot, the arch, the heel, the Achilles tendon, and finally, finally the top of the sock reached the calf of his leg.

He felt my glare of impatience. "I'm hurrying," he protested, picking up the second sock to repeat the procedure.

I walked out. I didn't have time for the nervous breakdown I felt coming if I stayed until he had tied his sneakers.

Actions that took me a few seconds took him several minutes as he paused to stare out the window, pick up and put down objects for no obvious reason, and have several reflective pauses. I have more rewarding ways to begin my day than to match my personal agenda with that of a dawdler.

I thought I was the only one with a child who marched to the beat of a different, much slower, drummer. I thought only I had a child who daydreamed about the future while the rest of the world rushed to make it happen.

Then I began talking with other parents.

One parent's only consolation is that both children have to leave for school at the same time. The lingerer does not like the penalties for missing the ride to school. (My laid back teen knew I meant it when I assured him that he would be riding his bike, whatever the weather, if he missed his ride.) However, while the slow pacer dresses and eats, the sibling does all that plus has time to play Nintendo or watch TV, study a bit and start his daily chores before going outside to wait for his slower sibling.

Our dawdling children do offer occasional insights to their world.

Another friend, exasperated with her child's progress, asked, "just who is president of your little world anyway?"

The minor looked up vaguely and murmured, "I don't know; I didn't get there in time to vote."

April, 10, 1995

Lawn Mower Motivation

USUALLY IF I HAVE TO wake someone, I try to be gentle. But kindness went out the window the morning I opened that three hundred dollar phone bill. I marched to my son's bedroom, yanked the covers off and harshly announced, "I don't care what time you went to bed last night; you are getting up right now and going to look for a job!" Since high school graduation he had been interfacing with computer bulletin board systems around the country into the wee hours of the morning.

"Awww, Mom!"

"Look at this phone bill. It is three hundred dollars and most of it after midnight. I know you don't have enough to keep up this lifestyle. Go find a job."

A couple of days later, he was mowing lawns with a man from our church who has a lawn service. Late nights at the computer were replaced with dewy, fresh morning departures. By late afternoon he returned, a tired, green-stained, funny-smelling creature. In time he paid off his phone bill and bought clothes for college.

At the end of his first year of college he mowed yards again. Before he went back to college that year, he said, "I do not ever want to have to mow lawns again. I've seen want ads for college students to work part-time at businesses around the university. When I get back, I am going to apply at some."

A couple of weeks later he called. "I have an interview to be a computer program tester. What do you think I should wear?"

After discussing various choices, he mentioned that his interview was on the thirty-eighth floor of the highest office building in New Orleans. His dad said, "Better wear a really nice suit and tie to that interview."

Later our son called back. "They have a very strict dress code, Dad. Nobody is ever to wear a tie or suit. Most of them come to work in jeans and casual shirts. There are free Cokes and coffee at the office. I have to work twenty hours each week, but I chose the daytime hours around my schedule."

He had entered part-time office work heaven. He loved it, and he flaunted it. "I bought a monthly commuter's ticket for the bus to my office. At my bus stop I buy a newspaper and cup of coffee to drink while I read my morning paper."

Eventually the job and commute pinched into his class time and study hours. For his last semester he quit work and pinched pennies so he could finish, take an extra class, and enjoy life before looking for full-time work.

When he came home this spring, we invited folks to visit. The lawn service owner stopped by for a few minutes, "Hey, are you going to be here for a couple of days? I need someone to help mow lawns," he teased.

"No way; every time I thought a class was too hard, or that it was forever until graduation, I thought about pushing that lawn mower, and I got busy studying. Thanks for the job, but I don't ever want to earn my living mowing lawns again."

"Glad to have helped you get your education," the lawn man said and lined up my youngest son to work the next week.

May 25, 1995

Resolved to Make Her Life Miserable

I MUST DO IT. I must be a better parent this year. A couple of weeks ago my daughter was practically begging me to be more attentive to her, especially in respect to discipline.

I did not see any need for discipline that evening. We had the house to ourselves for the evening. She had been curled up in the lounge chair most of the evening, working on one of a series of reports due in a couple of weeks. I was reading a book on the couch.

I guess she reached the end of editing the encyclopedia's information for that report and needed another book from the set. She slid out of her cocoon of knowledge, walked across the room to the bookshelf, and flopped in the rocking chair.

"I don't feel like doing any more reports," she sighed.

"Um-hmm. I know the feeling, but you will."

"But I don't want to," she said, picking up the reference book.

I reopened my book.

"Mom, make me do my homework."

I eyeballed her. She had to be kidding.

She wasn't.

I shrugged. "Okay, go do your homework."

"No. Really make me do my homework."

Sure, Miss Never Misses an Assignment needed me to "make her" do her homework.

"So, go do it."

"No, Mom, punish me, if I don't."

I sighed and closed my book. My daughter is really missing having her brothers around to pester.

"Okay." I felt ridiculous. "If you don't do your homework, I will take away your fish watching privileges."

"Oh, Mom, really, that's nothing."

"You're right," I thought a minute. "Okay, if you don't start doing your homework right now, I am not going to let you go to your friend's house for two whole years," I said magnanimously.

"Oh, Mom, you know you would never follow through on that," she giggled.

"Okay, if you don't go do your homework in the next thirty seconds, I will not let you visit her until after Christmas."

Her face lit up, "Really?"

"Yes. Really." I picked up my book.

She sat in the chair looking quite gratified.

"And if you don't get moving right now, I will add another week to the time."

She looked at me amused.

"I'm serious," I laughed.

She went back to the lounge chair. Before she opened her book, she studied my face. "You aren't really going to do that, are you?"

"Yes, I am. You asked me to make you do the homework. You wanted me to discipline you if you didn't. So I did. You can't go over there until after Christmas. And, if you don't settle down right now, you won't go until after the New Year."

"All right!" she said gleefully and returned to her homework. So she is not going to her friend's house. She went to school the next day and told her friend she could not come and visit and exactly why she couldn't come. Her finished reports were done on time and looked fantastic.

I finished my book and tore a page out of her notebook to record my only New Year's resolution: "This year I will make my daughter happier by giving her a lot more discipline." As much fun as we both had that night, it ought to be a really happy new year for the both of us.

January 1, 1996

The Day after Mother's Day

MOTHER'S DAY WAS SUCH A warm fuzzy day: breakfast in bed, Sunday dinner at the restaurant, and greeting cards.

Welcome to the Monday after Mother's Day.

The junior high student who wrote the fantastic card has to be reminded three times to bring his clothes to be washed. The teen who took Mom to get a burger is too busy to mow the lawn. And that darling sixth-grader who gave Mom a lovely coupon book good for setting the table can't be bothered to have it cashed in today.

That's how it is unless mothers go on strike as my friend did.

"I decided that moms have rights, too," she told me.

"The strike was an accumulation of things: their lack of helping out, not even bringing clothes downstairs to be washed. Their general attitude was that I didn't know anything and that they didn't have to do anything I told them to do. They assumed I had to help them, but they didn't have to help me. I finally had had enough of it. I decided if they don't have to do what I want them to do, then I don't have to do what they want me to do.

So she didn't.

She gave them an envelope of cash for the week's groceries.

"There's your money for your food. I will be using these dishes. Do not touch my dishes, not even if yours are dirty." She handed them a list of things they needed to do, and she went to her room.

"It was the most relaxing time of my life. I read books, watched movies, and slept. My blood pressure probably went down twenty points."

The kids went into shock.

Cash in hand, the four stumbled blindly to the grocery store. They all wanted a different kind of food. They didn't have enough money to buy half of it.

Terse, heated discussions were held in aisles four, five, six, and seven before they finally worked out a compromise.

Unlike when Mom did the shopping, their grocery sacks were filled with mixes and quick foods. The instant meals only lasted a few days.

Mom cooked her food in a cluttered kitchen. She shoved aside their dirty dishes. Mold grew over the mashed potatoes in a pan on the back of the stove. My friend saw it, took a deep breath, and walked away. It was their problem, not hers.

Friends told her children, "Moms don't go on strike!" When the child listed what they had to do, they begged, "Please don't tell my mom about this."

As reality set in, they studied the rotation system she had laid out: mow the lawn, vacuum the house, wash the clothes, shop for groceries, and fix meals.

They wanted to pick and choose the job. They swapped chores until the oldest sister realized she had the bulk of work. It only took her a couple of days of being a mom before she joined Mom on strike. A few days later the next younger sister joined them.

Three weeks and much talking passed before the entire family had negotiated a settlement with Mom. The strike ended, and Mom, with the entire family's help, returned to work.

May 13, 1996

Hungry for Math

HIS FINAL REPORT CARD SAID that in spite of a year of work and after school flash card drills, he had not learned his math facts. When we did flash cards, he hemmed and hawed, looked away, taking forever to answer.

Certain he could answer more quickly, my patience evaporated. Tempted to whack him on the head with the flash cards to pound a few facts into his memory, I resisted. Instead I vowed to make him spend his summer vacation studying math facts every day until he learned them.

The first day of summer we spent over two hours working our way through the flash cards. I was frustrated. I resigned myself to the fact that my tried and true method would not work. That night I sat in front of the computer and began typing. The next morning I handed him four sheets, one each for addition, multiplication, division, and subtraction tables.

"No more flash cards. Fill in the answers on these four pages. I have more copies. When you can do all four correctly in less than forty-five minutes for five days in a row, I will take you to the ice cream shop for as many flavors of ice cream as you want."

His older brother who never had a problem learning his math facts heard me and demanded the same opportunity. I couldn't believe him.

"Okay, fine," I conceded, "but you have to do the four pages in sixteen minutes for five days with no mistakes." He concentrated and scribbled out the answers in sixteen minutes every day. He had his ice cream by the end of the week.

Meanwhile I cleaned the house while his math deficient brother dawdled his way through the pages of math. It took him four and a half hours to complete the pages that first day. When friends came to play, they heard about my deal and begged to be included. I agreed and soon boys sprawled on the floor, chairs and couches scribbling numbers on their four sheets of math.

They did not come back. The next day he worked alone for two hours completing identical pages. By the end of the week he was finishing in about an hour with errors on each page. For the next several weeks he plodded on slowly improving. By the third week he said, "Mom, I am dreaming math facts every night."

"Great. That means your mind is figuring it out."

By the fourth week he knew his facts but could not quite finish in the allotted time. My husband watched him work one Saturday. He pulled out his stop watch and began timing each page. With time to rest and shift mental gears between pages he took nine minutes for addition, thirteen for multiplication, eleven for subtraction, and eleven for division. With the aid of a precise stop watch and time between pages, he could do it! His dad took over clocking him. By the last page on the fifth day, he had eight and a half minutes to do division. He went to bed full of ice cream, finished with his summer math, ready for long division and three column multiplication. I know it was a bribe to learn, but it was worth every penny we spent on ice cream.

March 8, 1999

Inconvenience That Child

THE BUMPER STICKER OF THE twentieth century was, "Have you hugged your child today?" For the twenty-first century, I propose a bumper sticker that reads, "Have you inconvenienced your kid today?"

Lots of hugs are good for children. However, a little bit of inconvenience goes a long ways towards increasing their loveable factor. Children need to know, just as adults do, that life often is just plain hard.

It was the hard work that twenty-eight of 118 biology students at Piper High School wanted to avoid last year when they collected leaves for their biology project worth fifty percent of their semester grade. They copied descriptions of the plants directly from the Internet. Seeing the same sentences over and over again, their teacher tracked down the Internet source and called the shortcut 'plagiarizing.' At the beginning of the year students and parents had agreed that the penalty for cheating would be a grade of zero. That zero brought their grades down to failure.

The kids thought that grade looked bad on their college bound transcripts. (What an inconvenience!) Through their parents they protested all the way to the school board. The teacher was told to make the project count a lower percentage of the semester grade, twenty-seven of the twenty-eight who cheated passed the semester after all. Twenty of the ninety, who did not cheat, averaged out to a lower semester grade.

Their teacher resigned, as did another teacher who resigned in support. The principal resigned at the end of the year for academic reasons saying, "Read between the lines."

The whole student body instead of just the twenty-eight was inconvenienced with the subsequent public reaction. The deans of Kansas State University sent a letter to the school reminding prospective students that they would be expected to follow the school's academic honesty code. At interscholastic events, other schools called anyone from Piper a "Plagiarist" all because a few mommies and daddies and the school board buckled under when the kids whined about a well-earned zero, rather than saying, "Tough luck, kid; next time do it right."

The whole incident reminds me of one of my son's friends. As a toddler he didn't like the inconvenience of chewing solid foods. He spat that nasty stuff out.

No one told him, "If you don't chew on this lumpy baby food, there will be nothing else to eat." To keep their poor darling from starving they allowed him to choose his diet. He subsisted on peanut butter, soup, sugar coated doughnuts, and vitamins until he was about ten years old when he developed a blue tinge under his fingernails. The doctor said, "Well, son, you either come in weekly for iron shots, or you start chewing a variety of foods." His family looked at the cost of weekly doctor visits. He looked at the pain of weekly shots. He began eating solid, chewy food.

I never understood what took them so long. The way I figured it, he was half their size, a fourth of their age, and a fraction of their weight. Why was he in charge? I respect children's feelings and opinions, but I expect them to respect mine as well and recognize that, being older, I know a lot more than they do.

I inconvenienced my children if it was necessary, as it was the day my grade school son came home with yet another report that he was not doing his homework. I had tried everything that worked for my other children. It all had failed to catch his attention. I thought about going to school and sitting beside him in class to make sure he did his assigned work. I rejected that idea. Why should I be so inconvenienced when it was his problem?

I found a way to inconvenience him: he had to get his teacher to initial a fresh index card every day with one of two choices checked, "completed work today" or "did not complete work today." If he brought home the card saying he had done his work, he got points towards a prize. If he didn't, he received extra work at home. There was no acceptable excuse for not coming home with a card every day. His level of inconvenience went way up; mine went way down.

He did his assigned work.

"Have you hugged your kid today?" Great, they need it! But also remember, sometimes they need the benefits of being inconvenienced to keep them really huggable.

September 2, 2002

You're Bluffing, Right?

MY SEVEN-YEAR OLD GRANDDAUGHTER DID not want to go to bed the night she stayed at my house. The clock and her tired whine said that she needed sleep.

I listened for a moment to her whiny protest, looked at the clock and then at her. "You can cry and whine as loud as you want for one more minute and then that's it. If you do not stop at the end of the minute, you will lose a privilege. It is your responsibility to go to bed so you can enjoy the privileges and fun tomorrow. If you do not take care of your responsibility, you will lose a privilege."

Still whining, the child looked at me in disbelief. I ticked off ten, twenty, thirty seconds, and warned her that she would have twenty more seconds before she lost a privilege, one that she really wanted.

"You really don't want to find out what privilege you are going to lose," I assured her.

The pitch of her whine lowered, her rhythm slowed a bit. I counted down the last ten seconds. She enjoyed her whine until nearly the last second, settled onto the bed, and was quiet.

"Okay. You still have all your privileges for tomorrow. Now just lay there and be quiet. That's all you have to do to keep them."

I turned out the light, stepped out of the room, and went to the kitchen where my husband was sitting at the counter.

"And what would you have done if she had kept on crying?"

"I don't know," I admitted with a rueful grin, "but I would have figured it out. A lot of this job is just bluffing one's way along. I have had my bluff called a couple times before a child realized I meant what I said."

I went to check on the child. She was asleep.

She is not the only one confronted with a choice in behavior.

I heard recently of an eleven-year-old boy who tested his mom's mandate that he had to turn in all of his homework. Sometimes even homework done at home under his mother's tutelage failed to reach his teacher's desk.

Exasperated with her son's willful forgetfulness his mother sought to capture his attention. Taking into account that he would post a "No Girlz Allowed" sign outside a clubhouse with his friends, she went to the store and purchased a very feminine pink T-shirt. As her son watched, she decorated it with the message, "It's my choice. I can either hand in my homework or wear this shirt."

Fear and trepidation filled his heart. This was one bluff he did NOT want to call. His forgetfulness improved. Homework reached the teacher's desk except for one assignment that he was sure he had turned in.

His mother took the T-shirt off the hanger, anyway.

He pled with his mother not to make him wear the shirt. She relented a bit. If his teacher would agree to a makeup assignment, he would not have to wear the shirt. "You have to have a grade reflecting work done," she insisted.

The kid missed a few meetings of the "Boyz Only" club, skipped a couple of recesses, and stayed after school to get the grade, but he didn't have to wear that pink T-shirt.

At the time he probably thought, as did my tired grandchild, that he had lost. It will take him a few years to realize that ultimately he won. He learned to hand in his work in a timely manner, a skill which will hold him in good stead for a long time.

March 27, 2006

Yes, you can!

SUCH A LOUD SCREAM FROM such a little kid: "I can't do it. It hurts!"

My heart went out to the child. And I would have believed the child with a cast on the leg broken at the playground except...except, well I just didn't think that a simple break disabled the entire body for a week no matter how awful it felt.

So I looked at the tiny tike in my care for the day and decided it was time for *The Little Engine that Could:* the engine that went chugging up the mountain puffing, "I think I can, I think I can," and rolled down the mountain singing, "I thought I could, I thought I could."

I looked at the pathetic puddle of pain, sat down on the ground myself, and cheered the whimpering one into trying a new way to move: Scooting along on her bottom with one leg pushing and the other up in the air.

Her younger sibling, just learning to walk, grinned, and joined us on the floor. We skedaddled as a trio down the hall to the bathroom and then the two slid around the house on their bottoms for the rest of the day. I heard no more about the horrible pain until their momma returned.

As soon as the door opened, that child reverted to whimpering, whining, and crying. She could not possibly go over to the other side of the room to greet her mother. That was just too hard. It hurt too much.

Although the mother had been tiptoeing around pain-filled cries for days, I reassured her that the child had smiled, laughed, and scooted everywhere on her bottom the entire day, but only the pathetic pleas caught her mother's ear. She scooped up her child and gently carried that pain-riddled child to the car and drove gingerly home.

It's easy to believe every pitiful whine from a child. Even with years of experience it happens to me all the time. I am swept away with their misery, their bold statements, and their emphatic insistences that they cannot do something.

My understanding of children's games began before I married. My fiancé supervised preschool-aged nephews preparing to spend a night at their grandmother's house. He told them to grab their little suitcases and take them upstairs to their bedrooms.

The four-year-old grabbed his little suitcase, threw it over his back, and holding it with one hand, he came whining to us in the kitchen, "I can't do it. I can't carry my suitcase."

I started to reach for the suitcase. My guy said, "He already is carrying it." I looked. So he was.

For months we heard and accommodated the pathetic story that one grandchild absolutely could not take her nightly pill without milk.

We figured otherwise, but pill swallowing can be an issue for some folks. Then we landed in a cabin at camp for the night with running water only and no milk in sight. In the blink of an eye, without one peep or query about milk, the child gulped that pill down with water without a whimper and went to bed. So much for that "I can't do it" when she was at our house, although I heard months later that she still maintained the same miserable mandate at home.

As a child my son refused, choked, vomited, and made quite a scene every time he had to take medicine. We got the medication down him when necessary, but mostly stuck with the universal cure of lots of fluids and plenty of sleep for his childhood illnesses. As an adult he developed a serious illness which necessitated he absolutely must take pills a couple of times a day. He took them every day, all without a whimper.

Years ago taking junior high students on a field trip, I mentioned the restaurant where we planned to stop.

"Oh, no! Not there! They serve just awful food," the most outspoken girl protested.

Mentally I veered away from that restaurant, but before I could say anything, the trip planner took us there anyway. As the kids unloaded at that "awful restaurant," I heard that same teenager say, "Well, they do have some nice baskets," which the child ordered and proceeded to eat happily and completely. And to think I almost asked to change our plans for her. Lesson learned!

I could go on, but I kind of enjoy being a grandparent, allowed to simply sit back, pretend I have it all figured out, and watch someone else teach the lesson of *The Little Engine that Could*.

May 31, 2010

Playing with the Big Boys

IF YOU WANT TO WORK with the big boys, you have to wear the clothes, as our three-year-old grandson knows. For a week he pulled on a fedora, clipped a tie to his T-shirt, grabbed a pad of paper and stuffed pens in his pocket and put on his heavy shoes so he could stomp around importantly, thrusting his head first looking for things because, "I am an investigator; I have to talk with people and then draw pictures about what they say."

For the week-long summer kids program, he topped off his attire on Monday with a magician's hat, telling everyone, "I'm a wizard." Two days he dressed as a fireman with the red jacket, red shoes, red hat, stethoscope, fireman's rain coat and a badge.

He carried a big tool box, because, "I have to have a lot of tools to help people who have an emergency." He finished out trying out the big boy jobs wearing Christmas pajama pants, red shirt; red, clip on tie; red bandana (he could not find a Santa hat) and carried around a black bag. "I am Santa Claus. I give toys to other people." But mostly he pulled out his encyclopedia book and read stories about dinosaurs to people.

If you want to party with the big boys, you have to pay your own way. The preschooler earned enough money for his first trip to the Dollar Tree to purchase one item. His parents took him to view all the things he could buy for a dollar. He knew what he wanted, the chewable pirate teeth. His mom and dad pointed out fifteen or twenty other things they thought he might like and asked him if he didn't want that instead. He stuck with his preference and took it to the checkout. His parents watched from the sidelines.

The clerk looked down on a customer barely able to see over the conveyor belt.

"Is it my turn?" he looked up at her.

"Yes, now is when you put it up here," she indicated the black counter, scanned his item and told him that would be $1.10. He carefully opened his billfold, took his dollar and dime and handed it to her. She slipped his purchase into a bag and handed it to him. Glowing like a thousand-watt light bulb, he left the store with his first ever earned purchase.

By the next day he had consumed nearly all of his candy. He had only one comment to his mom, "Why did you keep asking me if I wanted that?"

"Because it is not what I would have wanted," she admitted. If you want to play with the big boys, if you do the crime, you do the time. Last week big brother broke a rule for polite living and was sent to the time-out corner to reconsider his actions and choices. Taking it like a man, he trudged over to his time-out corner and sat down to wait out his sentence. Over on the other side of the room an almost two year-old baby his mom babysits stood up and screamed to declare his presence.

"Liam, we do not scream." Liam showed his budding independence, looked at the giant person telling him to stop, picked up a shoe and tossed it at her.

"Liam. We do not throw shoes. You need to go sit in time out." He did not go down easily, but the momma patrol captured him and sat him on a time-out stool.

Watching all this with total fascination, our fifteen month-old granddaughter grinned, looked at her mother, picked up a little shoe and flipped it across the room.

"Now, Caroline, you do that again and you will be in time-out. We do not throw shoes in the house."

Eyes twinkling with mischief as she looked at her mom and the big boys, the sweet little thing reached down, grabbed another shoe and every so gently tossed it just enough to count as throwing a shoe.

"Now you have to go to time-out."

Picking up the petite child, my daughter carried her over to a time-out stool. The little lassie sat there swinging her feet back and forth, grinning and flirting with her mother, quite pleased with herself for having gotten time for the crime just like the big boys.

August 9, 2010

The Babysitter Speaks

OKAY, SO THE WOMAN MADE a mistake. She had an affair with a married man. She says she did not know about the wife until she announced her pregnancy, and he said as a married man he had no interest in divorcing his wife and marrying the young woman.

He disappeared from her life as emphatically as he had arrived. She refused to even consider abortion but adoption perhaps. In the end, she chose to keep the child, a boy.

She did not, however, take the next step and embrace the mantle of motherhood. As an infant, baby, and preschooler, the boy needed her loving direction in his life and a sense of her commitment to him, but he did not feel it.

By the time he was three, after yet another person had given up on babysitting a child who screamed and threw tantrums, his mom went to a woman she had met at the church she had begun attending.

"No one wants to babysit him. They can't control him. Would you please babysit?" the young mother sighed in defeat.

The babysitter, a mother of three and grandmother of two, agreed to try.

The first day the preschooler was overwhelmed with the frustrations that every little kid experiences and began throwing a screaming temper tantrum.

The babysitter began singing, "Jesus loves me, this I know."

"Stop singing!" he screamed at her.

"You do not tell me what to do," she said bending down to look in his eyes. "I am fifty; you are three. I am the boss, not you. When you stop screaming, I will stop singing."

He looked at her dubiously.

He screeched. She began singing.

He stopped. She stopped.

He screamed; she sang. He stopped and looked at her. "You're the boss?" he asked tentatively.

"Yes."

He sank down inside himself to think about that.

He tried the scream a few more times and discovered she would not yield to his tantrum. He pretty much quit screaming around the babysitter.

The babysitter told the workers in the church nursery, "If he starts screaming, sing."

It was not all discipline for the child. This babysitter enjoys children. She spends her days interacting with them, playing, and even doing a bit of roughhousing and tumbling about.

"You want to play with me?" he asked, bewildered at this strange adult.

Yes, and she even encouraged him to jump on her second hand couch from Goodwill and to learn to fall into the cushions.

"But, I told him to be sure to ask before he did it at any other house because not everyone would want him to jump on their couch," she said.

He looked at her in astonishment. She didn't just want him to sit in front of the TV and just be good?

The mother told the babysitter she would not take her son out in public because he did not behave.

"Well, you have to train him how to act in public. He won't learn unless you take him," the babysitter said.

So the mom took her son shopping and was surprised at how well he behaved.

The babysitter was surprised at how long the mother held onto her guilt for having had an affair.

"Maybe I should have given my son up for adoption," the mother said one day as she wallowed in her misery.

"No. You made the decision. Now forgive yourself and choose to have a good time with him," the babysitter urged her.

"If I had given him up when he was born, I would not miss him," the mother mused one day.

"Yes, you would. Once you are pregnant, even if you never have the child, it changes you forever. Now grow up and become his mother."

During their daily visits the mother expressed astonishment at all that the babysitter knew. "I wish I knew how to do all that," she sighed.

"Look, I am a babysitter. I am a mother of three, and I have taken care of many more children. I just have had more time with more children than you have. You're a first time mom. You're not supposed to know all this. You are still learning. That is normal. You're supposed to ask questions and not know how to do it all. So ask, watch, listen, and learn. That is what you do at this time."

"I don't have to be the best?"

"No, but you do have to ask questions from experienced people. Talk with other moms; talk with teachers; and listen. They have had more time and experience. That's what it takes."

In the Bible older women are encouraged to teach what is good and to "urge the younger women to love their husbands and children." Titus 2:4 (NIV). Now may the younger ones listen and learn.

December 7, 2011

About the Author

In 1993 Joan Hershberger exchanged four long years of college science labs and calculus study sessions for the opportunity to write a weekly column at the El Dorado News-Times. Over the years she has served as news clerk, special sections reporter, hard news reporter and education reporter, as well as worked with page layout and photography.

When she married Joseph in 1972, she gained two sons. The family now has five sons, one daughter, five daughters-in-love and one son-in-love, seventeen grandchildren, three great-grandchildren and counting. They travel extensively to visit family and see the country.

Besides being an avid reader, Joan maintains a photographic record of her family and collects fabric and needlework at yard sales and thrift shops to make into quilts, aprons, and home décor. Each week she teaches Bible lessons to elementary students at her church.

CPSIA information can be obtained at www.ICGtesting.com
Printed in the USA
LVOW13s0251151013

356884LV00003B/3/P

9 781490 806686